ask
an **expert**

Issues from toddler tantrums and meltdowns
to peer pressure and teen self-esteem

ask
an **expert**

answers every parent needs to know

Dr. Claire Halsey,
Dr. Matthew Johnson, Dr. Joanna Grave

Foreword by Professor Tanya Byron PhD PsychD MSc BSc
Consultant Clinical Psychologist

DK

London, New York, Munich, Melbourne, Delhi

Project Editor Emma Maule
US Editors Shannon Beatty and Charles Wills
Designer Charlotte Seymour
Senior Art Editor Nicola Rodway
Senior Production Editor Jenny Woodcock
Production Editor Kelly Salih
Production Controller Mandy Inness
Creative Technical Support Sonia Charbonnier
Managing Editors Penny Warren, Esther Ripley
Managing Art Editors Marianne Markham, Glenda Fisher
New Photography Vanessa Davies
Art Direction for Photography Isabel de Cordova
Publisher Peggy Vance

Every effort has been made to ensure that the information in this book is complete and accurate. However, neither the publisher nor the authors are engaged in rendering professional advice or services to the individual reader. The ideas, procedures, and suggestions contained in this book are not intended as a substitute for consultation with your healthcare provider. All matters regarding the health of your child require medical supervision. Neither the publisher nor the authors accept any legal responsibility for any personal injury or other damage or loss arising from the use or misuse of the advice and information in this book.

First American Edition, 2009
Published in the United States by
DK Publishing
375 Hudson Street
New York, New York 10014

09 10 11   10 9 8 7 6 5 4 3 2 1

AD446—08/09

Published in Great Britain by Dorling Kindersley Limited.

A catalog record for this book is available from the Library of Congress.
ISBN: 978-0-7566-5147-3

DK books are available at special discounts when purchased in bulk for sales promotions, premiums, fund-raising, or educational use. For details, contact: DK Publishing Special Markets, 375 Hudson Street, New York, New York 10014 or SpecialSales@dk.com.

Printed and bound in Singapore by Star Standard

Discover more at **www.dk.com**

Foreword

Being a parent is the most wonderful, exciting, and incredible role that we will ever play in our lives. It is also, at times, terrifying. From the first moment we bring them home, to their first faltering steps; from their first day at school to their first time on a date, our children amaze us, enthrall us, and make our hearts race in a way never experienced before. The love we have for our children is unconditional and their love, in return, is pure and without question. They arouse the most extraordinary feelings in us and can bring tears to our eyes just by smiling. The instinct to nurture, protect, and love them is so powerful that it can leave us breathless. So, if this is all about the purest love and the deepest instincts, why do we need experts? Surely being a parent isn't something you ask advice on, it's something we all "just know"?

Well, as the mother of two (Lily, 13, and Jack, 10) and a professor who specializes in child and adolescent mental health, I am probably more qualified than most to tell you that sometimes even the most highly trained among us can feel completely out of their depth. Knowing what we should do, can often be at odds with what our heart drives us to want to do. Add into this the fact that there is often more than one person contributing to the parenting decisions—partners, grandparents, well-meaning friends, all offering differing views—then sometimes we really do need to be able to find the calm voice of reason that can cut through the confusion and help us to find the sensible way forward. *Ask an Expert* provides all parents and caregivers with this occasionally needed facility to find a way forward. Written by experts, beautifully laid out, and clear in its advice and information, this book will be invaluable to anyone who wants to make the right decisions for their child. It does not preach—it suggests. It does not prescribe—it empowers. It does not patronize—it engages. Whether your question is about specific techniques, for example how to feed a fussy toddler—or about bigger emotional issues, such as how to educate children about sex, *Ask an Expert* offers a holistic approach to tackling some of the greatest challenges of parenting.

Ask an Expert does not set itself up as being a manual for how to be a perfect parent—it allows us to accept that it is okay to feel out-of-our depth at times and it provides support as and when we feel we need it. If you want clear, no-nonsense, easy-to-access advice then this is your book. In fact, just having it on your bookshelf will be like having a wise friend in the corner—a friend who will never tell you how to raise your children but will always be there to offer non-judgmental and rational advice and support when it is needed. Enjoy the book, enjoy your children, and most of all enjoy being a parent—these truly are the best times of our lives!

Professor Tanya Byron PhD, PsychD, MSc, BSc, Consultant Clinical Psychologist

Contents

Babies a new life

Toddlers a little person emerges

School starters out into the world

Grade schoolers their lives expand

Preteens the middle years

Teens becoming an adult

You have started out on the most exciting, yet terrifying, path of your life: Raising and nurturing your child

Introduction

Nurturing your child from birth through to independence is a task that can inspire, yet daunt, even the most confident parent. Be assured that there is no such thing as the perfect parent—you'll be the best you can be by aspiring to do your best, being well informed, and seeking help when you need it.

What does my child need from me? This is the question that lies behind and guides the parenting decisions you make. Whether you're figuring out something as general as your parenting style or as specific as how to put your baby down to sleep, how to help your child with her homework or worrying your teenager is getting into risky behavior, this is this question you'll be answering.

What you offer your child can vary depending upon her age and stage. In the earliest years, she will need you to do plenty for her, from dressing and feeding to carrying and cuddling. As she grows in independence, your role is to do less for her but teach her more, for example, guiding her to dress herself, encouraging her studies, and giving her opportunities to be make friends and socialize. As she matures, she may value information from you as well as guidance, and ultimately as a teenager it'll be listening rather than advising that is most needed, along with your trust and confidence in her. There are, however, some things your child will need from you no matter her stage of development. She needs you to hold her in mind and to be aware of her emotional, social, and physical needs, and to be her champion and advocate for her as she moves from home to school then on to work—and as she negotiates studies, friendships, and relationships along the way. She'll thrive on your warm, firm, loving style and the physical affection you offer, as well as the consistency, boundaries, and values you pass on.

To help you in your role, *Ask an Expert* spans the ages from birth to 16, with a mix of information and answers to the questions you may be curious or concerned about. This is your personal resource, supporting and guiding you to make parenting choices that suit you, your child, and your family. Whether you dip in and out or read from cover to cover, you'll be presented with information and practical ideas about raising your child to satisfy your goal to raise a happy, healthy young person.

Parenting, even when surrounded by family and friends, can be a lonely business; the responsibility lies squarely on your shoulders. Many parents wonder if they're the only ones who feel uncertain, have difficulties, or sometimes get things wrong. We believe the questions and answers you encounter in this book will give you a sense that others have faced similar issues, as you find practical solutions that have helped others get through.

The information and ideas in this book will, on many occasions, reassure you that you've got it right, confirming that your parenting decisions are well founded. At other times, you may find a different perspective on an issue, an idea you hadn't thought of, or a clearer understanding of what to do and not to do. Remember, no matter what you try, give it time to work. Few parenting strategies are effective overnight, so persist for a few weeks before you try something else. Otherwise you'll find yourself stuck in the "I've tried everything" trap before you've given each idea a chance to work.

As you read this book and decide which ideas to use, try to put yourself in your child's place. Imagine you are experiencing being parented this way. Think about how this might feel, how you'd react, and what you'd learn from it as a child. If you'd feel safe and secure, respected, treated fairly, and loved even when boundaries and consequences were applied, then you can be confident you're on the right track.

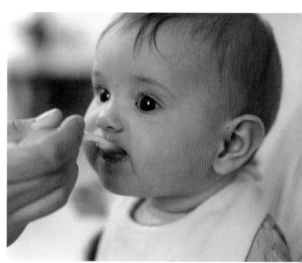

Babies
a new life

* **Welcome to the world**
  what your baby knows and feels

* **Bonding**
  your relationship from the start

* **Feeding, sleeping, and crying**
  how to raise a contented baby

* **Will we ever get better at this?**
  new parents' highs and lows

* **Early learning**
  giving my baby a good start

* **He's on the move!**
  keep him safe; let him explore

Welcome to the world
what your baby knows and feels

Q **Everyone is giving me advice about my baby. How do I tell them nicely to back off?**

When you have a new baby it seems everyone is willing to offer advice, whether you want it or not. Even complete strangers will approach you to offer their suggestions for colic, crying, and all else baby-related. There is no harm in listening to these well-meaning ideas, but don't feel under any obligation to try them out yourself. Simply smile and thank the person, then decide yourself what is best for your baby and yourself.

If the advice comes from closer to home, perhaps from your mom or best friend, it can be harder to handle. Some simple honesty should do the trick: Explain how much you appreciate their help but that sometimes, when they're giving lots of advice, it feels like they don't have confidence in you. Reassure them that you will turn to them if you have a question.

Q **I feel silly for always talking to my baby as if she understands. Am I wasting my breath?**

You may get a few funny looks while you're chatting away to your new daughter, but you're actually doing the right thing. Whether you give a running commentary about what you're doing, describe things around her, or sing a lullaby, the more your baby hears your voice, the better her ability to speak and listen in the coming years. Research has found that the babies of chatty mothers had 131 more words in their vocabulary by the age of 20 months compared to the children of quieter mothers, so all that talking really does make a difference.

You may wonder if you should be speaking in an adult tone or using the "sing-song" voice which probably comes naturally to you. Called "parentese," this is a musical way of speaking using a high-pitched tone of voice combined with strong facial expressions, long vowels, and short sentences. These features, and the repetitive nature of "parentese," promote your baby's speech more effectively than speaking in a normal adult voice. "Parentese" should not be confused with baby talk, which might substitute "woof woof" for "dog" or include nonsense words, and is less helpful for your child's developing speech.

Q **How can I take the best care of my premature baby?**

Caring for a premature baby brings feelings of love as well as mixed emotions for many parents. It's common to feel immensely grateful that your baby has survived, yet anxious about meeting any additional needs or wondering whether there will be long-term difficulties.

Keeping a watchful eye on your child's development is wise, so you'll be quick to spot any problems and get the help you need. What you'll probably find is that she'll follow the same sequence of milestones and patterns as a full-term baby and will have caught up with her peers by the time she is two if there have been no other complications. To gauge how she's doing, check her development against her corrected rather than chronological age. Her chronological age is measured from her date of birth, while her corrected age is her time since birth

> The more your baby hears your voice, the better her ability to speak and listen in the coming years

minus the number of weeks she was premature. So, at eight months old, if your child was two months premature, her corrected age would be six months, and the milestones she's achieving will be closer to those associated with the younger age.

Simply because of her prematurity, your baby may be less responsive than you'd hoped for during her first days and weeks. Her reactions will be milder when you speak to her, touch her, and feed her. This is to be expected because she's less able to see, hear, and move her body in response to you. However, she needs your input even more than a full-term baby as she has to cope with an environment that, physically, she's not quite ready for. You can help her ability to bond with you, and her development, by practicing kangaroo care (see p. 20). This involves skin-to-skin contact, usually on your chest or belly, just after the birth or within 24 hours. Ask the advice of hospital staff about having skin-to-skin contact whenever possible.

I've heard baby boys and girls differ in their development. Is this true?

There are some differences in development between boys and girls, but these tend to come out a little later, from toddlerhood onward. If you have a little boy and a girl, when you compare your children's first years you'll notice plenty of variety in their development. This is a natural result of their being two distinct individuals, rather than an effect of sex differences. Their separate personalities will make themselves felt, and they'll have their own habits and temperament, whether it's excitable, placid, alert, or easily overwhelmed. The latest evidence shows that it is largely parental expectations of boys compared to girls that affects our perception of their development. Without realizing it is happening, boys and girls are seen differently even from birth. For example, parents tend to describe girls as more delicate and boys as stronger. Any small variation in development based on sex is overridden at this early age by individual differences.

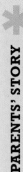

PARENTS' STORY

Baby language
learning to understand

When my son was born, I would hear his cries and feel like he was trying to tell me something but I couldn't understand what it was. It would be trial and error to figure out if he needed to be fed, go to sleep, or if something else was going on.

I tried to tune in to the different sounds he made: Sometimes he'd be howling; other times his cry was softer but still insistent. Over the first few days, to my surprise, I got much better at matching his cry with what he wanted. My confidence bounced back, and he seemed less frustrated because I wasn't changing his diaper when what he really needed was a nap.

There is one difference between boys and girls to be aware of: Researchers have found that boys are more vulnerable if there are difficulties in family life, such as parental conflict or depression. Reactions such as withdrawal, sadness, or aggressive behavior will be more marked compared to girls who tend to be less strongly affected and more resilient. It is not yet clear why this gender difference happens. But keep in mind that if you are feeling depressed or there are difficulties at home, getting help will benefit your children, especially your son, as well as yourself.

Is it better to stick to a routine or play and feed on demand?

There has been much debate among parents and childcare professionals on the topic of fixed daily regimes for babies compared to a more "play it by ear" approach where the baby sets the schedule. In reality, the ideal is a combination of routine and flexibility. Your child will thrive when he has regular but not rigid times for play, rest, visitors, bathing, and bedtime. Repeating a set sequence of events each day will give him a sense that his world is safe and predictable.

What's going on
Her brain and senses

Her brain: Your baby's brain, especially her higher brain (cortex), is developing at the fastest rate it ever will. During this period of intense activity it is using twice as much energy as it will in adulthood and by the time she is five years old, 90 percent of brain development will be complete. All this activity is not designed to increase the number of brain cells, of which there are over 100 billion, but to create the connections between cells through which information is passed and learning occurs. Your baby is born with plenty of neural cells already connected, or hard-wired, so she can perform essential tasks like turning her head, swallowing, and sucking right away. These basic survival reflexes will quickly be overridden by new neural connections, giving her increasing control over her body.

Neural connections: All that happens to your infant, everything she sees, each voice she hears or touch she feels is reflected in the firing of neurons in her brain, which in turn, forges connections between cells and creates learning. She will learn most quickly those things that are repeated often, simply because repeated use strengthens connections. When you talk and sing to her, the neural pathways for language are reinforced, giving her a head start in understanding speech and communication. Pathways that are seldom used fall away and connections can be lost. This is the brain's way of ensuring that the strongest, most effective pathways dominate. You can influence how your baby's brain develops at every moment by giving her plenty to look at, touch, and listen to in order to reinforce neural connections. When you hold her confidently, go to her as soon as she cries, and touch and speak to her with love, you are strengthening pathways in her brain which tell her she is safe and can rely on you.

Her senses: Your baby will be alert and turning toward sounds in her early days. At birth her hearing is more highly developed than her sight (for adults the opposite applies) and sight will become a more dominant sense than hearing as she grows older. She can see high-contrast items more clearly, so black-and-white toys and mobiles are good. A newborn focuses best at about 8–12 inches (20–30 cm) or so, which is exactly the distance between her face and yours if you cradle her in your arms, or when a mother breastfeeds.

At first, the pathways in her brain for different senses are not separated out. For example, when there is a loud noise she may see it as

REINFORCING: Speaking and interacting with your baby and holding her lovingly will all help to build pathways in her brain, telling her she is secure.

a disturbance of her vision as well as hear it, so it's no wonder she's easily startled. This joining of the senses is called synesthesia, meaning two or more senses are mixed—for example, hearing a sound and also seeing it as a color. It is not yet clear when the senses become separated; some say between two and four months of age, while others suggest a little later in the first year. For a tiny minority, between 1 in 100,000 and 1 in 25,000, some senses continue to be joined, and this becomes permanent.

Your baby will be born with a preference for sweet tastes over salty flavors. This hard-wired favorite is designed for survival, giving her a built-in appreciation for the sweet taste of breast milk. Her sense of smell is developing rapidly at birth. If you breastfeed, she'll be able to recognize the smell of your breast milk compared to that of another mother within a few days.

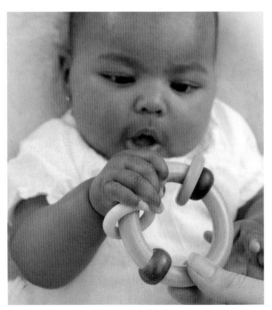

BRAIN-BUILDING: Playing with toys such as rattles helps develop neural connections, enhancing all aspects of learning, including hand–eye coordination.

It is just as vital, however, to respond to his basic needs for food, rest, and comfort immediately rather than wait until his routine tells you he should be hungry or sleepy. Reacting promptly with a cuddle or feeding tells him you are looking out for him, and that it's worth communicating with you because when he does, you "read" his cries or babbles and do something to help. Leaving babies to cry for long periods teaches them that they can't rely on the adults in their life, and also releases cortisol, a stress hormone. Prolonged exposure to this hormone in the long term can cause children to become sensitive to stress.

Recently I've noticed that the back of my baby's head has become flattened. Why is this?

What you're describing is known as Flathead Syndrome, also called Positional Plagiocephaly, which may affect up to half of children these days. This is probably the result of your baby spending a lot of time in one position, usually lying on his back. You'll be relieved to know that this difficulty does not affect the development of his brain.

You can help to relieve this flattening by increasing the time your baby spends playing on his tummy. But don't let him fall asleep like this: Babies should always be put down to sleep on their backs to reduce the risk of sudden infant death syndrome (SIDS). Try reducing his time in rigid seating, such as a car seat. When he's not traveling, take him out of his car seat or stroller and carry him in a sling, hold him on your knee, or give him tummy time. If he prefers to turn his head to one side only, try to alternate his position when you feed him or place his most interesting toys to one side to encourage turning. Special helmets or bands are available that allow a baby's skull to grow without pressure. It is not yet clear whether these help or not, but some parents say they've made a difference. For most children, the flattening eases without any treatment, especially once they're moving around. For a very few infants this flattening is a result of a more serious condition, so do consult a health professional to check this out.

Ages, stages, and milestones
What to expect

Your newborn is prepared for the most rapid period of development in her life, and you'll play a central role as caregiver and teacher. You'll also witness her growing relationships, communication, and physical development. Below are some of the milestones you can expect her to reach in the coming months.

Your newborn may...

✳ Know your voice and that of your partner and be comforted by them. She'll thrive on skin-to-skin contact with you in the hours after she is born. She may also like to be wrapped in a light, soft blanket, possibly reminding her of how warm and secure she felt curled up in the womb. If you gently stroke her cheek she'll turn toward your touch and suck if anything is put in her mouth. These reflexes help her take the breast or bottle.

✳ Focus best on objects nine inches (22.5 cm) away. This is the distance between her face and yours when you are cradling or feeding her; you're the center of her attention. She will stare intently at human faces and black-and-white pictures.

✳ Cry and make faces to communicate with you, although arm waving and kicking can also get a message across. You'll quickly tune in to her different cries, each one telling you what she needs.

✳ Appear to you to be constantly awake and feeding, but she is actually sleeping the day away; sleep experts have found that newborns need over 16 hours of sleep per day, having up to four naps and a longer sleep during the night.

In the first few weeks your infant may...

✳ Reward you with her first smile. She's becoming more mobile: She'll turn toward a noise, kick, and swipe at nearby objects—she really wants to grab those jangling rattles.

✳ Win everyone's heart by grasping their finger with her tiny hand.

✳ Show her personality: You'll know whether your baby is easy to please, excitable, or even a little grumpy. She may cry about two hours per day. Three to six weeks is her peak period for crying.

By three months your baby may...

✳ Communicate at every opportunity: She'll laugh, coo, and make expressions to tell you just how she feels. She'll cry loudly when things aren't to her liking.

✳ Love to be with you, thrive on cuddles and attention, and benefit from the predictability of a daily routine.

✳ Be motivated to reach out for her toys, especially those that make a noise. This leads to lifting her head when she's lying on her tummy.

✳ Begin to roll over in the next few months and put everything in her mouth, so child-proof your home now to safeguard your young explorer.

From six months your baby may...

✳ Want as many cuddles as ever and squeal with delight at tickles, but may occasionally push you away when she's concentrating or practicing her latest skill.

✳ Tune in to the emotions of others and respond to your tone of voice.

✳ Begin to react with distress to strangers and be soothed by your presence. This is separation anxiety, a normal phase of development which can last until your child is about three years of age. For some this will be mild while others will be more difficult to calm.

✳ Become a little chatterbox, imitating sounds and combining them, for example "ah-goo" and "ba-ba".

✳ Realize things still exist even when she can't see them. This concept, "object permanence," means that if she drops a toy and can't see it, she will search for it because she knows it is there to be found.

✱ Astound you with the speed of her physical development as she gains stability and can sit without support. She may start crawling or bottom-shuffling and will pull herself up to standing.

✱ Cry less, down to about an hour daily (usually in the evening), but more if she is overstimulated or tired.

At nine to twelve months your infant may...

✱ Move you with her first words, usually "mama" and "dada," and add gestures such as pointing and waving to her communication skills.

✱ Be curious about other babies. She'll look at them closely, but she's not ready to play with them yet. You're still the most important person in her life. She needs your touch, attention, and love as much as ever.

✱ Stand alone and side step along the furniture ("cruising"). Her increased mobility will delight her, and by 12 months she may be taking her first steps.

✱ Show off how well coordinated she is by picking up small objects between her finger and thumb.

✱ Cry if she sees others crying. She may find her own emotions overwhelming and need your calm reaction to show that strong feelings don't need to be scary.

Delayed development: There may be some clear indications that are picked up quickly by your pediatrician, but some difficulties emerge gradually. If you are unsure about your child's development, contact your doctor. Early detection and intervention are known to work best.

Consult a doctor if your child...

✱ Is having difficulty lifting her own head by three months; full head control comes later, but some control is important for many other developmental tasks.

✱ Is not sitting without support by nine months.

✱ Does not use gestures, such as pointing or waving, by 12 months.

✱ Has not progressed beyond one or two basic words by 18 months.

✱ Is not walking by 18 months.

HOLD ON TIGHT: Babies are born with a grasp reflex which they will lose as they progress on to further skills.

HANDY: Your child's coordination gradually develops so that she can pick up smaller objects.

NEARLY TODDLING: Pulling up on furniture is a sign that your baby will soon be taking his first steps.

Bonding
your relationship from the start

Where was the rush of love?

It is a common misconception that bonding always happens with an outpouring of emotion and joy as soon as your baby arrives. While many parents do have strong feelings for their baby at birth, it's just as normal for this to be a gradual process. If the attachment between you wasn't immediate, you may feel disappointed and even cheated—especially if circumstances such as exhaustion from a difficult labor or emergency treatment got in the way of your first moments. Like many parents you may find that your bond grows as you spend time with your baby, gain confidence as a parent, and get to know your newborn.

However, if you feel like you're going through the motions and not getting closer to your baby, try some ideas that are known to build closeness between parent and child. Skin-to-skin contact, baby massage, and quality time looking, talking, and touching your child can all help build up your relationship. Feelings of depression can also make you question your bond. If this is the case, seek help from a health professional, your family and friends, or a therapist as soon as possible.

My son was premature and is in an incubator. Will I miss out on the most important bonding time?

You haven't missed the boat to bond with your son—throughout his first year he'll be particularly tuned in and ready for the attachment to grow between you. Don't wait though; even while he's in the hospital neonatal unit there is plenty you can do to get close. Your touch will matter to him even if you can't hold him. Stroke, pat, or simply place your hand against his skin as much as you're allowed. Keep talking and singing; the sound of your voice will soothe and reassure him. You may have less time with your baby

than you would like, so leave a recording of your voice so he can hear you even when you're not around. Do get involved in his routine—feeding him and changing diapers are part of his daily care, and helping out will prepare you for taking him home.

If you are daunted by the busy medical environment or the equipment being used, ask the nurses to explain it all to you. They can also advise you on how to touch and care for your newborn without disturbing any tubes or devices being used.

I've heard of something called "kangaroo care" for babies. What is it and how does it help?

Skin-to-skin contact between mother and newborn, also known as "kangaroo care," means placing your baby on your chest or tummy, with skin touching, just after her birth or within 24 hours. It works best when you are feeling relaxed and hold your newborn lightly but confidently as she lies against you. Cover her back with a blanket to keep her warm. The timing of this care in the first few hours makes a positive difference to your relationship with your baby. You'll find it easier to bond, she will cry less, and it is known to make breastfeeding easier. There is no time limit for skin-to-skin contact; you and your partner can continue in the weeks to come as one of the many ways the three of you can become close.

Your newborn is ready for the most important relationship of her life, the one she shares with you

ESSENTIAL INFORMATION: BABIES

Creating a connection
Building strong bonds

The bond between you and your child can start before birth, with a rush as your baby is born, or more slowly over the first year as you get to know each other. This relationship will form the basis for her sense of security, give her the confidence to explore her world, and guide how she relates to other people throughout her life.

✱ Stay close: Keep your baby with you or your partner as much as you can after she's born. Resist sending her away to the nursery unless there is a medical reason to do so.

✱ The power of touch: At first it may seem your newborn is so small and vulnerable that she might break, but in reality she needs you to be in physical contact with her most of her waking hours. The more you touch, stroke, and get used to handling her, the more confident you'll become.

✱ Communicate: Look into her eyes, smile, talk softly, then wait to see how she responds. You'll be rewarded as she turns toward your voice. Don't worry if she doesn't seem to focus clearly on you—her eye muscles are still developing.

✱ Hold her with confidence: Your newborn has been held securely inside you for nine months and can find the open space and lack of enclosure a shock at birth. Help her feel secure by holding her close, skin to skin if you can. Try swaddling: This recreates the sensations your baby experienced in the womb. Make sure that she doesn't overheat if you swaddle her.

✱ Tune in: Learn your baby's habits, likes, and dislikes through observing her every move. You'll soon be aware of how she communicates, what soothes her, the times of day she's ready to play, and when she's at her crankiest.

SECURELY HELD: When your baby snuggles into your body and you hold her firmly against you, she feels safe and protected.

GIVE AND RECEIVE: Simple exchanges of physical affection are ways to express your growing relationship with your baby.

PRECIOUS MOMENTS: The more time you spend with your baby, the closer your bond will be. Make every minute count.

Mirroring your child's emotions

In her first year your infant will experience her feelings mainly as physical reactions in her body. You'll probably notice that when she is angry she'll look red and hot, with her face screwed up, and her hands balled closed, and she'll be waving both her arms and legs at you in frantic gestures. Your baby can easily be overwhelmed by all the physical sensations that swoop through her body when she has strong emotions such as frustration, love, dislike, and fear. It's up to you to show her that you accept her feelings, that they don't scare or overwhelm you, and that she doesn't need to feel afraid of them. You may be doing this instinctively when you mirror her emotions.

According to attachment experts, mirroring involves reflecting your child's emotions, but in a milder, less intense version. As you look at her you may also slightly tilt your head to the side, which denotes understanding. Holding her while a feeling grips her can reassure her that she is safe. Help her put a name to her feelings by talking about what is going on.

For example, when you say "You look angry" or "Is that a sad face?" you are helping her to label her emotions. You can mirror your child's emotions from birth and your steady reaction will give her confidence that feelings need not overpower her.

My baby arches away from me and is much less affectionate than I expected. Is something wrong?

Most babies love physical affection, but they can have preferences as to how they are held and touched. Try different positions—when he's alert and wants to look around, use a front baby sling so you can hold him close while he faces away from you to watch the world go by. Check your timing too; if he's awake and ready to play, a close cuddle with you won't be his first choice, so give him some time under his baby gym or playing with toys, then try again when his need to be busy has been satisfied.

It's also possible that he is reacting to a lack of confidence in the way you hold him. He'll feel safe and secure when you support his head and body well with your hands, lift him slowly without quick or jerky movements, and hold him against your body for a cuddle. If he's resisting your touch in general, try to build up his tolerance by starting small, holding his hands or feet, for instance. Once he's used to that, increase the contact to other parts of his body. This is worth addressing now, as his ability to give and receive affection throughout life can be shaped by these early experiences.

Will giving my baby a pacifier make it easier to comfort him when I leave him to go back to work?

Not all babies need or want a pacifier, whether you are returning to work or not. Some infants become very attached to a pacifier, depending on it to fall asleep or calm themselves when they're upset. Others will prefer to suck their thumb, hold a favorite blanket, chew on a soft toy, or stroke or pull at their own hair as a way to self-soothe. Before you offer the pacifier, check to see if your baby has other ways to comfort himself. If you do offer your baby a pacifier, bear in mind that speech and language therapists recommend you get rid of it when he's between eight and twelve months old. It's possible that continued use past the age of one can have a negative effect on speech development by restricting and changing the pattern of tongue movements and altering teeth positioning. Pacifiers are not recommended if you are breastfeeding, since they can cause confusion when your baby is learning to suck and reduce the time he wants to nurse.

In deciding whether or not to give your baby a pacifier, you may also want to take into consideration a small but carefully conducted study from 2005 that found that using a pacifier at night reduced infants' risk of sudden infant death syndrome (SIDS). While pacifier use did not automatically guarantee less risk, it was found to be strongly associated with a reduced chance of SIDS.

I come home tired from work every day. How can I have more energy for my partner and son?

Moving your focus from the work to the home environment can be hard, especially when there's a new baby to take into consideration. On the commute home, try to put work thoughts aside and begin to imagine your partner and your baby and what they've been doing while you were away. This means you are tuning into them in advance. Do expect to be pounced upon as you arrive home with tales of the day from your partner and an urgent need for hugs and cuddles from your baby. Remember staying home alone with a baby all day is equally, if not more, exhausting than a day at work.

The more quickly you give your attention, the more successful will be your homecoming. Young babies cannot wait while you go get a drink of water or relax; their need is immediate. Give yourself over and you may find your tiredness makes way for pleasure as you enjoy the new relationship. Make sure you choose low-key, quiet activities with him to promote the calm that is needed before bedtime. Avoid rough-and-tumble and tickling games, since they may cause your baby to become over-excited,

and he'll find it more difficult to sleep. You won't be too popular with your partner, either, if your baby's well-planned bedtime routine is spoiled.

Is a forward- or backward-facing stroller preferable?

It is common for babies to spend between 30 minutes and two hours every day in their strollers. For most children, that time is spent facing away from their caregivers. While this gives a baby a great view of his surroundings, it does limit your ability to interact with him, comment on what he is seeing, and monitor his face and body language to see if he is tired, entertained, or overstimulated. New research emerging directly links backward-facing strollers with improved communication skills. Speech and language experts recommend them, since they allow you and your child to make eye contact and speak and listen to each other while you're on the move.

It's up to you to decide on which stroller is best. Whether your baby is forward or backward facing, it's your conversation with him as you travel that makes each journey a learning and bonding experience for you both.

Too many visitors
feeling overwhelmed

PARENTS' STORY

After my baby was born I felt like an exhibit at the zoo, with well-meaning family and friends visiting in droves. My husband and I had hardly any time alone with our baby to get to know each other and start our new lives as a family of three. In the end we drew the line and gently but firmly asked people to visit during one hour a day while we got our routine figured out. Our parents were a bit disappointed but respected what we'd asked, and now, when they do come over, we're glad to have them because we get time on our own as well.

ESSENTIAL INFORMATION: BABIES

Baby massage
Beneficial for you both

Baby massage has long been associated with improved parent–child attachment. It's an activity that allows you to focus on your baby, calm her with touch, and tune in to her body language. As a bonding activity, it is ideal if you're a working parent and want to reconnect with your child.

Studies tell us that massaging babies under six months old means they cry less, sleep better, have lower levels of the stress hormone cortisol, and gain relief from colic and gas. The parent–child relationship is improved—especially if you have postpartum depression. It's suitable for premature babies too, who have been found to gain weight more quickly if they receive baby massage.

What's involved? Baby massage is essentially a simple method of touch involving smooth and gentle stroking of your infant's body. It works best if you are relaxed yourself and have the time (ten minutes is often enough) to fully concentrate. Your baby can be naked for the massage, or wear light clothes, which she may prefer if she doesn't like being undressed. She'll need a warm room and a soft mat or towel to lie on. Dim light can enhance the sense of calm. Have a diaper or cloth nearby in case of an accident during the massage. Avoid massaging within 30 minutes of a feeding, since stroking a full belly can be uncomfortable for your baby. You can be taught: Most areas have parent-and-child classes where you can learn some basic techniques. Not every infant likes baby massage. If yours doesn't, she'll let you know by turning away, squirming, or crying.

Which massage oil? Experts recommend edible, or plant-based, oils rather than those with a paraffin base. Do not use products that are likely to cause an allergic reaction or have added fragrance; edible oils such as sesame or peanut oil may not be suitable. Avoid essential oils.

STEP ONE: Lie your baby securely on your lap or a soft mat. Start with gentle strokes over his back.

STEP TWO: Move onto his limbs; stroke his hands and feet using soft yet firm pressure.

STEP THREE: Turn him onto his back and massage his chest using your fingertips.

Feeding, sleeping, and crying
how to raise a contented baby

When will my baby sleep through the night?

Like most parents, you may be eager to know when you can expect a little more nighttime sleep from your baby and for yourself. The good news: About 70 percent of babies sleep through the night by three months of age, usually lasting from their late night feeding until their next one in the early morning, giving you a precious few hour's slumber to recharge your batteries. A full night's sleep comes a little later, at about six months old, when you can expect a relatively undisturbed 10 or 12 hours of rest for your baby and yourself.

Will my little girl go to sleep more quickly if I exhaust her with play every day?

It is a common misconception that you need to wear your child out through play and activity right up to bedtime so she will fall asleep from utter exhaustion. It is worthwhile to give her plenty of playtime and stimulation during the day, but not close to bedtime. As you prepare her for sleep, your baby needs less nervous-system arousal, which means calming, quiet routines. Your aim is to have her fall asleep through increased relaxation, avoiding getting her over-excited. There is evidence that the more daylight she's exposed to, the better she'll sleep at night. It's also known that being in a natural environment improves adults' sense of well-being, so a walk in the park or playtime in the backyard will help her sleep at night and elevate your mood as well.

I can't cope with my constantly crying baby. What can I do?

A crying baby who seems inconsolable no matter what you do can stretch any parent to breaking point. Things can get especially difficult at night, when you are most tired, and you're probably conscious that other family members or neighbors might be woken by the crying. It's common to feel at these times that you're not good enough as a parent no matter how hard you've tried. Try to cast out any thoughts that you're failing, reassure yourself that you've tried every soothing trick in the book and that you couldn't do any more.

If you feel unable to continue trying to soothe your child, try passing her to someone else for a while. It often happens that a new pair of hands will be enough to calm the crying. If you don't have someone to support you at the time and must have a short rest from soothing your baby, place her safely in her crib and take a few moments to compose yourself. Have a cool drink, stand on the doorstep for some fresh air, relax your muscles by letting your shoulders droop, shake your hands and arms to release tension, or phone a parenting helpline to express how you feel. She won't come to any harm if you leave her for ten minutes or so, as long as you are close by. When you go to her again you may find she'll respond to your renewed calmness.

If the crying becomes so stressful that you fear you might shake your baby or harm her in some way, put her down in her crib and get help immediately from your partner, family, friends, or a professional. If you have to wait for help to arrive, don't leave your baby alone in the house. If she's in her crib, check regularly that she is okay.

> A crying baby who seems inconsolable can stretch anyone to breaking point

ESSENTIAL INFORMATION: BABIES

Soothing a crying baby
Why they cry and what to do

Crying is your baby's most important way of communicating with you, especially in the early days. She's trying hard to help you understand what she wants and needs. Crying tends to be at its most frequent (about two hours per day) when your infant is three to six weeks old.

Common reasons your baby cries...
* Being hungry or thirsty
* Having a wet or dirty diaper
* Being too cold or too warm
* Needing reassurance that you are around.
* Boredom and wanting to play or the opposite—being overwhelmed by too much going on
* Being overtired
* Being in pain and needing help
* Colic

If your baby is crying and you've ruled out illness, and practical solutions such as feeding, a diaper change, and more or less clothing haven't worked, then hands-on soothing strategies are the next step.

* **Hold:** Feeling securely held can be calming in itself. Position your baby firmly against your body; either in your arms, upright and supported against your shoulder, or in a baby sling.
* **Sing:** The sound of your voice is naturally soothing to your baby, so humming, singing softly, or murmuring can help reduce her state of arousal. If you speak to her, keep to a low, steady tone, rather than your usual "sing song" voice.
* **Pace:** Hold your baby close and simply pace the room. Make sure you are not too abrupt as you turn and choose a dimly-lit room with nothing else going on, particularly no TV, loud music, or other people moving around.

COMMUNICATION: When your baby cries she is trying to explain to you that all is not right in her world and she is asking for your help. It is up to you to determine what she's trying to say.

* **Wrap her up:** Swaddling your child by wrapping her firmly in a soft blanket can recreate the reassuring feeling of being held tightly that she experienced in the womb.
* **Gently rock:** Repeated, smooth rhythmic movements can have a settling effect. Keep your baby's head well supported and rock her in your arms side to side or up and down.
* **Massage:** Touch has a powerful soothing effect. Softly patting her, rubbing her back, or gently holding her hands or feet may help. Try baby massage (see p. 22) which is known to reduce episodes of crying; don't do this while she is distressed though, wait until she's calm and relaxed.

✱ Machinery: Oddly enough your baby may be calmed by the rumble of machinery, such as the washing machine, vacuum cleaner, or dryer. She may also like tape recordings of heartbeats or other rhythmic sounds. These sounds mimic the noises of your body that she heard before birth. Sounds of nature can also be soothing, such as recordings of birdsong.

✱ Take a break: It can be very distressing, not to mention exhausting, trying to soothe your crying baby. It's important to recognize your tolerance levels and seek help from your partner, family, or friends before you reach the breaking point.

✱ No relief? If your baby's cries persist no matter how hard you try to soothe her, and you judge that she is in pain that you can't relieve, seek medical help from her pediatrician.

Colic: trying to understand The specific cause of colic is not known. Experts suggest a range of explanations, from food intolerance to gas to overstimulation. Its effects are well known to many parents; up to one in five babies will go through it. Crying as a result of colic can last for several hours and is worse in the early evening. Your baby is likely to graduate from cries to screams, and her body will be involved. She may pull up her knees, clench her fists, pass gas, and show facial expressions of pain. Colic and its associated crying usually start at around two or three weeks of age and will often have abated by 12 weeks. Since a colic spell may last for hours and is difficult to soothe, it is intensely stressful for both you and your baby. To manage your colicky baby, try all the usual techniques to calm crying.

Other suggestions include laying your baby face down over your lap and gently patting her back, encouraging her to suck on the breast or bottle, and practicing baby massage when she is calm. Through trial and error you will find the combination of strategies that work best for your child. If colic seems worse in the evenings, one possibility may be overstimulation; soothing measures such as swaddling and dim lights may help, as well as a calmer daytime routine.

Getting a break from soothing your colicky baby is crucial, since coping with her distress is exhausting in itself. Be reassured that by the age of four months, very few babies still experience this condition.

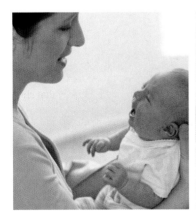

LULLABIES: Singing or speaking softly to your distressed baby may calm her, since your voice is familiar and naturally soothing.

BACK AND FORTH: Gently rocking your baby in your arms or pacing the room with her may help; she'll enjoy the rhythmical motion.

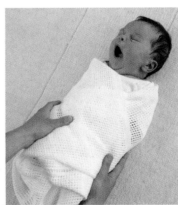

ALL WRAPPED UP: Swaddling calms and reassures many babies, because the gentle pressure recreates the feeling of being in the womb.

MYTHS AND MISCONCEPTIONS

Is it true that...

✳ **I will spoil my baby if I pick him up as soon as he cries?**
No! Your baby is crying because he needs you and his only way to call too you is to cry. When you go to him right away and wrap him in your arms, you are teaching him that he is safe and secure, that he is important to you, and that you're there for him. Studies have shown that babies who are responded to quickly when upset grow up to be happier, more confident children.

✳ **It is easier for me to hear my baby when he wakes than my partner?**
Mothers do seem to be more sensitive to their baby's cries and will wake up very quickly when the baby stirs in the night. Although you'll tend to be first to notice her, both you and your partner will feel a sense of urgency to go to your crying infant. This is specific to your child and you won't get the same sensation if you hear another baby cry.

✳ **The more babies sleep, the more they sleep?**
This is entirely true. Each time your baby successfully nods, off she is practicing how to go to sleep. Reducing or eliminating daytime naps in a desperate attempt to have your infant sleep at night only causes overtiredness which often makes sleep more difficult to achieve.

ESSENTIAL INFORMATION: BABIES

A good night's sleep
An impossible achievement?

Go to any parent-and-baby group and the most common topic of conversation is sleep—usually the lack of it. There is no doubt that the amount of sleep you get takes a dive once your baby is born. You'll be up in the night to offer feedings or comfort, and you may wake up to her every snuffle even when she remains blissfully asleep.

In her first few days, your focus will probably be on developing your confidence with your new baby, and her sleep won't be in any sort of routine. However, bright daylight and plenty of things to look at in the daytime, combined with less excitement, dimmer lights, and plenty of calming cuddles in the evening will gradually get her into a day-and-night pattern that suits family life.

When your baby is a few weeks old, you may be ready to tackle her sleep patterns. At first you can expect her to need more than 16 hours sleep per day, with up to four naps and a longer sleep during the night. By three months old she'll want about 13 hours' sleep, which includes three naps per day, reducing to two naps by about six months of age. This pattern of reducing need for sleep will continue; at one year old she'll average just under 12 hours and will need only one nap.

✱ **Read the signs:** Learn your baby's ways of showing she is tired—maybe pulling at her ear, twirling her hair, or rubbing her face. Settle her to sleep as soon as you notice these signs, before she is overtired (when getting to sleep is harder).
✱ **Get the light right:** Try for dim light and low noise where your baby sleeps. Bright light and a lot of activity will keep her awake. No noise at all, however, can be a problem, as she's more likely to be woken later when the silence is broken by other family members getting ready for bed.

✱ **Routine, routine, routine:** Follow the same pattern every night; for example, bathe then feed her before sharing a story and putting her in her crib. Always putting her to sleep in the same place will help her link this place with sleep time.
✱ **Repeat yourself:** Work out a simple bedtime message, such as "night-night, sleep well" and repeat this each time you put your baby down. This is another cue to tell her that it is time to sleep.
✱ **Touch:** Your baby may be soothed by gentle patting or stroking as she lies in her crib. Even a calm hand placed on her head or body reassures her that she's safe and can sleep.

KEEP IT THE SAME: A regular bedtime routine, at the same time every night and with calming routines, can help your baby learn the difference between night and day so she'll know it's time for sleep.

ESSENTIAL INFORMATION: BABIES

Co-sleeping
Safe for baby?

Many experts recommend that your baby sleep in your room with you for the first six months. You might want to co-sleep: to share your bed with your baby. The debate about the benefits versus dangers of this method rages among parents and professionals with pros and cons on each side. Some research suggests that you should not co-sleep with a baby of less than three months

✱ **A quiet night:** Co-sleeping can result in your baby waking less often and going back to sleep more quickly, so there may be extra rest for you.

✱ **Laid-back night feeds:** It's certainly easier to breastfeed if you are simply turning over in bed to do so, rather than getting up to your baby. You're likely to breastfeed for longer if you co-sleep.

✱ **Building bonds:** Sleeping together means more time nestled up with your baby feeling close. However, it's the love and attention you give her when she's awake that creates the

strong attachment between you, so she'll still develop her sense of security whether she sleeps snug in her crib or cozy in bed with you.

✱ **You, your partner, and your baby:** Having your baby in your bed can be an effective, if unintended, contraceptive by making sex an impossibility. Sometime or other you're going to want your physical intimacy back, and a baby in bed doesn't allow for a sex life.

✱ **Co-sleeping safety:** Some experts state it is never safe, while others offer safety guidance. Don't co-sleep if:

✱ You take medication that makes you drowsy.

✱ You smoke, even if you don't smoke in bed.

✱ You have any alcohol or drugs in your system.

✱ You are very tired or have a sleep disorder.

✱ Your baby was premature or weighed less than 5½ lbs (2.5 kg) at birth or is under three months.

✱ You're sleeping on a sofa, armchair, or waterbed.

✱ Other children share the bed with you, too.

BONDING: Babies who co-sleep have been shown to sleep better and breastfeed more. You'll appreciate the time together to reconnect with your child if you're out at work all day.

KEEP IT SAFE: If you have doubts about co-sleeping, another option is a specifically designed bassinet that attaches to the side of the bed, or a regular bassinet elsewhere in your room.

Q Will using cloth diapers mean my baby is more likely to wake up when she wets in the night?

Sometimes it can be a hard decision to balance what's best for the environment with the need to keep your baby undisturbed by dampness in the night. However, don't dismiss cloth diapers as a nighttime option as they've evolved considerably since the terry square and safety pin design. Pocket diapers, which contain absorbent inserts, can work well at night as padding can be added and they do move liquids away from your baby's skin to avoid the sensation of wetness.

However, no matter which diaper you choose you're likely to have to change your infant at least once a night in the early months. Minimize disruption by laying out all that you'll need before she goes off to sleep, have a night light to illuminate the task, and avoid turning on the main light which can wake your baby further. Work calmly and confidently and she may hardly rouse as you change her.

Q I'm concerned my baby will wake my other children when she cries in the night. Am I worrying needlessly?

It's true that your children may have their routine and even their sleep disturbed occasionally by your new arrival. Minimize disruption by maintaining your older children's existing bedtime and wind down routine. Perhaps you could enlist your partner or a family member to help with the baby while you put the others to bed. Unlike adults, your children will usually enter a phase of deep sleep soon after falling asleep. This will last a couple of hours and is achieved again during the hour or two before waking in the morning. During these periods of deep sleep, your children are unlikely to be roused by your baby, or anything else for that matter. In the middle of the night there will be times of lighter sleep and a noisy baby may be a problem at first. However, children should soon become accustomed to new nighttime noises and are less likely to be woken once these become familiar sounds.

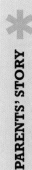

PARENTS' STORY

* Well fed
how to tell if it's enough

I breastfed my baby and constantly wondered if I was giving her enough to drink. I was always envious of bottle-feeding moms who could tell you exactly how many fluid ounces their baby had each time. I worked out in the end how to gauge it for myself. I kept an eye on her diapers to check she was having enough wet ones each day. If she had five or six wet diapers a day and her urine was pale yellow, she was getting enough to drink but if it was less or her urine was dark, then I needed to breastfeed her more often.

Q Should I breast- or bottle-feed?

The bonding and nutritional benefits of breastfeeding are well documented, and it's a good option if you feel you can do it. It is not always an easy choice: Some mothers' initial attempts to breastfeed are so painful or nonproductive that bottle feeding is introduced. For others, the prospect of being watched while feeding is off-putting, while in some families it is discouraged so that others can share in feedings

Feeding your baby is a special quiet time when you can hold her close, make eye contact, gently caress her, and relax as she lies in your arms. Breastfeeding mothers can make the most of skin-to-skin contact too. If you are bottle-feeding, make sure that all, or almost all, bottles are given by you or your partner in the first few weeks. If other adults are feeding your baby, too, she'll miss out on this prime bonding time with the two of you.

Whether you breast- or bottle-feed, dads can get involved. Expressed breast milk allows dads to play a role. Picking up some night feedings can be especially helpful to the mother. Bottle-fed babies get the benefit of being held close by both parents, which can even out the balance of the baby's experience of both caregivers.

Your breast milk is made specifically for your baby. It transfers your antibodies to fight disease, and provides all the nutrition your baby needs up to the age of six months. Formula is also designed to provide a good nutritional balance, as long as it is prepared exactly as described on the packaging. Do not add any other ingredients or use cow's milk in your baby's first year.

What are the challenges for breastfeeding mothers?

Breaking a family tradition of bottle-feeding may be one of the challenges you face as a new parent. You may have little support from family members if no one else has breastfed and they can't offer advice on the best methods. There may even be resentment for keeping the feeding to yourself when others are eager to enjoy the closeness of offering a bottle. It will take plenty of resolve to resist these pressures. Support from your partner is crucial: When they take a role in defending your decision to breastfeed and responding to pressure to bottle-feed, you can concentrate on the important task of feeding itself.

PARENTS' STORY

Bottle-feeding
fighting disapproval

I feel so judged by other parents for bottle-feeding my baby. Some mothers, and even some health professionals, tell me breastfeeding is better or imply I could have tried harder before switching to the bottle. I do wish I had breastfed for longer than six weeks, but it simply proved too painful, and my baby was constantly hungry. I'm lucky that I had a supportive pediatrician, she did want me to continue to breastfeed, but gave me good advice when I made the decision to change. She reminded me to be sure to hold my baby while I bottle-fed, to make the most of that time to bond, and to limit the number of others who wielded the bottle.

> Your breastmilk is made specifically for your baby and transfers your antibodies to fight disease

Breastfeeding can be an immensely satisfying experience, but it does entail giving yourself over to your baby, which may lead to the feeling that your body is not your own. At these moments, your consolation can be in knowing you are giving your baby the best nutritional start in life, that each feeding gives you the skin-to-skin contact that enhances bonding, and that breastfeeding can help you lose your baby weight.

When should I wean?

Breastmilk or formula should meet your baby's nutritional needs until he's six months old. Weaning used to be recommended earlier, but the prevailing opinion is now that solids should not be given before your baby is four months old, since the digestive and immune system is not yet fully ready.

When you introduce solid food, expect a mess. Your baby will want to squish it, spread it, and, if you're lucky, get it into his mouth. He's exploring new textures, so let him experiment and keep a damp cloth handy for clean-up. And expect some tears and refusals. The feel of the food on his tongue will be different from the smooth sensation of milk, and since he's used to a steady flow of fluid, he may be surprised at the gap between spoonfuls of solid food.

Do go at his pace and never force-feed him. If he's becoming unhappy, stop and try again next time. That way he will come to see mealtimes as a pleasure rather than an ordeal. Don't give up on a new taste; even if he rejects something, try again next time. It takes at least ten tries before a new food becomes familiar, so perseverance is the key. Always stay with your child while he is eating.

Will we ever get better at this?
new parents' highs and lows

Q My baby seems to cry all the time—I feel completely useless. Why can't I get anything right?

New parents tend to set such high expectations for themselves that, unless everything is going perfectly well all of the time, they feel as if they are failing in their role at some time or other. It's very easy to criticize and blame yourself, particularly if you are not getting much sleep and are at home alone with your child all day. The truth is that you are doing all you can, and this is just a phase. Spending time with other parents will help you see that you are not alone in how you feel and give you the opportunity to share hints and tips, and talk about the difficult times, too. Speak to your pediatrician to find out what parent-and-baby groups are available locally. Learning to do baby massage may also help to relax your baby and improve her sleep—and yours. If there are no suitable groups available in your area, you could always consider starting your own. If groups are not for you or it's difficult to get out and about, and you have access to the internet, try logging on to the discussion forums hosted by many parenting websites, or start your own blog on a social networking site. No one gets everything right all the time—aim to do your best, ask for help when you need it, and you will be good enough.

Q I love my baby, but she's taken over everything. When will I get my life back again?

A new baby impacts hugely on your life. You undergo changes on a physical, emotional, and practical level. After giving birth, your hormones are fluctuating as your body tries to recover, which can cause all sorts of emotional upheavals. At the same time, you and your partner are striving to find a balance between the joys of becoming new parents and the responsibilities of caring for your newborn. It is, therefore, not unusual to feel overwhelmed, anxious or even distressed at times. You might feel like you're losing all sense of self as your priorities change and you spend every hour dealing with the demands of your newborn. Those on maternity leave may feel totally removed from their previous lifestyle as a career woman. A small number of women (and men) may slip into postpartum depression, in which case it is advisable to seek professional help. The first few months are the most taxing. You may not have the time, energy, or motivation to pursue the same activities that you did before becoming parents. This is a time when you should be able to count on the support of family, friends, and, of course, each other. As your baby grows and your relationship develops, you will gain confidence in your new role and begin to see the opportunities that parenthood opens up, such as making friends with other new parents. It will eventually feel perfectly natural to think of yourself as a parent, and this new identity will become a part of the person you were before childbirth, adding to your sense of self.

Q My relatives keep interfering. How can we explain to them that we want to do it our way?

It's only natural that family members want to help by offering the fruits of their experience. However, even when given with good intentions, advice can conflict with your own attitudes, or sound confusing and even overbearing. However, it is important to keep the family peace, and avoid the risk of upsetting relatives by brashly rejecting their pearls of wisdom. First, agree with your partner how you are going to approach the important issues, then present a united front and discuss your plans with family. If you want advice, try saying, "What are your thoughts on…?"

ESSENTIAL INFORMATION: BABIES

Involving dads
Creating a partnership

Ideas about a father's role in the family have changed a lot over recent years: Many men now feel that it is important for them to be equally involved in day-to-day childcare tasks. Becoming a father is one of the most exciting and life-changing events in any man's life.

What are the benefits? Research suggests that, over time, children with involved fathers tend to have better emotional health, perform better at school, engage in less anti-social behavior, and have more successful relationships. With your support, your partner will benefit from being able to take a well-earned break; she is also less likely to suffer from postpartum depression, and may be more successful at breastfeeding. You will build a stronger, closer relationship with your baby, improve your childcare skills, gain confidence, and experience a greater sense of satisfaction with your parenting role. Successful parenting is a partnership, and sharing the workload—in whichever way you choose—will help to maintain a strong relationship and keep stress levels down.

What can I do? As a new dad, you can engage in any of the childcare tasks except breastfeeding, and even then you could get your partner to express her milk so you can feed your baby with a bottle. Examples of things you could do include: feeding, bathing, changing diapers, putting your baby to bed, helping out with the night shift, and entertaining and playing with your baby. A father can be just as sensitive to his baby's cries and needs as its mother. In fact, dads may find it easier to soothe a breastfed baby, since they won't have the distracting smell of breast milk around them.

Read a babycare book, so you're up to speed with all the latest guidance. If your partner won't let you help out at first, talk to her and negotiate to find ways in which you can support her.

FAR LEFT: Feeding your baby with expressed breast milk or formula is great for bonding and can give your partner a break when she needs to rest.
TOP RIGHT: Bathtime can be fun for you and your baby. The more time you spend handling and interacting with your child, the more confident you will become, and your child will feel secure, too.
BOTTOM RIGHT: Learning to change a diaper takes a little practice, but it's an essential childcare skill.

rather than, "What do you think we should do about...?" This approach will ease the pressure and lead to a discussion where you can open up a conversation about how parenting practices have changed. You could mention key differences in modern babycare, for example putting babies to sleep on their backs, when to wean, and the potential harm of leaving a baby to cry it out. It will reassure them that you are being thoughtful and responsible, and that you are not rejecting them, despite disagreeing with some of their ideas.

Finally, expect to make mistakes—being a parent is not about getting everything right the first time.

I feel scared to take my baby out for the first time. Is this normal?

Leaving the safety and security of your home for the first time can be a daunting experience when you consider that you've been confined to the four walls of your house since your baby's arrival. However, going out can really lift your mood, and will help structure your day by giving you something to focus on. Your baby will delight in the stimulation provided by new sights, sounds, and smells.

Keep your journeys simple at first; maybe start off with a short walk, increasing the distance as your confidence grows. Remember that as you travel further from home, you will need to take more equipment with you, so plan in advance to ensure you have everything you need.

Why haven't we had sex since our baby was born?

Lots of couples find that it can take time for them to resume their sex life after the birth of their child. This does not mean that the relationship is breaking down, just that both parties are under considerable pressure and having to adjust to life with the new addition. After carrying a child and then giving birth, women often feel self-conscious about their changed bodies and not particularly sexy. They might be feeling overweight and unattractive, so their partners will need to be complimentary and help to rebuild their confidence. There also may be pain and soreness due to stitches. Women who are breastfeeding may not want their partner to touch their breasts, especially if their nipples are sensitive or because they may leak. Sleep deprivation is common, which doesn't help. Some couples are uncomfortable with the idea of having sex in the same room as their baby (in which case the obvious solution is to have sex elsewhere). There is also evidence to suggest that fatherhood decreases testosterone levels and raises prolactin levels to help with the bonding process, so a new father may experience a fall in libido due to hormones. The issues could be myriad, but whatever they are, it is important that you talk to each other about your concerns, how you feel and what you want from each other. If one of you, or neither of you are ready for sex yet, make time to be intimate in different ways: Enjoy time alone, find a few quiet moments to talk and be affectionate with each other by holding hands, kissing, or cuddling on the sofa. You can have sex whenever you feel ready, but some women prefer to wait until the postpartum checkup at around six weeks to make sure everything has healed.

PARENTS' STORY

Making new friends
avoiding isolation

When my husband went back to work after our little girl was born, I was really happy to be staying at home. However, I began to feel more and more isolated and cut off from the world, and things really started getting me down. I knew there was a woman nearby who had also had a baby around the same time as me, and I really wanted someone to talk to during the day but just could not pluck up the courage to say "Hello!" One day I decided to go for it and stopped to speak as our paths crossed in the street. Now we meet up regularly for coffee, a chat, or a walk in the park. It's amazing what a difference it's made to how I feel, and my daughter seems happier too.

ESSENTIAL INFORMATION: BABIES

Baby blues & postpartum depression
Why am I upset?

Your baby has just arrived, and you're feeling on top of the world. So why are you crying? You are simply at the mercy of your hormones as they adjust. Like the majority of new moms, you're going through a tearful phase and may feel overwhelmed by the thought of your new responsibilities as a parent. But be reassured, this is known as the "baby blues" and happens to most mothers about three days after the birth, as hormonal changes wreak havoc on your emotions. It should ease within two weeks, but if you continue to feel upset, you may be experiencing postpartum depression.

Postpartum depression Feeling distressed as the weeks go by, having a sense that other mothers can cope but you can't, or feeling low during your baby's first year means you may be experiencing postpartum depression. This can continue from a few weeks to several months, but getting professional help will shorten the time you feel depressed and make your recovery smoother.

You may be feeling:
* Exhausted even when you've just woken up.
* Empty, sad, and tearful often.
* Guilty and ashamed that you're not happy or that you don't love your baby enough.
* Anxious for yourself or fearful for your baby.
* Scared of being alone or going out.
* Irritable, angry, and agitated.

Who gets postpartum depression? You may think you're the only one feeling this way, but it's not true. One or two mothers in 10 will go through postpartum depression. You're more likely to suffer if you've been depressed before or had a stressful pregnancy or labor. Seek help from the following:

DON'T SUFFER ALONE: Postpartum depression can get in the way of your relationship with your baby and your partner. Ask for help as soon as you can.

Health professionals: Your pediatrician will ask you how you are feeling at your well-child check-ups—speak openly about your emotions and fears. Your doctors are trained to recognize postpartum depression and know how to get you help; they may link you into local services to support new parents. Your doctor may also recommend that you take medication such as antidepressants, and will need to know if you're breastfeeding in order to choose the best ones to suit you and ensure that the medicine does not affect your baby. He or she may also recommend you attend some psychological therapy. This usually involves meeting one on one, or in a small group with other new moms, with a qualified psychologist or counselor who will try to help you understand why you are feeling this way.

Wider family and friends: These people can support you by listening to your worries. Let them know you simply need to talk, and ask them to avoid treating your concerns as trivial—this can become frustrating when it doesn't match how you feel at that time. They could also help you make and get to appointments with doctors and assist with day-to-day tasks such as shopping and cleaning. Helpful relatives may be tempted to take over the care of your baby to give you a break. However, this can deepen your sense that you're not good enough as a parent, so ask them to keep you company and help with practical tasks rather than whisk your baby away.

Your partner: As well as offering you love and commitment, a partner can care for your baby while you take a little time to care for yourself. Partners: Remember that depression is an illness and people can't just "snap out of it." If others are likely to take this view, you can help by defending your partner from such unwanted and unsympathetic "advice."

Different types of therapy: Your doctor may recommend that you attend some psychological therapy. Cognitive behavioral therapy (CBT) or interpersonal psychotherapy (IPT) are common approaches. These usually involve meeting one on one with a qualified psychologist or therapist about once a week. Appointments are usually held in private at a doctor's office, since it is easier to speak openly away from the usual interruptions of home life. Another option is to have non-directive or listening support from a counselor who will encourage you to talk and help you express yourself. This can happen at a clinic or in your home if you prefer. This is an opportunity for you to explore any worries that come to mind.

What does each therapy offer?
✱ **CBT** is based on the idea that how a person thinks affects her emotional reactions. It aims to help people challenge their current thinking patterns, therefore altering how they feel and behave. It is often effective after four to six meetings.

✱ **IPT** focuses on the relationships in a person's life, and is based on the belief that social context can affect psychological difficulties, so working with people on their history and interpersonal skills will assist their recovery. The exact length of treatment varies from person to person.

✱ **Non-directive therapy** (also known as client-centered or Rogerian therapy) is based on the premise that through exploring your thoughts and feelings with a warm and empathic listener, you can understand and resolve your difficulties. Little advice or direction is given during this therapy, and it is your choice what areas you consider. The length of treatment varies considerably; when to finish is a personal decision.

GET ENOUGH REST: Let your partner, or friends and family help out while you recover from the strain of giving birth. Getting enough sleep will help your body and hormones recover more quickly.
SYMPATHETIC EAR: Talking to a counselor or therapist is an effective way of tackling depression. Look for state licenses or certification when choosing your listener during this challenging time.

Q I've been feeling miserable since my baby was born. Can men get postnatal depression too?

Taking on the responsibilities of caring for a baby, changes in your relationship with your partner, dealing with the added financial pressures, and going out to work each day feeling exhausted from a lack of sleep are all bound to take their toll on you physically and emotionally, so it's perfectly reasonable to be feeling at a low ebb during this time.

If you find yourself increasingly tired, upset, hostile, and unable to cope, it is possible that you may be experiencing depression. Opinion is divided as to whether or not this should be called postnatal depression but research indicates that between five and 10 per cent of dads feel this way. If you are a first-time father, are not getting along with your partner, or are unemployed, you are more likely to get depression. If your partner is suffering from depression it also increases the chances since human beings tend to synchronize their emotions. Depression left untreated can have a harmful impact on your relationship with your partner, your career, and how you bond with your child. Don't ignore your feelings or hide them from your partner. Talk about it and, if the problem persists, seek professional help. Make an appointment with your doctor or an accredited counsellor and address the issue head on.

Q Since the baby's arrival there seems to be no time for our relationship. What can we do?

In the first few months it is fairly typical for new parents to find that caring for their new baby leaves little time for anything else and the relationship can become neglected. However, as routines become established and you both become more confident and skilled in your parenting roles, it should be possible to reclaim a little time for yourselves. It is important to keep your relationship on a strong footing, not only for your own wellbeing but also because your child will pick up on any tensions between you. Remember that you are partners as well as parents so make time to talk to each other

daily and try to get out on your own as a couple – go to the cinema, for a walk, or out for a meal. Staying indoors is certainly easier but there's always something to do around the house, the baby is nearby, and it is difficult to switch off. What's more, family and friends will appreciate the opportunity to help out by babysitting so take full advantage – go out and try to rekindle the things that brought you together in the first place.

Q I've heard about postnatal psychosis. Am I likely to get it?

Only a very small number of women, about one to three in 1,000, may develop this condition. It occurs within about a week of their baby being born. As well as being severely depressed, symptoms may include delusions (believing everyone is conspiring against them or thinking that they or others are possessed), hallucinations (seeing and hearing things that are not there), and being unable to think clearly. In some cases the mother may reject her baby. Up to 65 per cent of women who suffer from postnatal psychosis have a family history of severe depression. This condition is usually treated with antidepressants or anti-psychotics. With medication and counselling, for example cognitive behavioural therapy, the psychosis can usually be treated in a few weeks. For some women psychosis can recur after another pregnancy. However, 70 per cent of women will be fine the next time round.

Q I am constantly worried that my baby is not developing as she should. Am I being over-anxious?

Almost every parent asks themselves "Is my baby okay, are they developing normally?" This is a hard question to answer as there are wide variations as to when individual babies achieve each milestone. In some cases missing out a stage is not of concern. For example, some babies shuffle on their bottoms, rather than crawl, with no ill effects. One way to avoid anxiety is to check your child's age and stage in child development books. It is natural to compare her to other children of her age but, if you do so,

Keepsakes: creating memories

When you are wrapped up in the day-to-day demands of caring for your baby and every new experience seems special and important, you think that you will never forget these times. However, children grow and develop so fast that, unless you take the time to record things in some way, you are unlikely to remember every detail. A little effort now will bring you and your family endless pleasure for years to come.

✱ Buy a quality newspaper to show what was happening in the world when your child was born.

✱ Write down your birth story.

✱ Buy the number one single/album in the charts.

✱ Keep small mementos, for example, your baby's first outfit, a lock of hair, a selection of greeting cards, but be sensible—you cannot keep everything!

✱ Keep a baby book or simply take a few minutes to write down what your baby is doing, how you feel, and how you are spending your days—it's these little things that you will forget.

✱ Take plenty of photos and videos. Digital photos have a number of advantages: They save you time and money in processing, you can email them to friends and family, and you can date-stamp them so you know exactly how old your baby was at the time.

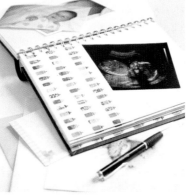

PRECIOUS REMINDERS: When things are not going as well as you hoped, looking at your keepsakes and reminders will help you appreciate how far you've come as a family and how much you have achieved as parents. Keepsakes can help you realize that some of the worst times are really just very short phases. They may also be fascinating to your children when they are older.

remember that normal development covers a wide spectrum, and there is much natural variation. If you have checked her milestones and do believe that there is something to worry about, talk it over with others to see if they have the same concern. If they've noticed delays, too, then make an appointment with a qualified health professional right away to check this out. Fear of being labeled overanxious might hold you back from raising these important questions. However, it is part of your job as a parent to be cautious about your baby's health and development, and to speak up for her so she gets all the help she needs. The sooner you obtain assistance the better;

intervening early is known to get the best results. Whether your concern is confirmed or not, it will always be helpful to stimulate your child's development. Give her playtime in different positions; on her tummy, in your arms, and on her back. Present her with interesting, noisy toys to listen to and reach out for to promote coordination and body control. Encourage speech by chatting and storytelling.

When you notice and respond to her babbles, smiles, and first words, you're helping her learn the two-way nature of communication, while at the same time strengthening her bond with you.

Early learning
giving my baby a good start

Q Sometimes my baby cries and turns away when I give him a toy. What does this mean?

Timing is everything when you introduce a new toy or game. If your baby is ready to sleep or has been playing for a while, a new activity is likely to be overstimulating, and he may cry and turn away rather than play. Don't be disheartened; simply wait until he's well rested and gently introduce the item again later.

Take it slowly when you bring a toy into view. If you move something noisy or colorful too quickly into his line of sight or place a bright mobile very abruptly overhead, your baby could be startled and upset. Just imagine if something half the size of your body was suddenly put within a few inches in front of your face, and you'll understand how he feels!

Q I have less time to spend with my baby because I work. Will this affect her development?

There is much debate about whether it is the quality or the quantity of parent–child time that is important to your baby's development. The answer is simple: Your baby both needs intense periods of playtime with you, and will appreciate simply snuggling up doing very little, or watching you as you go about your chores. It is only if you find yourself at one extreme or the other—avoiding interacting with her, or being a slave to stimulating her every moment of the day—that you need to review the situation and adjust the balance.

You can make the most of your time together by concentrating on what your baby is doing. Research tells us that, during playtime with your baby, she will benefit most when you are focused on her rather than trying to do two things at once. For example, if you are joining in with her activity but watching TV over her shoulder or chatting on the phone, her play will be less complex and she'll be aware that your attention is not wholly on her. One technique to keep you "in the moment" with your child is to give a running commentary of what she is doing. This simply involves describing, rather than making suggestions—for example, saying, "Oh, you're putting the cars on the mat" but avoiding prompts like "Why don't you line the cars up over there?" This way she is leading her own activity but is fully aware that you're with her as she does so.

Q My baby hates bathtime. How can I make it fun?

Often bathtime distress is related to the sensation of being undressed, feeling a little cold, or having a sense of falling or being out of contact with you as he is placed into the water. Increase his confidence by keeping him wrapped up until you've got everything ready for his bath and making sure the room is warm. Undress him quickly and calmly, and hold him firmly as you put him in the water. If he cries, hold him close and keep talking in a slow and soothing tone. You can also try getting in the bathtub yourself, with your baby on your lap. If bathtimes are very stressful, reduce them to once every two days and "top and tail" your baby in between. Don't give up: As he develops more control over his body, he'll feel safer in the bath and may grow to tolerate (if not enjoy) the experience. From the age of three months onward,

> You are your child's favorite playmate—she delights in your attention

ESSENTIAL INFORMATION: BABIES

Communicating with your child
What about "baby signing"?

Learning to communicate is a complex and exciting process which progresses at great speed throughout your baby's first year. You'll experience highs and lows, the elation as she offers her first smile and the frustration of trying to correctly interpret her cries. It's no wonder, therefore, that baby signing, also known as symbolic gesturing, has been so popular in recent years as its proponents promise easier communication with your baby.

What is baby signing? Baby signs are based on a system of sign language developed originally to assist communication when people suffer deafness or, in some cases, learning difficulties. In baby signing, these have been adapted into a program of hand movements specifically for babies, each gesture representing a word or idea.

Baby-signing practitioners suggest starting to teach your baby at around six months of age. Classes, DVDs, and books are available to help you learn this method. Baby-signing practitioners report that the program allows babies to express themselves earlier than they otherwise would, and to experience less frustration. For example, she will be able to tell you she wants a drink by giving you the sign for "milk."

Is it really necessary? There is great debate about the value of baby signing. Gestures, facial expressions, and speech are a crucial part of any parent–child interaction and occur naturally in the communication process. Replacing them or focusing a lot of attention on a system which concentrates closely on hand movements is of concern to a significant group of speech and language therapists. Many recommend that the frequent use of natural gestures and quality interaction is best for language development.

If your child is at risk for delayed speech and language development, for example as a result of hearing or other difficulties, then sign language can be a valuable addition to her care. Discuss this with your speech and language professional.

What to do? Your most important tool in the development of your baby's communication skills is your own frequent interaction with her, using eye contact, gestures, touch, speech, and song to encourage and teach. It is up to you whether you choose to add baby signing to the range of skills you teach your baby. If you do try this system, include it as an additional area of learning.

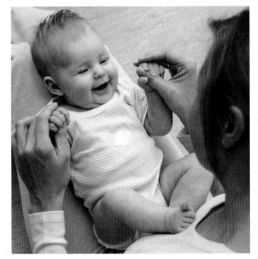

TALKING TO YOUR BABY: Gestures, facial expressions, and verbal communication are all part of the two-way conversation with your infant. Baby signing can add to this, rather than replace it.

ESSENTIAL INFORMATION: BABIES

Best toys for babies
Helping your child develop

When your baby is born, you're on a learning curve like no other. Alongside the focus on feeding and sleeping, you may also be wondering what she needs to learn and develop well.

Toys to cuddle: Every baby needs plenty of cuddles from you and they'll love the comfort of a small soft toy, too. Cloth animals that are easy to grab, suck, and chew make ideal comfort toys for your baby. For safety's sake check that any soft toys are suitable for newborns, and don't overwhelm your child with too many.

Toys to make noise: Mobiles, musical toys, and rattles are great for getting your baby's attention. Shaking a rattle to one side teaches her to turn her eyes and body to find things. Mobiles overhead motivate a young baby to reach up and practice coordinating her movements.

Reading: Speaking to your baby frequently promotes language development and gives a sense of closeness as you cuddle up for stories. As soon as your baby is born, you can begin reading or telling her stories about her environment and family. Begin your baby's love affair with books by giving her cloth books from her earliest weeks, and board books during her first year. Don't worry if books are scrunched and chewed at first; this is normal.

Playmates: It is too early for your baby to be interested in playing with other babies, but she'll adore having you to play with. You hold a powerful interest for her, and your attention, interaction, and playfulness will be her delight. Whether you use rhymes like "Mary Had a Little Lamb," make a game out of picking up the toys she's thrown out of the stroller, or read to her at bedtime, you will be her favorite playmate.

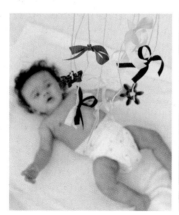

LOOKING UP: Looking at a brightly colored mobile will help your young baby focus and encourage her to reach up and swipe.

ALL ABOUT BOOKS: Reading to your child helps develop language skills, and is also good for bonding as you cuddle up together.

COMFORT: A soft toy may be used as a security object, providing comfort and soothing when you're not around.

Positions: Your baby will enjoy playing from all sorts of different positions—being held in your arms, on a rug on her tummy, lying on her back, or in a bouncy chair. Each position allows her to practice using her body differently as she plays. From five months, play a game of rolling around on the floor (on a rug or carpet) to strengthen her body in preparation for crawling.

Games: Your baby at a few months old will love playing games such as peek-a-boo with you. Try draping different fabrics on her body or gently on her face for her to pull off, and see her delighted reaction as you come back into view. Once she can sit, games such as rolling a ball to her and getting her to roll it back teach simple turn-taking.

Bold and beautiful: In her early weeks, your baby's sight is fuzzy, so she will prefer high-contrast, bold, black-and-white designs on mobiles and in books. She'll like looking at human faces, since the visual pathways in her brain respond well to strong patterns. She's primed to prefer faces over other images.

INTERACTION: Playing games such as peek-a-boo will help your baby understand concepts such as object permanence, which means understanding that objects remain in place even when hidden.

you might bring a playful element into bathing by introducing some water toys. Start with simple plastic ducks and floating toys that are suitable and safe for his age. From six months old, add plastic cups for filling and pouring. Children tend to love containers with holes, such as those used for packing berries, because they empty out in an interesting fashion.

Remember: Never leave your infant alone in the bath for even a moment. A baby can drown in under a minute, and in less than an inch (2.5 cm) of water.

Q Can I turn my baby into a genius through extra play?

You can certainly help your baby develop by providing him with plenty of age-appropriate toys and activities, and by speaking and singing to him. Remember that much of what he can achieve in his first year is dependent on the gradual acquisition of skills, such as physical coordination. For example, while you can stimulate reaching and grasping by supplying plenty of attractive toys, your infant must have gained voluntary control over his arms to make the most of this activity. Overstimulating your child—by presenting him with things to see and do when he is tired or needs comfort—can lead to distress. Wait for your baby's signs that he wants to play, and then he'll make the most of the toys and activities you offer. As your baby grows, he'll be able to stay awake and concentrate for longer periods, so be realistic about what you can do with him at first. A newborn can only maintain the alert state that is ideal for learning for about 30 minutes at a time between sleeping and feeding. The range of educational material available for babies, such as training DVDs and baby flash cards may give you a sense that traditional play isn't enough to give your child a head start. Research suggests otherwise. It has been found that infants presented with baby-training DVDs have ten percent fewer words in their vocabulary than those who don't watch this material. Watching a screen is a very passive exercise: It is your time, attention, and a wide variety of play, speech, and stimulation, given without pressure to perform and achieve, that creates the best start for your infant.

He's on the move!
keep him safe; let him explore

Q My baby is crawling everywhere. Should I be worried about hygiene?

When your child is on the move and putting everything he finds into his mouth, hygiene can be quite a challenge. It is best to try to prevent him from putting leaves and dirt into his mouth, especially in the playground or park. At home, as long as you keep your floors moderately clean, a little bit of dirt will not hurt him and can actually help to build up immunity against infection. In fact, according to the latest research, though your baby may have a few more colds now than his peers living in spotless environments, he may be less likely to suffer chronic problems with asthma and allergies later in life. This has become known as the "hygiene hypothesis." Try to use safe cleaning fluids rather than toxic bleaches. If you are worried, rather than denying your child the freedom to roam and explore for fear of getting dirty, make a play space by covering the floor or ground with a large blanket. This will give you peace of mind when you cannot be sure the surface is clean enough.

Q My son has a never-ending curiosity, but I've run out of suitable, safe play ideas. Any tips?

Your son's desire to be "into everything" allows him to build up knowledge and experience of the world. Encourage curiosity by creating your own treasure basket, such as a plastic bowl or soft drawstring bag, filled with household objects of different shapes and textures. Include objects such as a wooden spoon, a lemon or orange, plastic containers, some different fabrics, and some noisy toys such as rattles. Change the items regularly to keep his interest. Another favorite, once your baby is mobile, is to let him explore one of the kitchen cupboards. Pile it full of plasticware such as containers, tumblers, and mixing spoons, and let

him pull everything out. You might label it "his" cupboard to prevent him learning that all the kitchen cupboards are for him to play with. Remember, he will be putting everything in his mouth to taste and feel, so supervise him at all times and don't include anything sharp, with rough edges, or small enough to cause choking.

Q Can I take my young baby to the local swimming pool?

Babies have a built-in affinity with water, and introducing her to a swimming pool can be a safe, stimulating experience. Stick to the baby/toddler areas, which are usually warm and shallow and not too loud and splashy. Bringing along a familiar bath toy may help make the transition from bath to pool. Start with shortish periods of time (20 minutes) and build your time up gradually, always ensuring that your baby is not getting cold or tired. Allow her to enjoy her natural confidence in the water while holding her securely. If you can be calm and confident, she will have a wonderful time. If you are unsure of water and swimming yourself, try joining a moms and babies swimming course to help you manage your own anxieties.

Q Do children and pets mix?

If you already have a pet before you have your baby, you have to think carefully about the needs of both and be prepared for your pet to feel a bit neglected. This can mean that a dependable family dog can behave in uncharacteristic ways, including being aggressive. This is rare, but it is essential that you never leave your baby alone with a pet. If you have a choice, it is probably better to wait a while before getting a pet, until your toddler is steady on her feet, and not putting everything in her mouth. Pets do present a wonderful opportunity to teach your child about kindness, gentleness, and

Safety-consciousness or overprotection?

Helping your child feel safe and secure and, as a consequence, facilitating his easy development toward independence, is a step-by-step process. His early fears of being left alone, of strangers and of the unknown, engender great distress. Your role as parent is to comfort and diminish the enormity of the fears. In the case of being left or separation anxiety, you say, "I was just in the other room, I wouldn't leave you" and make sure that you're true to your word. His distress will gradually disappear, and soon he'll learn to trust that you will return and happily be able to function in your absence. As he grows into toddlerhood and beyond, your explanation of things such as loud noises or looming shadows will help him learn to contain his fear, increasing his confidence and allowing him to explore his world with impunity.

COMFORT ZONE: Your child will use you as a base to explore from. A "securely attached" child (meaning she has strong bonds with you) will find this easier and be more willing to leave your side.
KEEPING AN EYE OUT: Close supervision around potential dangers, such as stairs, is needed since your child will be quick to explore.

caring for others. Even babies need to learn not to pull tails or interfere with feeding time. Teach them caution around animals, especially unfamiliar dogs. Don't let animals lick your baby's face, and protect her against the possibility of dog and cat feces being passed from hands to mouths to prevent dangerous infections.

How can I teach my child about safety without frightening him?

It is never too early to start to teach your child the difference between what is safe and what is not. This is not to instill unnecessary fear and caution in him, rather to clearly point out things that are "hot" or "sore" and show him how to respond to them appropriately. Learning not to touch at an early age is an important lesson that is always best backed up by safety equipment, so that no real harm comes to youngsters who need to find out for themselves. Part of teaching safety in a measured way is making sure that you are a good role model. Your child will try to copy the things he sees you do, so don't balance on rickety chairs to reach the top shelf in front of him, or cross the road when a red light is showing. If you are overly fearful and cautious in certain situations, however, your child will copy that too. Studies of 12-month-olds have shown that when a child is unsure whether there is danger or not, he will look to his mother for cues and will respond accordingly.

Although you do want to teach him sensible caution, you may not want him to grow up thinking the world is treacherous, so it may be worth putting on a brave face in your own feared situations and teaching your child the response you wish you had.

ESSENTIAL INFORMATION: BABIES

Safety in the home
Things to be aware of

From around six to eight months, as your baby's physical development accelerates, his motor skills will start to match his burgeoning curiosity. He can wriggle, kick, roll, crawl, grab, pull, "bottom shuffle," and eventually walk and climb. In order to safely encourage his exploration and learning (without constantly having to warn him not to touch), now is the time to make your home and surroundings as hazard-free as possible.

In the US accidents are one of the biggest causes of death in children, and many of these are in the home. Every week hundreds of preschoolers are admitted to accident and emergency rooms due to falls, burns, and suspected poisoning.

Your small child will be intrigued by things that are kept locked away or put on high shelves, especially if they are in brightly colored bottles or shiny wrappings. Child safety gadgets range from helpful to essential, but can never be a substitute for your attention and supervision. Do not leave your child unsupervised in any room in your house or in your yard (or in anyone else's). Always know where your child is and what he is doing. Lots of interesting activities and games to keep him busy are the best prevention against unwanted risks.

Try getting down on your hands and knees and crawling around your home from ground level to do a safety check space by space:

The kitchen This is a hazardous place and probably where you and your baby spend a lot of time. You can't be watching him all the time, so it is worth considering the following points.
* Store knives, sharp objects, lighters, and matches out of reach. Turn saucepan handles toward the back of the stove and use the back burners.

Put hot drinks out of reach, and don't drink or pass them over your baby's head. Ensure that cords from toasters and other countertop appliances are tucked away. Keep plastic bags out of reach.
* Mop up spills immediately and keep floors clear and clutter-free. Keep household chemicals out of sight and reach. Alcohol, aromatherapy oils, cigarettes, perfume, and mouthwash can all be poisonous to children. Remember that child-resistant lids aren't entirely childproof.
* Use a barrier or playpen while you are cooking. Use safety covers for electrical sockets, safety corners for sharp edges, a stove guard, and child-proof locks for low cupboards. To prevent choking, keep anything small out of reach—including coins, and hard foods such as pieces of raw carrot.

The bathroom This is probably the next priority in your safety audit. A frequently used space for water play, bubbles, and stories while you are toilet training, it should be safe and anxiety free.
* Store medicines in a high cupboard with a child-resistant catch. Be extra careful with pills in shiny, colorful blister packs. Never leave them lying around, and if you need to take medication do so when your child is not around, because he will copy you. Don't keep medicines on your bedside table, or in your handbag. Put lids back on bottles and put them away immediately after use. Take left-over medicines to the pharmacy for safe disposal.
* Run the cold tap in the bath first and then add the hot water to prevent scalding. Use non-slip mats in baths, showers, and on the bathroom floor.

Your hall, stairs, and landing Can present you with some unsuspected hazards on your endless trips from room to room and floor to floor.

✱ If the gaps between your banisters are more than 2.5 inches (6.5 cms), cover them up with boards or safety netting, as a determined youngster could squeeze herself through. Think about fitting safety glass in doors and windows or cover glass with safety film.

✱ When carrying your baby downstairs, always have a hand free to hold on to the bannister, and keep stairs clear of clutter. Use gates at the top and bottom of stairs. Teach your child how to climb down stairs safely when he starts to be more mobile.

✱ Never allow a small child to carry a baby downstairs.

In bedrooms and living areas Toys and play tend to feature day to day in these places. Bear in mind the following points.

✱ Secure heavy furniture to the wall to prevent it from toppling over. Avoid having furniture under windows and fit window catches. Doors and doorways can be made safer with door wedges and other gadgets to prevent little fingers from being jammed in them.

✱ Fit smoke alarms and fire guards, and get all heating appliances safety checked.

✱ Never leave candles or tea lights unattended.

✱ Change your baby on the floor, preferably, and never leave him unattended on a raised surface.

✱ Keep an eye on his crib toys—once he can get up onto all fours, he can use them to climb out of his crib.

Your outdoor space This presents a treasure trove of exploratory possibilities, and will be fascinating to your child. It needs a careful safety once-over.

✱ Tools and equipment need to be stored securely and put away after use. Your child will be less interested in your garden and home-repair tools if he has a set of his own (use play tools designed for children).

✱ Paint, mineral spirits, pesticides, and antifreeze must be securely stored out of sight and reach, under lock and key. As with indoor chemicals, always keep them in their original containers to avoid any confusion.

✱ Enclose and cover ponds and pools, and take extra care around bonfires, barbeques, and garden lanterns and candles.

✱ Do a first-aid course, learning infant CPR and how to deal with minor injuries, in case of accidents.

SAFETY CHECK: Be careful in other people's houses, especially those without young children—they may not have taken the same precautions.

OUT OF REACH: Store medication out of reach and preferably where your child cannot see it. Dispose of leftover medicines at the pharmacy.

NOT A GAME: Toddlers frequently see the stairs as an adventure course to be explored, so install gates at the top and bottom of your stairs.

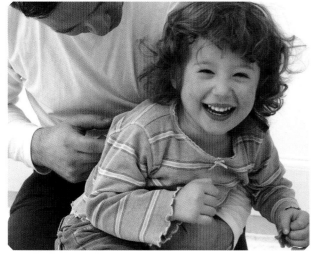

Toddlers a little person emerges

Toddler challenges
behavior and discipline

Q **My daughter makes us late all the time because she wants to be independent. What can we do?**

"I do it" is your toddler's way of telling you she is ready to be more independent. She's experiencing a drive to use her growing dexterity and coordination to practice new skills and to keep trying until she has something mastered. This is worth fostering, since her enthusiasm to learn and try new things will be an advantage throughout her life.

On an everyday basis, the delays caused by her practice sessions can be frustrating, and you may be tempted to take over. However, this may take even more time, since you'll have to battle her for control. Instead, try some practical remedies, such as leaving more time for each activity. As she gets better at each task, she'll be quicker to complete it and there will be less delay. You can enhance her learning by actively teaching her some key self-help skills, such

> The more attention you give your toddler, the less time you'll spend managing misbehavior

as putting her clothes on. Set up practice sessions when there is no time pressure—weekend mornings, for instance. Break down tasks into small steps and go through each one, telling her what to do and guiding her physically if she needs help. A few learning aids can help her learn—and help speed up the process. You can sew a tab into the back of pants to help her get them on the right way, and pair socks so she can easily pick up two that match.

Q **How can I get my child to share?**

Children ages two to four see themselves as the center of the universe. Your toddler thinks everything belongs to her, and that her needs rule the daily lives of those around her. This is a normal egocentric stage of development, and your child finds it almost impossible to see things from anyone else's point of view. Being aware of this stage can be useful in understanding her behavior. For example, it makes sense that she is distraught when another child takes the fire engine from her at play group, because she sees this toy as being her own. For an adult this would be the equivalent of someone walking over and taking your handbag or wallet or driving off with your car. You can help her develop the social skill of sharing by praising her whenever she does offer a toy or food to another child, but do expect this to be a gradual learning process.

PARENTS' STORY

Just a phase
bring on the tantrums

I used to feel like a hostage to my toddler's tantrums, always walking on eggshells to avoid setting them off and giving in to keep him happy. After letting my son stay up late yet again just to head off an explosion, I realized that this needed to change. To teach him to accept the rules and routine, I had to learn to love those tantrums, to let him show me his anger while I stood my ground. I got through it by thinking to myself, "Bring on the tantrum, I can cope." Now I'm more confident, my boy knows the rules and that no amount of fussing will make me give in.

ESSENTIAL INFORMATION: TODDLERS

Toddler meltdowns
Key tips for tantrum survival

Tantrums are embarrassing, noisy, hard to ignore, and a normal part of your toddler's development. They often occur as an expression of strong emotions, when a toddler doesn't know how to communicate his feelings in words. You'll notice tantrums are often triggered by frustration, having to share, and being told "no." They're more likely when your child is hungry, tired, or overstimulated. The good news is that each tantrum gives you a chance to teach your toddler how to handle frustration in the future. There are ways to minimize and deal with these pint-sized explosions.

Tantrum prevention
✳ **Distraction:** Redirect your child's attention and praise him for good behavior if you see a tantrum brewing.

✳ **Timing:** Hunger, thirst, and tiredness make tantrums more likely to occur, so schedule activities that have a high-tantrum risk when your toddler is well fed and rested.

Once a tantrum starts
✳ **Don't give in:** If you give in or offer a treat, you'll teach your toddler that tantrums work and he'll be more likely to try it again.
✳ **Remove:** Take the toddler out of the situation to a quiet spot, and wait for him to calm down.
✳ **Stay close:** Strong emotions can be scary for your child, so stay nearby.
✳ **Stay calm:** Your reaction can demonstrate that strong emotions don't need to be overwhelming.
✳ **Stay quiet:** Do not react or try to reason with your toddler until the tantrum subsides.

FAR LEFT: Following a tantrum, a mother picks up her toddler and acknowledges his feelings of anger or frustration. This helps him begin to label and understand his emotions.
TOP RIGHT: A toddler takes the opportunity to express her emotions through a tantrum. Most tantrums simmer down when parents stay nearby but don't interfere.
BOTTOM RIGHT: A father stays by his daughter while she is upset in order to provide support. She may feel overwhelmed or afraid as she experiences these strong new emotions.

ESSENTIAL INFORMATION: TODDLERS

Getting the behavior you want
Why toddlers act the way they do

What motivates your toddler?

The number one motivator for your toddler is your warm, loving attention. She wants to please and will work hard to be noticed, get your approval, and snare a cuddle or hug into the bargain. Most toddlers have a very high need for attention, although this varies according to temperament and how quickly you've responded to her in the past. Generally, if you've been quick to notice and meet her needs then, paradoxically, she'll be less concerned about having your attention all the time, since she knows you are keeping her in mind.

If your child is not getting the attention she needs by cooperating, her second-best strategy will be getting you to notice her through misbehaving. She'd rather be in the spotlight for mischievousness or misbehavior than not be there at all.

Getting the behavior you want

✱ Praise: Warm, honest, simple praise tells your toddler you notice her and you like what she's doing. It makes her eager to do more of the things you like, and helps her feel good about herself.

✱ Pay attention: It's the small ways you notice your child that matter—ruffling her hair as you go past or waving as she goes down the slide. These tell her you are keeping her in mind even when you're not playing together.

✱ Supervise: Being able to play alone for short periods is common at this age, but your child still needs you to supervise her closely for safety reasons, companionship, and to give her praise.

✱ Keep busy: Boredom is the starting point for mischief. Your toddler has a brief attention span of around three to four minutes.

YOUR APPROVAL: Getting a sticker for good behavior shows your toddler you like what he's doing and raises his self-esteem.

REWARDS: Sticker charts work well as motivators for behavior. You could also have them for other members of the family, or pets.

NOTICE THE GOOD: Showing that you notice your child when she's playing means she won't need to misbehave in order to gain your attention.

Managing the behavior you don't want

For your child's safety and to help her learn to be cooperative and helpful, there are times when you'll need to manage risky behavior or misbehavior.

✻ Up close and personal: When you want your child to stop what she's doing, whether it is jumping on the furniture or getting too close to the hot stove, make your message count. Squat down to her eye level, look her in the eyes, and tell her calmly, clearly, and firmly to stop. Specify exactly what she needs to do, for example "Stop jumping, please sit on the sofa" rather than "No."

✻ Short and simple: If you need to give your toddler a consequence for misbehavior, make it brief and relate it to the problem.

✻ Consistency: Your toddler needs to know what you want her to do and what she should not do. She'll learn this when you apply the same rules and values consistently, every day. If you give mixed messages, she'll be confused and will find it harder to behave well.

✻ Right away: If you need to manage misbehavior, do it immediately: the link between behavior and consequence is then clear. Delayed consequences are ineffective, since your toddler will have forgotten what she did wrong.

✻ Stay calm: No matter how irritated or exhausted you feel, never punish in anger. You may harm your child either emotionally, through your words, or physically. If you are ready to explode, then walk away, delay, and try some calming strategies for yourself.

✻ Ignore: This strategy is only useful for behavior that is irritating but not harmful or dangerous. Ignoring means withdrawing your attention for a short time (seconds to a minute) while your child does something like play with her food or pester for a cookie. Once she's stopped, that's the end of the matter.

✻ Respect: Maintain your child's dignity by making sure, if you have to correct her, that you do so in private and not in the presence of adults or her friends. When she's misbehaved let her know what the problem was, rather than comparing her to "better" children. Always be sure to refer to choices as "good" or "bad," rather than calling children "good" or "bad."

EYE TO EYE: Make sure your child gets the message when she's misbehaved by getting down to her level to talk to her.

OUT OF MISCHIEF: You'll need a steady stream of activities to keep your child entertained, otherwise he'll find something else to do.

BE REALISTIC: Your child has not yet learned to share, so expect her to get angry or upset when things don't go her way.

MYTHS AND MISCONCEPTIONS

Is it true that...

✳ **You need to give four or five times as many positive comments to your child as negative?**

The exact number of positives to negatives is debatable, but it is definitely true that for good self-esteem and a positive relationship with you, your child needs to hear your praise and compliments many more times than your censure. Try describing what she's done well as a praise method.

✳ **Toddlers live up their reputation as "Terrible Two's"?**

This is how many parents feel as their toddler reaches a stage called differentiation sometime from 16 months to two years of age. At this point your child recognizes herself to be a separate individual from you, able to make her own choices, even to disobey you. As she struggles to assert herself it is normal to have tantrums at least once a day, hence the label.

✳ **My child will respond better if I tell her what to do, rather than what not to do?**

This is true for children and adults alike. Your toddler will find it easier to do as you ask if you frame it in the positive, for example when you say "Please hold my hand as we walk" she is clear about what to do. If you say "Don't run away," she knows what you don't want, but may still be at a loss as to what to do instead. This is especially important when it comes to hitting—"Don't hit" is important to say, but parents often forget to model what is okay to do, instead.

Q Will I spoil my toddler if I keep rewarding him for being good?

You can't spoil your child by giving lots of genuine, warm praise when he behaves well. The very best form of reward is your time and attention, and in the early years your son will benefit from as much of this as he can get. Through your approval he's gaining a sense of security, growing in confidence, and learning exactly how you want him to behave. By contrast, frequent use of sweets or toys to reward him can backfire, since he may come to demand material incentives for each achievement and react by misbehaving or sulking when they aren't forthcoming every time. A healthy diet of praise, affection, and the occasional treat will encourage positive behavior with no risk of spoiling.

Q When our son throws a tantrum, my partner screams and shouts back. Is this a good idea?

Reacting emotionally to a tantrum will escalate the problem rather than soothe it. Talk over and agree some tantrum-calming strategies you can both use, such as staying quiet and waiting out the storm, and speaking slowly and softly afterward. Find some time to discuss parenting in general and how to control negative reactions. It can help to try imagining how you'd like to be treated if you were a small child.

If you can't agree on these issues, ask your pediatrician about parenting classes or other services in your area.

Q When my child bumps into things, she smacks them and says "bad." Why is this?

This interesting stage in child development, labeled "animism," occurs roughly from age two to seven. During this phase your child will see inanimate objects as having life, being able to feel, react, and act. It enables your child to find real comfort in a toy such as a stuffed animal or doll as she can attribute emotions to that toy. It is one way of explaining her experiences, such as bumping into things, and it allows her to practice reactions such as scolding a

"naughty" table. This is nothing to worry about, and over the next few years her understanding will grow, until she is able to accurately judge what is animate and what is not.

Q I complain about my child, then feel guilty. Am I overreacting?

Talking to other adults about life with your toddler is a positive move to offload your stresses (as long as you do it out of your child's earshot!). Problems occur, though, if all your stories are unfavorable, since you may be shaping a negative view of your daughter. Frequent horror stories of the latest tantrum in the supermarket or the biting incident at day care mean family and friends will begin to see her as difficult—and this label, once formed, can be hard to shift. A negative view of your child can be self-fulfilling. If she is labelled "naughty" then, when there is a problem, she is more likely to get the blame whether or not she was responsible. To give everyone a balanced view, remedy the situation by pointing out her good points and achievements too.

PARENTS' STORY

Praise
a positive development

I knew I was supposed to praise my son but I just couldn't find a good word to say about him. He resisted everything from eating his breakfast to putting on his coat, and both of us were miserable. I decided to try a praise experiment to see if I could change things around. For one day I praised every little thing I could think of, from getting out of bed to having one bite of his toast.

It worked like a charm—I had a different boy. He was smiling and seemed to do what I asked to see if I would notice. My day was much better, and I felt positive in myself. I've kept this going as well as I can. It doesn't always work but now I can't imagine having nothing to praise.

Is my child ready?
venturing into the wider world

Q **Should I stay at home with my son or take him to day care?**

Many parents feel guilty and worried about taking their child to day care or leaving them with a nanny. However, good-quality childcare, balanced with loving and nurturing time at home, can bring huge benefits. At this age your child is increasingly interested in other children and will be starting to play more cooperatively with them (rather than in parallel alongside them). Children learn through play, so being with other children helps them develop. Research suggests that children who go to day care may be better at sharing, working together, and understanding others' feelings. This time will also help to develop your child's confidence and independence in preparation for school.

Childcare (whether day care or a nanny) provides a much-needed break for parents, so you will have plenty of time and energy for your child when he returns. Many parents now choose to take their child to day care or hire a nanny for part of the week even if they are not returning to work. However, if you do choose to stay at home with your child, make sure that you give him plenty of opportunities to be around other children of his age.

Q **My daughter cries and says she won't go to day care without her favorite bear. Should I let her take it?**

Leaving the comfort, safety, and security of home to spend time at a new place with unfamiliar people makes some children anxious at first. Holding onto an object from home will help your daughter feel safe and allow her to cope better with this change. If she insists on bringing her teddy bear long after she has settled in, or if it prevents her from joining in with activities, you may want to help her leave it at home. Don't ask her to give it up immediately, which

may make her even more anxious. Speak to the day-care providers and see if they can find somewhere for your daughter to put teddy away when she is settled. As she becomes more confident, encourage her to hand her teddy bear to a staff member as you arrive, then the next week to leave it with you at the door, and eventually to say good-bye to him at home. To avoid any upset, you may want to purchase an identical teddy for home—just in case hers gets lost.

Q **It is so hard to say good-bye to my son. What might help?**

Having spent so much time together at home, it's bound to be difficult when you have to wave to your child and leave them in someone else's care—particularly if your child is upset, too. With emotions running high for both of you, it can be difficult to say good-bye properly. However, a consistent routine will help both of you cope better with the separation and allow your son to get on with the important task of having fun. So don't sneak off without saying good-bye leaving him to worry where you've gone, and don't drop your son at the door and then leave quickly. Take a few minutes to settle him in when you arrive, then give him a hug and kiss, and say clearly, "I'm going now"—but let your son know when you will be back to get him. When you have left, avoid the temptation to watch him through the window. However difficult saying good-bye may be at first, saying hello at the end of the day will more than make up for any upset in the morning.

Q **My child is very unsettled at day care and says he does not want to go. Should I make him?**

Starting at day care is often the first major transition that a child needs to deal with. We are all different in terms of how well we cope with these life events, and

ESSENTIAL INFORMATION: TODDLERS

Choosing the best day care
Things to think about

In most cities and towns, there are lots of day-care centers to choose from. Listen to personal recommendations from friends, then go and visit the ones you are interested in. Remember, the most expensive is not always the best. A happy, successful placement depends on four key things: the staff who will be working with your child, the activities available, the general atmosphere of the day-care center, and the environment itself.

Staff: Staff should be well trained, enthusiastic, friendly, and interested in your child.
You may want to ask:
* What is the ratio of staff to children?
* What qualifications and training do staff members have?
* How long have they been working there?
* Do they enjoy working at the day care?
* Will your child have one primary caregiver?
* Will staff members record your child's activities and achievements for you?
* How is difficult behavior handled?

Activities: A good day care should offer a range of stimulating activities and have plenty of toys and equipment for your child to play with.
You may want to ask:
* Are activities planned out each day?
* Will your child be able to choose some of his or her activities?
* What will your child eat and drink?
* Is there an outside play area?
* Are the children taken on trips?

General atmosphere: Your child's time at day care should be all about learning through fun. Do the children (and staff) seem happy and content?

Did you feel welcomed? Did staff members listen to you and answer your questions? How did your child react to the visit?

Environment: The building should be clean and safe for your child to play and explore. Location, access, and security are also important. All day care centers are regulated, so ensure that you ask for a copy of their most recent inspection report.

CHECKING IT OUT: Your child should enjoy her time at day care, maximizing her learning. Watch how staff members interact with the children—do they pay attention to them and get involved with the activities, or stand back? Do they seem happy to be there? Inspect the resources and toys to make sure that they are clean, safe, and well cared for.

how long it takes us to adjust and move on. Your son could just be getting used to things at his own pace. If he is as upset now as the day he started, there may be issues at day care that are making him unhappy. Ask your son what he likes and dislikes about school, and speak to his main caregiver to get her view on how things are going. Find out how he spends his time there—what activities does he like best? Does he play with the other children? Having one or two children that he gets along well with can really help, so see if there are any opportunities to meet up with other families on the weekends. At home, remind your son about the fun things he does there. Keep the lines of communication open with staff, and ask for a regular update on his progress—out of your son's earshot. If things don't improve, it might be that the day care is not meeting his needs, and you may want to consider an alternative setting.

I want to potty train my son. How will I know if he is ready?

Starting potty training too early will result in frustration and upset for you and your child, so ask yourself these questions to see if he is ready to begin. Does your child have control of his bowels at night? Does he have the balance and coordination needed to squat down on a potty and get up again, or to climb up and hold himself on a toilet seat? Can he pull his pants up and down without help? Does he tell you in words or gestures when he wants to urinate or defecate? If the answer to these questions is yes, then your son is probably ready to take the next step. Start off by letting him pick out a potty or child toilet seat that he likes. Adult toilet seats are too large and can intimidate children. Children's seats are the right size for a toddler, and some also have handles for extra security. If you are using a potty, leave it out in the same place. Get into a routine of sitting your son on the potty or toilet for a few minutes when you are changing his diaper. Providing a small step will allow your child to get on to the toilet independently. Give him lots of praise and encouragement—good sitting and results will follow! Make sure your son has plenty to drink and allow him some time without a diaper on.

This will give him lots of practice and make it easier for him to go when he needs to. Most importantly, stay calm when things get messy. If your child feels pressured to get it right first time, he will hold back from performing, so support your child's efforts when things don't quite go according to plan. Allow him to learn at his own pace, and it should all fall into place eventually.

I don't want my daughter to go to day care because I'm scared I'll miss her growing up. Is this silly?

Whether your daughter goes to day care or not, the truth is that children develop so fast at this age that, try as you might, you are bound to miss at least one new achievement. Day-care staff will be prepared for this, and usually provide you with a record of your child's progress. They may even be able to record events on video, or you could buy a disposable camera and leave it with them—just in case your daughter decides to do something momentous in your absence! It is rather frustrating to find out that you put in all the hard work only for someone else to reap the benefit of seeing your child do something for the first time. However, your daughter will take great delight in showing off her new skills, and in years to come you will witness many more of her achievements than you miss.

My child has a very settled routine. Will going to day care or a nanny upset it?

It is quite likely that, whichever childcare arrangement you choose, some of the caregiver's daily routines for feeding, sleeping, playing, and resting will be different from your own. This does not mean that all of your hard work was in vain, since your child will still benefit from the security of clear boundaries and a consistent approach. Speak to the day-care center in advance to let them know about any important routines you have at home, and to find out how their practice differs from what your child is used to. You may want to think about changing some of your routines to fit more with the routine at day care to

Separation anxiety

Separation anxiety is the distress shown by children when you leave them in the care of someone else. It begins at around six to nine months—the age when your child first becomes aware of strangers. Showing signs of separation anxiety is your child's way of trying to keep you close to make sure her needs for food, warmth, protection, and loving care are met. Your child may cry inconsolably and cling onto you, begging you not to leave her. This can be very upsetting for parents and makes it difficult to say good-bye. Don't be surprised if your child also cries when you return to pick her up. This does not mean that she has been terribly unhappy without you—her tears are simply a result of the rush of emotion she feels on being reunited.

Is it normal? All children experience some separation anxiety; how much depends on your child's temperament, and on the strength of her bond with you. Children who are calm, confident, and securely bonded are more likely to cope better with change, and so settle more quickly when you leave them.

What can I do to help?

✱ Leave your child with family and friends so she has some practice at separating from you.
✱ Prepare your child by driving past the building and talking about all the fun things she'll get to do there.
✱ Have at least two settling-in visits at day care, and stay with your child at first. Take along a favorite toy.
✱ Say good-bye confidently, even if you feel distraught! Your child is sensitive to your emotions, and if she picks up on your anxiety she may be even more upset.

help your child settle in more quickly. If you choose a family day care, you may be able to request that they follow your own routine if there are only a few children there. Don't forget that your child will be one of a group, all doing the same thing, and their growing interest in copying others' behavior can make it much easier to establish new routines.

My son gets upset if I leave him for even a minute. How will he cope when he starts school?

Your son may be sensitive to change in his social environment and need longer to adjust to new routines. If he is anxious about meeting new people or being in unfamiliar places, his instinctive reaction will be to stay as close to you as possible because he knows that you will protect him. To help prepare him for school, let him spend time with friends and family to gain some positive separation experiences. Games of peek-a-boo can help him learn to tolerate disappearances and expect reunions. As he comes to realize that being apart from you always ends with your return, his anxiety and clingy behavior will reduce. Give him plenty of notice before taking him out—tell him where he is going, who he will see, and what he will do there. Take along some favorite toys to occupy him and to provide familiar activity. Once he is playing happily, withdraw quietly, but don't go too far at first. Check back in with him regularly so he can see you are still around if he needs you.

Over time, as he grows in confidence, you will be able to withdraw more quickly and venture further afield, eventually leaving him in the care of someone you and your child both trust.

What kind of parent are you?
exploring parenting styles

How can we parent as a team?

No two people agree entirely on every parenting decision, so it's natural that your toddler will check with each of you to see which one will let him have what he wants. Being aware of this means you can present a united front. Friction can be caused if you undermine each others' decisions, even if this is done unintentionally. For example, your child may be in the habit of asking one of you for a treat, then, if he gets told "no," going to the other for a different answer. To avoid this situation (called "splitting"), make a habit of checking with your partner to see if a decision has already been made. If this can't be done easily, delay giving your answer until you've had a chance to talk it through. This way your child sees you as a parenting team who will back each other up. If you do disagree, and this is bound to happen sometimes, do it away from the children and then let them know your joint decision.

PARENTS' STORY

Parenting
getting the balance right

I was determined not to parent like my mother. She was very strict, imposing a rigid timetable of homework and chores. With my son I tried to be the opposite. I wanted to be a playmate and thought if I set limits or a routine he wouldn't love me and would go wild later, as I had. I was surprised and hurt when he behaved badly all the time, and, at my wits' end, I asked his pediatrician for help. She pointed out that he needed both playtime and limits to teach him that I loved him but that I was in charge. I realized then that setting a routine didn't make me a bully.

> There are patterns and habits in almost everything we do, and this includes bringing up our children

Why does my child try to wind me up when she knows I'm tired and busy?

It must seem that your toddler picks her moment to have an outburst but, developmentally, she does not yet have the ability to judge whether you are stressed or not. She can pick up on basic emotions, but she simply doesn't have the sophisticated reasoning to be calculated about when she cries or is uncooperative. Unfortunately, the times when you are most stressed tend also to be the times she is overwhelmed or tired, too.

Take a moment to see the situation from your child's point of view. For example, difficult behavior at dinnertime, such as refusing to eat her meal, spilling a drink on the floor, and screaming, could be a result of her being tired. She might also have missed your attention when you were occupied with making the meal, or possibly she is not used to the food tastes and textures you're asking her to try. Rather than being a deliberate attempt to upset you, she is simply expressing strong needs.

Seeing things from her point of view allows you to be sympathetic, and gives you ideas to remedy the situation. For example, you may decide to make her mealtime earlier so that she's less tired, have some playtime with her beforehand so she's had your attention, and offer her fewer new foods to try.

Old-school parenting
Looking back to your childhood

The greatest influence on your values, aspirations, and parenting style is likely to be your own parents and upbringing. Whatever your experiences as a child, how you raise your child will be affected by how you were brought up, whether you want it to or not. It's worth noting that most parents, when asked, would choose to go to family and friends as their first choice for parenting advice; a demonstration that much of the time the last generation got child-rearing right.

Blast from the past: How often have you heard yourself say something to your own child exactly as it was said to you, even down to the tone of voice? Depending on your experiences you may be pleased to repeat something that made your childhood special, or disappointed that the memory of a negative comment has broken through your resolve to parent differently. The powerful nature of learning through experience means that these automatic reactions will intrude unless you actively try to control them. At times of stress you're most likely to copy the parenting you experienced as a child. If you're anxious to avoid these reactions, then identify situations when they're most likely to arise and practice alternative responses. Creating new patterns of behavior will help override habits from history.

Rejecting the past: One reaction to a difficult childhood can be to apply the opposite parenting style when raising your own child. For example, if your upbringing was strict or harsh, perhaps now you put in place very few rules or boundaries, or buy your child all she asks for to compensate for having had very little yourself. A common fear in these circumstances is that, if you start to use discipline, then you will lose control and go too far, repeating the patterns from the past that hurt you. Unfortunately, in rejecting everything from your childhood you may be going to a different extreme, which means your child doesn't have the limits and regulation she needs. If you don't have a positive role model, effective ways to establish your own style are to read parenting books, observe others, and attend parenting courses.

New challenges: Your child will face a different world and present you with new dilemmas. She's taught to challenge your opinion rather than go along with it, she is exposed to more technology than you were, and later in life, she will face choices and pressures that weren't present for you.

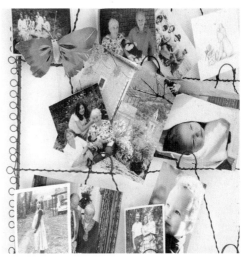

MOVING FORWARD: Looking back to previous generations can remind you that the underlying principles of caring for your child—predictable, loving parenting—still applies.

Do I have a parenting style?
Elements you may recognize

There is no one correct parenting style, but some approaches are more likely than others to create the rich, loving relationship you want with your child. You may find your parenting approach is a collection of ideas accumulated through reading books, watching others, your values and experiences from childhood, and trial and error. Being able to identify and challenge how you parent allows you to cut out unhelpful ideas and stick to those that suit you and your family best.

Elements of your parenting style

✱ **Playful:** This is a quality to be cherished. If you have this type of parenting style, you'll dedicate many hours to your child's development through play and stimulation. This style works well when you also provide the routine your toddler needs to feel safe and secure. Although you can be her playmate, avoid the temptation to be her best friend, since this makes it difficult to apply the limits she needs.

✱ **Warm:** This encompasses the many ways you show your love to your child. It is in the physical affection you show, your gentle tone of voice, the softening in your expression when you see or think of her, and the unconditional love you feel. If you were raised not to show your feelings, to be embarrassed about them, or to believe that telling a child you love her will spoil her, you may feel limited in the expression of warmth that is needed in your relationship. Speak to a counselor or parenting expert if your beliefs about expressing affection are getting in the way of warm parenting.

✱ **Firm but fair:** You establish a clear routine for your child but don't apply it so rigidly that she misses out on play dates or other activities. You have a few simple house rules but don't go overboard with a long list of do's and don'ts. Most of the time you say

COMPARING NOTES: Parenting is a big job, and you may need some help to do your best. Be open to exploring new ideas with other parents.

"yes" to your child but you're not afraid to impose limits when it's for her own good—for example, you set a reasonable bedtime even though she protests.

✱ **Consistent:** A predictable routine and the same rules and rewards applied regularly means your child knows where she stands. She can be confident about what comes next and understands what is expected of her. What may seem repetitive to you equals security to her.

✱ **Confident:** You have the confidence to make parenting decisions and stick to them. You do not fear losing your child's love when you apply consequences for misbehavior, since the bond between you is strong. While you usually get your parenting decisions right, when you need to apologize you do so quickly and honestly and this builds your child's confidence in you.

✱ **Team player:** Whether you parent with a partner or have your own parents or friends helping you raise your child, it is helpful to discuss and agree your parenting values, discipline strategies, and rewards. If your styles are poles apart—for example if one parent is "soft" and one parent "tough," difficulties can arise, and resentment may build between you if one feels undermined by the other. It may not be possible to reach full agreement, but discussion and negotiation bring you closer together.

Parenting styles to avoid

✴ Volatile: You try to stay calm, but there are times when you shout and fume. No parent is expected to stay perfectly calm at all times, but feelings of anger directed at your toddler can be distressing and unsettling for your child. The reasons you are angry often have little to do with her. If you already do or feel you may express your anger through shouting or unkind words, long periods of ignoring your child, or physically hurting her, seek help immediately.

✴ Permissive: A style which gives little or no routine, few limits or guidance on behavior, and no parental authority can be very frightening for a young child, since their world does not feel predictable, safe, and secure. It leads to misbehavior and, in later years, may result in lack of respect for parents or authority, which goes on to affect educational achievement and respect for the law, other people, and property. Often permissive parenting comes about as a reaction to having been strictly or harshly parented yourself and not wanting to repeat that pattern. It may also be the result of feeling so stressed, overwhelmed, or depressed that you have no motivation or energy to apply rules and routine.

✴ Authoritarian: You may have high aspirations for your child, but these translate into expectations of her behavior which are almost unattainable. You tend to be distant, with warmth and acknowledgment dependent on achievements rather than being an integral part of everyday family life. This style teaches your child that her self-worth is dependent on what she achieves rather than who she is in herself. She may become highly critical of herself and be vulnerable to low self-esteem if she does not reach her goals. This style should not be confused with authoritative parenting, which means being firm but fair, assertive, and warm, and has clear rules, boundaries, and expectations which match a child's age and level of development.

✴ Neglectful: A small number of parents cannot or will not recognize the physical and emotional needs of children. Not providing enough for your child to eat or drink or leaving her alone and unsupervised, can place her in immediate danger and is punishable by law.

TEAMWORK: Parenting as a team will make your child feel secure, since it will form part of her consistent and predictable routine.

FUN AND GAMES: Giving playful physical affection is an essential element of parenting.

FIRM BUT FAIR: Having consistent rules and consequences is important for children.

Why is he obsessed with blue?
fads and habits explained

Q Since my partner and I broke up, my son is sucking his thumb all the time. Have we damaged him?

Thumb sucking is a very common comfort habit. It is a useful and effective form of self-soothing, which on its own is not a sign of emotional disturbance. It is not unusual for even a school-age child to suck his thumb at bedtime. The most common concern about thumb sucking is the effect it has on growing teeth.

However, if your son is spending a lot of time sucking his thumb and you think that he is upset by your breakup, you need to take some action. If his self-soothing isn't working, he may need more comfort from you and his father to have some of his fears allayed. Children find parents' conflicts especially difficult if they don't understand what is going on and if their familiar routines change. Research shows that children who keep good relationships with both their parents do best (see advice on coping with divorce, pp. 190–95).

Q My child can't bear to be without his "blanky" comfort blanket. How can I break the habit?

Clinging to a special blanket is a habit developed to manage with times when you are not there. If security blankets are relied upon heavily, particularly for getting to sleep, they can prove to be somewhat problematic. If they are forgotten or lost, you can be faced with a distressed child and a sleepless night.

With a blanket you can gradually make it smaller and smaller by cutting it in half and then quarters, so your child gets used to its changed shape slowly. It is worth keeping a piece in reserve for emergencies. It might be a good idea to have "blanky"-free zones such as playgroup or day care, and to gradually restrict its use to home and then bedtime.

Q What can I do about nosepicking?

Attempts to stop a small child from picking her nose usually results in an increase in the habit. In the process of exploring all the nooks and crannies of their bodies, toddlers discover what a treasure trove their noses are. They often pick their noses when they are bored or tired. They also discover that they get a big reaction out of the adults around them, which is unfortunately likely to make them do it more.

Nosepicking is best ignored completely. If you really cannot do this, try giving her something else to keep her hands occupied, such as some play dough or a small toy in her pocket to fiddle with.

Q Why does my son want me to read the same story over and over again?

There are a number of possible explanations for this common feature of toddlerhood. On the whole, toddlers do not like change. Repetition is an effective way of learning new information and new words, and knowing chunks of the story by heart is a great achievement for him. It may be that some part of the story touches him emotionally and possibly reflects something from his own experience or aspirations. Rhythm and repetition are soothing, a central theme in toddler habits. One method of making it more

Central themes in toddler habits are rhythm and repetition, as they find these to be soothing

interactive and interesting is to involve him in the reading, getting him to find characters in the pictures or play a part by saying a character's lines. You can try introducing another story rather than replacing the current one. In time he'll probably want that one ad nauseum!

Getting dressed in the morning is a battleground. Any tips?

Toddlers often focus their quest for some control on the process and choices associated with getting dressed. (This also explains why they can become obsessed with one color.) The fact that this is a time when everyone is in a hurry may not be coincidental. Whether there is a pattern to her resistance, such as wanting to do it all herself, or it is a random rejection of your choices, here are a few helpful tips.

Start out positively and on good terms, perhaps with a pre-dressing cuddle. Then play a game or tell a story to detract from the focus on dressing. Make sure her clothes are easy to put on, with a minimum of buttons and snaps, to limit the number of opportunities for a meltdown. Perhaps she can be dressing a stuffed animal while you dress her. Select clothes that are less likely to bother her on a sensory level—toddlers can be hypersensitive to synthetic fibers, scratchy seams, and itchy labels. Give her choices, but not too many: Put out-of-season clothes away to prevent having to fight over flip-flops and bikinis in winter. Finally, praise her successes to make her more willing to try again next time.

What can I do about nasty habits picked up at playgroup?

When your child joins a playgroup, it is inevitable that he will copy things he sees and hears other children doing. This could be any number of things from mildly irritating to downright disgusting. High-pitched screeching, blowing spit bubbles, hitting, and swearing are probably the worst of them. Balance this experience with all the lovely things he will learn from others as well. You may be able to ignore some of your toddler's bad behavior or divert his attention. As with many bad habits, your

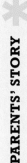

PARENTS' STORY

"I dressed myself!"
a child's determination

When she was about three, my daughter's love of girlie pink things became an obsession. She would only wear pink, only dresses, and only a particular shade of pink. I can honestly say I had no idea that a small child could be so inflexible and so determined. I found myself developing a sort of sixth sense, scanning clothing rails and catalogs for this particular shade of pink dress. Eventually my friend gave me some advice: to buy her some leggings in her particular shade of pink and a very pale pink dress and give her the choice. She explained that I needed to stay calm and to help her see that it was a win-win situation.

By not teasing or criticizing her, and by encouraging her to choose between two options, I was able to gradually expand her categories of color and type of clothes.

child will thrive on the reaction he gets. So if howling or blowing bubbles go unnoticed, they will probably die down and be replaced by something new the next time he goes to playgroup. Do make sure your toddler knows that there are consequences for unsafe or unacceptable behavior.

My toddler masturbates! Should I stop her?

It is normal for both male and female toddlers to explore their bodies and, at a time when they are getting out of diapers, they will inevitably discover their genitals. Your child may also discover that touching them gives her a good feeling, thus ensuring that she will touch them again. This is entirely innocent, and you do not need to worry about it. Scolding her or nagging her to take her hand out of her pants may not be successful and may actually make the behavior seem more attractive.

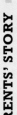

PARENTS' STORY

"But it's broken!"
establishing control

We went through a phase when Sam would have a tantrum if his food wasn't whole—if I'd cut his sandwich or there was a corner missing from his cookie. "It's broken!" he'd wail and refuse to eat it. He'd rather have nothing than have food with a piece missing. At first I thought he was being deliberately difficult, and we had terrible battles that I never won.

Then someone told me that it was his way of establishing some control over his life and, for some reason, he had chosen whole food! He was a perfectly happy little boy the rest of the time and he would eat most things, just whole. So I went along with it. It really wasn't very hard. Funnily enough when he went to day care he ate sliced-up apples with all the other children.

A child with lots of love and attention is unlikely to have a problem with excessive masturbation. If you find her putting her hand in her pants when you are in public and you feel that you must act, offering an alternative activity with her hands may help to stop it, possibly something in her pocket to fiddle with, or a comfort object. Making a distinction between "public" and "private" in relation to her body and her behavior may help her to understand this is a private thing to do which is not banned, but should only happen at home. Some children play with their genitals when they are bored or unhappy. If you think that this is the case, you may need to address the underlying issues before tackling the masturbation.

My son stutters and stammers. Will he always do this?

When children are first learning to speak, they often stumble across unfamiliar sounds and jumble their words up in a desire to be heard and a rush to get their message across. At this time repeating sounds, syllables, or words is common and it is, in fact, more frequently found in boys. It is not necessarily a sign of tension or anxiety. The best way to support your son's quest to communicate clearly is to show him that you are interested in what he has to say, to show him that you are in no hurry, and that you will let him express himself without your interference. By paying attention to what he is saying you avoid focusing on how he is saying it, and in this way you do not add any extra pressure to his performance.

Should his stammering continue and become more frequent with associated emotional upset, it is worth seeking professional help from a speech and language therapist. Your pediatrician can direct you to a local specialist.

How can I prevent my child from saying "poo-poo head"?

Given some of the main developmental tasks of this age—learning bowel and bladder control—it's not surprising that the toilet and its contents feature frequently in the language of the toddler. As with many other nasty habits, it is best not to react too much nor to laugh at this new-found ability. As well as providing a method of mild rebellion, toilet humor amuses preschoolers, so they laugh at each other, thus making it a difficult habit to break.

You may want to curb name-calling in general and have a talk about how much names can hurt people's feelings. It often helps to name the emotion behind the name-calling, by saying something like: "I can see you are angry with your sister for taking your toy but I don't like you calling her names." Try offering a small reward, such as a sticker, as an incentive for a name-calling free day.

You may also want to check that you and others are setting a good example in the language that you use in front of her, especially when you are driving or being overheard on the telephone. Whatever you do, "poo-poo head" will not last long in her vocabulary. but at least you can be well prepared for the challenging language that may follow it when your child enters the preteen years.

Why play?
links between play and learning

Q I've banned guns in my home, but my son "shoots" people with a stick. What should I do?

The war toys on sale are so frighteningly realistic, it is understandable that parents try to protect their children from them. However, banning things tends to make them more attractive, and whatever you do, boys seem to want to play with guns.

Perhaps you could compromise and allow the use of obviously unrealistic weapons such as water pistols and light sabres while encouraging his imagination in fashioning guns out of whatever comes to hand. At the same time you can teach him kindness and tolerance and the message that real guns hurt people. On the whole, children are quite able to tell the difference between pretend and real life. They are more likely to learn aggression from the behavior of the people around them so, through your own actions, you can show him how to resolve differences and deal with disputes in a peaceful way.

Q My daughter has an imaginary friend. Should I be worried?

Imaginary friends are very common in children from about two and a half onward, and they can become quite established for several years. The presence of an imaginary friend on its own does not signal loneliness or anxiety. Many happy healthy adults remember their own imaginary friends.

Imaginary friends can act as many things; they are often blamed for misdemeanors, used to express difficult emotions, hold the moral high ground, or are just a good playmate. They can take the form of people or animals, have names and intriguing characteristics and, sometimes, children have more than one. Again none of these things represent anything sinister in themselves. In fact, if there are other signs of worry in your child, the role and characteristics of "the friend" may be a useful insight into the problem. As with all play, imagination is to be encouraged and, as a parent, you are best taking your lead from your child. If requested to do so, lay a place at the table or hold the car door open for the friend, but don't try and take over or outsmart your child by using their friend against them. Accept and welcome them into the home and family and in time they will disappear quite naturally.

Q My son never wants to stop playing. How can I stop our playtimes from ending in tears?

If your child knows that playtime with you happens every day, it will be easier for him to stop. Make time in your day to play and relax and enjoy the time together. Create an expectation of something he can look forward to after playtime. Give him a warning a few minutes before playtime is up and then stick to your plan and walk away. If you give in to his pleas and extend the time, he will learn that there is always a chance for more and you will get more tears and whining. Let him know that you like playing with him and are looking forward to the next time.

Q I bought my son a doll, but he calls it Super Baby and throws it around. Will boys always be boys?

At around the age of three, children's gender identities start to set, and boys are more likely to be found playing with traditionally boys' toys and girls with girls' toys. Even before this age, although they may play with a wider range of toys, they may still express their gender in the way they play with them, such as your son throwing the doll as opposed to feeding it. We do see that children are influenced by their playmates' choice of games and toys, as well as by older siblings' games and by the behavior of the adult males and females in their lives.

ESSENTIAL INFORMATION: TODDLERS

Different kinds of play
Physical and pretend

Toddlers are discovering the sheer joy of using their bodies. This is a time for physical play—running, jumping, skipping, and play fighting. Puppies, kittens, and little humans all have a "play face" indicating this activity is just for fun. Parents and their toddlers will develop their own tickling, throwing, and hiding games, all accompanied by squeals of delight and excitement.

Rough-and-tumble play is common from three years on into adolescence. Children are very good at differentiating between play fighting and real fighting. Rolling over and wrestling games often find one toddler on top and then the other having his turn as the victor. Unlike real fighting, neither one is meant to get hurt and they are oblivious to onlookers, this is just for each other.

Along with the enjoyment of growing physicality, we see the first signs of pretend play.

This develops in an intricate sequence in which a one-year-old pretends to be asleep or eating, much to her own amusement. By about 18 months she can be seen feeding her teddy bear, or parent. At two years old, she might be getting her doll to feed her teddy. The ability to use her imagination to substitute objects for real things in play comes a little later, so by three or four she may happily use an acorn shell as a cup. A classic sign of this stage is the use of a stick or a block as a gun. Parents can help with developing this imaginary play because it is mostly social, and up to about four years, it is typically a parent–child activity. There is a shared quality to it, with neither parent nor toddler taking charge. In time, other children start to be involved in the pretending, and the stories get more complicated, following familiar themes such as cooking dinner or shopping.

CONSTRUCTION: Children love the challenges presented by toys to assemble: Completing them enhances self-esteem.

FAMILY GAMES: Playing with your child, perhaps developing your own physical games, is a great way of bonding.

LET'S PRETEND: You will see more sophisticated role play, such as dressing up, emerge around three to four years of age.

Consequently modern boys may well copy their fathers doing housework or caring for babies, they may play "house" with female playmates, or copy older sisters' quieter and gentler games.

Nonetheless, we are often surprised to find that gender stereotypes are pretty resistant to change. Psychologists have argued about the nature–nurture debate since the 1900s, but now think that nature has a strong role in defining gender roles, even while recognizing how pervasive and subtle nurture can be in setting up expectations based on gender stereotypes. Even before birth, there is a tendency to think about baby boys and baby girls differently because our society and culture conditions us to.

Providing a little boy with a doll and a little girl with a car may not lead to them playing with them, but you can still teach emotional literacy and, crucially, you can show that you value equally the strengths of both genders.

My toddler draws on the walls. What should I do?

First decide whether this is creativity gone too far or a deliberate act of defiance, because your response will be somewhat different. If he is really proud of his artwork and shows no signs of knowing it is wrong, then don't come down on him like a ton of bricks. You might admire his lovely picture but be sad that it's in the wrong place and will have to be cleaned off.

Take the time to show him the right place to draw and make this as accessible as possible. Pieces of paper move when you draw on them and walls don't, which may be why your child is using them. It might help to have a black or white board or to tape large sheets of paper to a table or the floor. In order to ensure that he learns this lesson, supervise him closely and praise his ability to keep on the paper as well as his artistic prowess. When you can't be around to supervise, keep art materials out of reach. Finally, exhibit his work in a prominent place for all to see and admire. It might be worthwhile to get him to help you clean the wall, not as a punishment but rather to further reinforce the lesson.

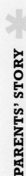

PARENTS' STORY

Laughing together
enjoying silly games

There is nothing I love more than the sound of my daughter's belly laugh. She and I can be having a really bad day and then I manage to get her to laugh and both our spirits lift. She finds it really funny when grown-ups make mistakes. We have this silly game in the mornings when I pretend to forget which piece of clothing goes where and I put her tights on her arms and her underwear on her head—she chuckles delightedly and puts me right. The other thing we do is hunt for parts of her body, or even funnier, her dad's body, but in the wrong place. I'll just say, "Where's Daddy's tummy?" while looking behind his ear, and she starts to giggle. Dad can make her roar with laughter by leaping up in mock surprise to find his nose on his knee!

The last time I arranged a play date for my child it was a disaster. Maybe she is too young?

It is true that she is only just learning to share her toys and her mommy or daddy, and to play nicely with someone her own age, so play dates can be quite a challenge. However if you do a little preparation and stick to some simple guidelines, you both may have a better experience next time. Keep it short, an hour and a half maximum. Time it when your daughter is at her best—well rested and fed. Decide with your daughter which toys can be shared and put those that cannot away for the occasion. Supervise the toddlers constantly to keep them happy and safe. Playing alongside each other is normal at this age, so don't try and force them to play together. Be prepared to take charge and play with them if they are struggling to play alone. Have a plan for dealing with trouble and agree on it with the other child's parent. Try to synchronize nap times

ESSENTIAL INFORMATION: TODDLERS

Does play aid development?
I'm only playing...

Since the end of the 19th century, play theorists have stressed the importance of play in children's development. Some think it's more important for emotional development, some for thought and creativity, and others still, for mastering general life skills in a safe context. The most radical theoretical position is that play has no ultimate developmental goal at all: It is purely for fun, and the learning along the way is secondary to the enjoyment of it. Some argue that play has been idealized in our child-focused society, and point to other cultures where less emphasis is placed on play with no detriment to children's development.

Finding links: Modern theorists draw links between both pretend play and creativity, and between role play and social-skills development. There is some evidence to link pretend play with greater creativity and fewer behavior problems. It is difficult to separate learning from any aspect of a child's development and easy to see how physical play, pretend play, and language play offer a multitude of opportunities for a child to learn what he can do, who he is and how to interact with his family, friends, and environment. Rough-and-tumble games that have no obvious rules or goals teach social skills such as turn-taking, negotiation, and making and keeping friends. They also teach competitive and cooperative skills. More complex, goal-directed play such as construction, drawing, and puzzles, which emerge in late toddlerhood, tend to develop a child's cognitive skills such as problem solving and hypothesis testing.

All children play, whether they live in the Amazon jungle or first-world suburbia, whether they have cupboards full of toys or a car made out of tin cans, and significantly, despite how much emphasis and energy their parents invest in their play. While the jury may still be out on what type of play and how play is linked with cognitive, social, and emotional development, what is indisputable is the profound link between play and the positive experience of shared pleasure.

I'M A BUILDER! Role playing and dressing up marks an important stage in your child's development: It means he is thinking about how other people see the world.
NOISY GAMES: Your younger toddler will love making a noise and mess with the contents of your kitchen. Create a special cupboard full of safe implements such as pots, pans, and sturdy plastic boxes for him to explore.

How to play: letting your child take the lead

Lots of adults have forgotten the pleasures of play or are so caught up in the desire to teach their youngster something that they end up directing and commanding their child in how to play properly. Unfortunately this often takes the joy out of the game. It's sometimes tempting to finish a puzzle or correct it at the end, but this could rob your child of any sense of completion and achievement. You might check if your child thinks it is finished and if she does, congratulate her on her effort and leave it at that.

Playing is a shared activity, and parents will have more success in encouraging play if they let their child take the lead. If you join her in a game and let her tell you what to do, your involvement is assured. Don't try and take over by imposing your own ideas and rules. If you're building a house, there's no need for it to look real, and there's no reason why the bath shouldn't be in the dining room. Try not to rush games and pay special attention to your child's creative ideas.

with the other child's parent to optimize the chances of two fresh toddlers. Don't try it too often: Once a week is plenty at this stage.

How do I know which toys are good for toddlers?

The best guide to choosing toys for toddlers is to match them to the different kinds of play that dominate this age. So for physical play and development: Toys and equipment to develop their skills such as climbing frames, trikes, sit-on cars, and fire engines are all perfect. For pretend play and social development, try dolls that can be fed and changed; a dressing-up box full of hats and costumes for familiar roles; characters and puppets from stories and movies; cars, trucks, and airplanes; and toy equipment to enhance fantasy play, such as a telephone, a cash register, or a tool box. Use arts and craft materials for creative play. Toys to avoid might be those that limit imagination and interaction, such as battery-operated toys that you just watch or dolls that talk, as well as toys that are not appropriate for the age and ability intended.

How can I get my daughter to play on her own?

It can be hard to get the balance right between being available to play with your child and encouraging her to play independently. If you always give in to her demands at the expense of your own needs, you may be setting yourself up for many battles ahead.

It is an important lesson for her to learn that Mommy has to do her own work sometimes and is not always available to play. If she has not shown any inclination to play alone, you may have to start small and build up slowly. Sitting at a table together but each with different "work" to do for a few minutes might be a good start. She can draw or paint while you do your paperwork. You could cook, read, or garden in this parallel arrangement. You will need to frequently observe and reflect on what she is doing and marvel at the fact that she is doing it on her own. She'll learn that this is something you approve of so will want to do it more frequently in order to gain your praise. It will be a slow process, since toddlers are not naturally solitary, but you are right to establish this first small step toward independent activity.

My toddler bites!
coping with an aggressive child

Q Our son keeps biting the other children at day care. Why is he doing this?

Day care is a fun but challenging place. Your son is learning to master new skills, and he has to share toys, games, time, and attention from staff, all of which can lead to feelings of frustration. The best solution is to figure out when tensions are rising and step in before things escalate. Ask your child's key caregiver(s) to watch closely, and if she sees your child becoming frustrated, for example, trying to take a toy from another child, to act quickly and distract him with a different activity. If biting happens, she should say firmly, "No biting—it hurts," then remove your child from the play area and keep him with her for a couple of minutes. The child who has been bitten should also receive some positive attention. Make sure that your child gets plenty of praise and encouragement when he behaves appropriately. Biting is a very common behavior in young children, but very few continue with it once they start school.

Q When we visit my friend, my daughter hits her children. Should I cancel our play dates?

Avoiding the situation will not help your child learn how to behave appropriately, and may actually reinforce her aggressive behavior. Being in an unfamiliar environment could be making her feel insecure and hitting is an effective way to gain your attention. If your daughter finds it difficult to be with new people, try inviting your friend (and her children) to your house first so she can get used to them on familiar territory. When she seems confident with this, introduce gradually longer visits to your friend's house. Spend some time sitting with your child at first—don't just send her off to play while you catch up with adult friends. Settle her into an activity with the other children, and stay with them for a little while. Check in regularly and make sure to give her plenty of praise and encouragement when she is playing nicely. This will build your daughter's confidence and social skills, encourage more of the behavior you want to see, and let you keep in touch with your friends!

Q My child seems so rough. Will he grow up to be a bully?

Boys tend to engage in more rough-and-tumble play generally. As long as he is not hurting the other children, it's probably nothing to worry about. If your son does hit, it will be in the heat of the moment;

PARENTS' STORY

Little nipper
an embarrassing episode

When I went to pick my son up from his first day at day care, my joy at seeing him quickly turned to embarrassment and shame when they told me he'd bitten another child. Although he'd nipped me a couple of times at home, I couldn't believe what he had done and just wanted to disappear. The staff were really understanding, though. They explained how they had taken him aside for a couple of minutes to calm down, then helped him join in again with the activities. I tried it myself at home and he got the message really quickly. My son gets on much better at day care now. He still gets upset sometimes over sharing toys, but we have no more biting, so I don't have to worry about what his caregivers will report when I pick him up.

he is too young to think about doing so on purpose. Bullies act the way they do because they have learned that being aggressive is an acceptable way to get what they want. Start your son off on the right track by setting some clear, simple rules so he knows how you expect him to behave, for example: "Keep your hands and feet to yourself," "Play nicely—no hitting," and "Use your words, not your hands." Praise him for following them. When there are arguments, step in and show him how to resolve things appropriately, since children learn by watching and copying their parents.

Q When he's upset my son bangs his head against the wall. I'm worried he will hurt himself!

Seeing your child behave in this way is upsetting, but try to stay calm. Head-banging is probably your son's way of dealing with very strong feelings of anger and frustration that he does not understand yet. Your best strategy is to calm the child, help him label the emotions he's feeling, and help him identify other acceptable outlets. Most children will quickly realize that this behaviour hurts and will soon stop. If you give in and panic, your son will use this behaviour all the more to get what he wants.

If your son is banging his head at other times and not just when he is having a tantrum, this may be a sign that he is sick or in pain. Look for any other signs or symptoms and ask your pediatrician for advice. As your son's language skills improve, he will find other ways to let you know how he is feeling.

Q My daughter has been kicked several times by another child at day care. What should I do?

Offer your daughter plenty of reassurance and lots of hugs, and let her know that you are going to take some action. Unless you know them, try to resist the temptation to storm in and tackle the situation yourself by speaking to the child's parents. This could make things worse and create lots of bad feeling. Remember that if your children end up going to the same school, you will have to

Hitting, biting, kicking
Some reasons why

✳ **Boredom:** If a child lacks stimulation, hitting is an effective way to get some attention—even negative attention in the form of scolding. Try to keep your child entertained with fun activities.

✳ **Tiredness:** None of us is at our best when we are tired. At these times your child is much more likely to lash out to let you know he's had enough.

✳ **Hunger, thirst, or illness:** Young children whose language skills are just developing may struggle to communicate these basic needs. Look for early warning signs to prevent things from escalating.

✳ **Copying others:** Children learn a huge amount by imitating the behavior of other children and familiar adults—particularly their parents. If children see someone else get what they want by being aggressive, don't be surprised if they try the same strategy themselves.

✳ **Frustration, anger, or upset:** Young children want everything "now!" and have poor impulse control, so when you set limits they will respond by showing you how they feel. As language skills develop, your child will be able to tell you how he feels, and aggressive behavior will reduce.

✳ **Needing attention:** Aggressive behavior is almost guaranteed to get a reaction from parents, so can be used very effectively by children.

✳ **Overstimulation:** Too much excitement can result in overenthusiastic play, and children may hit in the heat of the moment. Giving everyone a few minutes to calm down can help.

✳ **Trying to get something:** If aggressive behavior has been successful in the past, it is far more likely to be used again. This pattern can be changed by setting firm limits and responding consistently.

✳ **Trying to get out of doing something:** Hitting or kicking usually results in a child being removed from a situation. If your child doesn't like a particular activity, he may act in a violent manner to avoid taking part.

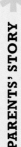

PARENTS' STORY

Calmly confident
a different approach

We always wanted our daughter to stand up for herself, so if another child was aggressive toward her, we used to encourage her to "Hit them back!" However, when she pushed her little brother over, we realized we had created a problem and needed to change our approach. We agreed on some simple rules and praised her for following them. Things are much calmer at home now. Our daughter is really confident, gets along well with other children, and knows how to stand up for herself without being aggressive.

share the playground for several uncomfortable years! There may be lots of reasons why this other child kicked your daughter. He or she may have hit or kicked at other children, too. If she isn't doing so already, tell your daughter to steer clear of this child for the time being. Speak to the day care staff— share your concerns and check back to see what they are doing about the situation.

Q Should I make my toddler apologize when he hits?

Apologies should be heartfelt and genuine, letting the other person know that you are truly sorry for what you did and how it made them feel. As a young toddler, your son is only just beginning to understand the impact of his actions on others. It will be some time before he is fully able to put himself in someone else's shoes and understand how they feel. If you force him to apologize, he will of course learn to say what you want to hear, but he is not yet able to mean it. Making a child apologize, particularly after an upsetting incident, when emotions are running high, also runs the risk of creating another problem as they may genuinely feel they have done nothing wrong. Explain to your

son what he did and how the other person feels, and model apologizing yourself when you make mistakes. In time he will genuinely feel and say "I'm sorry" when he is more able to see the world from someone else's perspective.

Q Ever since her sister was born, our daughter has become really unpleasant. We've tried buying her gifts but it doesn't help.

A new addition to the family is bound to upset the balance of your daughter's world. She is used to being the focus of everyone's attention and is not going to be happy about sharing the limelight she has been basking in alone until now. Buying gifts can help to let your daughter know you are still thinking about her. However, a word of caution: Your daughter is probably feeling a little displaced, and is acting up to get some attention. If you then shower her with gifts, you will be rewarding this behavior, and she will do it all the more. Try to spend some quality time with her alone and ask her to help take care of her sister. When you do reward her, make sure it's because she deserves it and not because you feel guilty.

Q I'm worried about my three-year-old son copying his older brother. Should I keep them apart?

Children learn a huge amount by watching and imitating other people, particularly those they are close to. Unfortunately, you are not going to be pleased with everything your child learns this way. By the age of three, most children can distinguish between fantasy and reality, so your son will be aware that his older brother is only playing if he is acting out violent scenarios or play fighting.

However, if you really don't want your son to be around when his brother is enjoying some rough-and-tumble play with his friends, draw your younger child's attention to another activity rather than telling your older son to change what he is doing. Before long, you will probably be encouraging them to play together and you don't want your older son to start resenting his little brother for ruining his fun.

MYTHS AND MISCONCEPTIONS

Is it true that...

The best way to stop biting is to bite back?

No! This is a very risky strategy and may seriously hurt your child. Clear rules and plenty of praise are safer and far more effective at helping children learn how to behave.

My child's aggressive behavior is just attention seeking?

For younger children this may well be true—although there are lots of other reasons for aggressive behavior. If your child is attention seeking, the important question to ask is "Why?" Children need attention for a reason, so look at what you can do to help them.

Some children are just more aggressive than others?

This is certainly true, but it does not mean that children are born that way. If children learn that aggressive behavior is acceptable and the best way to get what they need, then they will continue to use this approach as they grow up. If your child seems to be very aggressive, consider who he spends time with: He may be imitating this behavior from the people who care for him.

I should practice what I preach?

Yes—you are your child's most important role model. If you correct aggressive behavior but behave aggressively yourself, you give mixed messages and undermine the lessons you are trying to teach.

How do I expand his diet?
fussy eaters

Q Food seems to go flying everywhere when my daughter eats. Is this bad behavior?

Your daughter is naturally curious about how food looks, tastes, and feels. She's making a mess because it's a hit-or-miss process figuring out how to feed herself, and she's exploring the sensation of food in her hands and mouth. This is not bad behavior—it's a step toward greater independence and a welcome sign of curiosity. If too much food is being wasted this way, try giving her a small amount of food to play with while you hold the bowl she's eating from. At this stage it's a good idea not to wear your best clothes at mealtime! You could also put a mat down under her chair to make cleaning up easier. With a little bit of practice and lots of encouragement, your daughter will soon master her self-feeding skills and develop her interest in food. Add in plenty of praise for eating nicely and avoid a fuss when food goes flying, and she'll get the message about what you prefer.

Q My 18-month-old is too busy to stop and eat, and he seems to be losing weight. Should I worry?

Children put on significantly less weight in their second year than they did in the first 12 months of their life. So, while it might look like your son is losing weight, he is actually just growing more slowly than you are used to. Running around and exploring will also burn plenty of calories, so his body shape will be changing, too. Offer him healthy snacks between mealtimes to keep his energy levels up. Avoid sugary or fatty things such as cookies and sweets. Stick to regular mealtimes, but don't force him to eat. This is a battle you will not win, and could lead to eating problems when he is older. Don't overwhelm your child with a large meal—this will not make him eat any more.

Offer smaller portions of food instead—there is always the option to ask for more if he is still hungry. Your son will eat what he needs, so focus on providing him with regular, healthy options, and his interest in food will develop.

Q My three-year-old son wants to eat his meals in front of the TV. Should I let him?

TV is distracting and likely to draw your son's attention away from his meal. If he does not eat enough he may be asking you for snacks later to fill in the gaps. Children at this age are also targeted by TV advertising. Colorful packaging, loud music, and cartoon characters may spark his interest in inappropriate foods and undermine your attempts to encourage healthy eating. Sitting in front of the TV instead of around the dinner table means that your child will miss out on the social aspect of mealtimes, too. Eating as a family allows you to share things about your day, helps your child learn more about food, and gives him the opportunity to develop other skills such as table manners.

Children who eat at least one meal a day with their family have also been shown to have better vocabularies. The occasional meal in front of the TV is unlikely to do any harm, but it is best to avoid this becoming a habit.

Your child may need to try new foods at least 10 times before he will accept them

Q My daughter will only eat canned spaghetti. Help!

Don't worry—you are not alone. Around 20 percent of children under five are known to be fussy about their food at some time. When your daughter keeps asking for the same food meal after meal, this is usually referred to as being stuck in a "food jag." When you are working hard to encourage healthy eating, this can be frustrating and worrying.

Try to stay calm, and avoid unhelpful strategies such as threats and bribery, which will only make things worse. If your child seems happy, healthy, and has plenty of energy, she is probably getting all the calories, vitamins, and minerals she needs from her diet. Offer her healthy snacks through the day and keep preparing her favorite foods, but introduce new things alongside them for her to try. Don't challenge your daughter on her pickiness— focus on the positives and give her plenty of praise when she tries other foods.

Q My child just picks at her food. How can I make her eat more?

All parents worry at some time or other that their child is not eating enough. The truth is that most children will eat what they need, and negotiating this with parents is good for their developing independence. Don't force your child to eat or make her stay at the table until she has cleared her plate. This can make things worse, and could lead to eating difficulties when she is older. Clear the table after 30 minutes—praise what she has eaten and ignore what she has left. Just make sure your child is not filling up on treats afterward! If she's still hungry, this suggests that either she does not like what she is being given or how it's presented. Try including your daughter in the choosing and preparation of her meals. Be careful to limit her choices to two options—both of which you are happy with. Let her help out in the kitchen and make food fun by preparing simple meals together, such as pizzas that she can decorate. Let her see you enjoying the same foods. If you have a garden, you could also try growing a few things together: Children love eating food they've grown themselves.

Introducing new food
How to break the deadlock

Many parents dread presenting their children with a new meal, knowing they will make a fuss and perhaps refuse to eat anything at all. There is a way through this deadlock, though. Start off by putting a tiny amount of the new food on the side of your child's favorite meal. If he complains, don't give in and take it away. It can be hard to see your child upset, but this won't last long, and it is important that he gets the message about who is in charge at mealtime. When your child is okay with the new food being on his plate, encourage him to play with it, put it to his lips, taste it, and finally, eat it. Your child may need to try new foods at least 10 times before he will accept them—so don't give up after a couple of attempts. If he really does not like what is being offered, try something else from the same food group that has the equivalent nutritional value; for example, if he refuses to eat yogurt, try offering cheese instead.

Snack happy
filling up on treats

My son was always happy to eat during the day, and I was pleased he enjoyed his food. He had a good breakfast and then wandered around with his bottle of milk snacking on whatever took his fancy through the day. When it came to his evening meal, though, it was a very different story. Getting him to eat anything was such a battle it often ended with either me or him in tears. Eventually I realized that topping up his bottle with milk whenever he wanted and allowing him to snack freely on cookies meant that he was just not feeling hungry at the right time. I decided to give him water sometimes instead of milk and swapped his cookies for fruit slices and vegetable sticks. He protested at first, but he got used to his new diet in a few days, and it seemed to do the trick. Our evening meals are much calmer now, and my son is more than ready for his food.

Is it OK to reward my child for eating?

You certainly won't be the first parent to say, "Eat your peas, then you can have some ice cream." While this might seem like a good way to motivate your child, research shows that statements like this actually result in children eating fewer peas and valuing ice cream more highly in the long term.

Rewards do help, though—as long as you use them in the right way. Rather than offering a tasty treat, research shows that the most effective reward is to give plenty of praise and encouragement when your child is eating healthy foods. This will make her feel good about what she is doing rather than teaching her to eat just so she can have that dessert. Using rewards in this way will help your child develop healthy eating habits that will last her a lifetime.

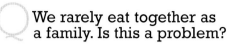

We rarely eat together as a family. Is this a problem?

Modern life is very busy, and it can be hard to get everyone together at the right time to sit down and enjoy a meal. Family mealtimes are an important social event, though, and your child will gain a huge amount from taking part. Conversation around the dinner table promotes speech and language development. Watching how you prepare, serve, and eat your food helps children learn the skills they need to become independent. Eating together also teaches children good table manners and the social skills they will need in school.

Perhaps most importantly, mealtimes are a great opportunity for you to spend quality time with each other as a family. It may not be possible to achieve this every day, but even if you only manage it two or three times a week it will be well worth the effort. Turn off the TV, sit down, share a meal, and enjoy each others' company.

My child refuses to eat his vegetables. Should I hide them in something else?

Young children are much more sensitive to bitter flavors than adults, so it's important to understand that vegetables particularly can taste very different to them. Hiding disliked vegetables in other foods may be successful in getting your child to eat them and so make you feel less anxious. However, if your child does not know he has eaten carrots, he is very unlikely to ever eat them out of choice. Also, if you tell your child what he has just eaten, he may well feel that you have tricked him and will be less likely to trust you on other issues.

Rather than hiding foods, it's best to be open and honest with your child about what he is eating. Try changing how you present the vegetables—serve them raw, cut them into interesting shapes and sizes, or serve them with a sauce to take the edge off their flavor until he is used to the taste. Try different types: If he won't eat spinach, try kale. There are lots of vegetables to choose from, so get your child involved in deciding which he would like to try.

Is she OK?
your child's development

Q My child can't do half the things other parents say their children can. What am I doing wrong?

It is worrying to hear other parents talk about how far ahead their children are—particularly if your own child appears to be slower to develop in some areas. It is important to remember, though, that each child progresses at his or her own pace and in their own unique way. For example, some might walk at an early age but be slower to develop speech and language skills. What matters is that you support your child to make sure she is developing to her potential. Comparing yourself and your child to other families is inevitable (and may make you feel good sometimes), but there will always be someone out there who seems to be doing things better than you. Talk to other parents and you will no doubt discover that they too have worries and concerns about their own children and may be grateful for your advice. If some of your daughter's playmates are more advanced in certain areas, spending time with them will help her to learn their skills too.

Q My son seems lazy—should I push him to do things that I think he's capable of?

Children can only develop as fast as their bodies, and brains, will allow. However, social interaction with parents, other adults, and peers will help a child who is ready to move on to the next challenge. Children learn best when you give them new experiences and challenges that are just beyond what they are currently doing, but still within their capabilities. Some children need more encouragement than others to attempt new tasks, but try not to take over too much. Help your child learn by showing him how to do things, then getting them to repeat them, making suggestions about how to solve problems,

and breaking things down into simple steps. One good example is to get your child to dress himself while you offer a running commentary of what should come next, helping out where necessary. However, pushing your child too hard will result in feelings of frustration and failure—for you and him. Having realistic expectations is the key to success.

Q My partner thinks I'm overanxious, but I'm worried about my son's progress. Should I get him checked out?

Parents know their children better than anyone else, so you are in the best position to judge if something does not seem quite right. Talk to your partner and explain the reasons why you are worried. It may be that he is concerned, too, but is anxious about taking things further in case there is actually a problem. Parents share lots of similar concerns about their children, so discussing things with family, friends, or other parents may be all the help you need. However, if you are still worried and have reason to believe there is a problem, check things out with your pediatrician, who will be able to direct you to further consultants or health professionals if anything is wrong. It is better to worry too much than too little, and if there are any concerns about your son's development, then getting the right support and help early on could make a big difference.

Q My son keeps having nightmares and wakes up very upset. Should I let him sleep with us?

As your son's knowledge and understanding of the world expands, so too will his imagination and the ability to scare himself. If he's getting anxious about going to bed, make this event as relaxing as possible. Spend time with your son in his room before the light

ESSENTIAL INFORMATION: TODDLERS

Early developmental difficulties
How common are problems?

Most children will demonstrate some sort of difficulty during their early years. Problems ranging from nightmares and bed-wetting to fussy eating and behavioral problems are common and a natural part of your child's development. Significant developmental and learning problems such as autistic spectrum disorder, Down's syndrome, and learning disability affect a very small number of children. Overall, boys tend to have more difficulties than girls. The exact reasons for this difference are not clear, although it has been suggested that girls' XX chromosome pattern is a protective factor so boys are more vulnerable to the effects of stress. Behavioral problems may be more common in boys because of the effects of the male hormone testosterone and the fact that society seems to condone more physical and aggressive behavior.

What should I look for? It is helpful to have some idea of the milestones and challenges that your child is working toward at particular ages (see pp. 82–83). Don't worry if she does not hit these targets exactly. Development is a slowly unfolding story, and each child follows her own individual path—some skills emerge early, some may be late or slow to develop, and some may arrive out of turn. For example, persistent bed-wetting may not be a cause for concern in your three-year-old child, but if it is still happening at age five, she may need some specialist help to master this skill. However, even at this age around seven percent of boys do not have full control of their bladder at night.

In these early years, children are progressing through a complex set of processes affecting their physical development, thinking skills, speech and language, and social skills. Difficulties in one area will have an effect on other aspects of their development, and may make things seem worse than they really are. A child who is slower to develop speech and language skills, for example, may get frustrated at being unable to communicate, have more temper tantrums, and find it more difficult to interact than other children do.

When should I get help? Most problems are very short lived, lasting for only a few weeks or months. If you have concerns about your child's development, write them down and check things out with your pediatrician. Make sure that you

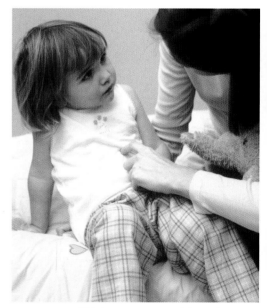

BED-WETTING: This is a common problem, since young children learn bladder control gradually. However, if it persists or starts again after a dry period, something may be troubling your child.

attend regular well-child checkups. If your child has been struggling with a particular issue for six months or more, or you are worried that your child appears to have difficulties in several areas—for example, if she has little speech and language, limited play skills, shows a lack of interest in other people, or displays repetitive or unusual behaviors—it would be advisable to seek professional advice.

Worrying about your child's development is a major source of stress for parents, but remember that in most cases, it's just a phase. It is difficult to accept that your child may be struggling, but for those children who do need additional support, early intervention will lead to better outcomes. In the meantime, a good strategy would be to offer your child plenty of extra playtime and practice in the areas she struggles with, along with lots of praise.

IN A RAGE: Tantrums occur a lot over the toddler years, as your child starts to exert her independence.
NIGHTMARES: Comfort and reassurance when your child has bad dreams will help her to feel secure.

goes out, read a bedtime story together (nothing scary!), and leave him with lots of positive, happy thoughts. If he wakes in the night, listen to his fears and give him plenty of hugs, and reassure him that it was just a bad dream and everything is OK. Settle your son back down in his own room, and avoid the temptation to cuddle up with him in your bed. This will make it even more difficult to get your son into his bed the next night, and will not help him to deal with his nightmares. If your son dreams about a monster under his bed or in his wardrobe, it's fine to turn on a light and go hunting to prove that he's alone. Be careful what you say to reassure him though. Reporting, ''The monster's gone now,'' will make your son's dream even more real because it suggests there was one there in the first place. Try ''See, there's nothing here,'' instead.

Everyone has nightmares from time to time, but if your son's bad dreams continue, try to find out if there is anything worrying him that might explain why his sleep is being disturbed in this way.

My child rocks back and forth before she sleeps. Is she upset?

Body rocking is normal behavior in toddlers, who seem to find the rhythmic movements soothing and sleep inducing. It's similar to the way a child may suck her thumb or twirl her hair to fall asleep. A few toddlers may rock to distract themselves from pain— from an ear infection, for example. The behavior usually starts in the first year, and most children outgrow it by the age of three or four. Your toddler may rock back and forth on all fours or sit up to rock.

Although you may not want to ignore it completely, try to take a low-key approach. If your child perceives that you're trying to stop the rocking, she may take it as a challenge and persist in it, or the added attention may encourage the behavior. A soothing bedtime ritual, such as a warm bath, a story while cuddling, or a gentle backrub, may help her unwind without rocking. If your child starts rocking for the first time after 18 months of age or exhibits similar behavior during the day, or if it lasts past the age of four, bring it up with her pediatrician.

ESSENTIAL INFORMATION: TODDLERS

One to three years
What to expect at each stage

Over the next two years, your toddler will strive to be increasingly independent. He will become more mobile, learn about his environment, himself and other people, and develop speech and language skills. Be prepared—your child will start to have opinions and want to do things his way. Support your child's efforts at independent thinking, and his self-confidence and self-esteem will increase, giving him the skills he needs to succeed in the big wide world.

At 12–18 months, children may:

✻ Be walking on their own. Children may still fall occasionally, but they can move quickly and love to explore. Make sure that their environment is safe: Use stair gates and check that furniture is stable.

✻ Learn to feed themselves with a spoon and use a cup to drink from. You will soon be able to tell if your child will be left- or right-handed.

✻ Look for favorite toys they can't see. Your child is forming a stronger mental picture of his world and can think about things that are not in his immediate environment. This includes you too!

✻ Know their own name and turn when called— unless they are busy!

✻ Enjoy listening to nursery rhymes and sitting on your knee to look at books and pictures. Sing and talk to your child as much as you can.

✻ Start to use single words. By using these words in a different context, changing the intonation of the voice and using gestures, "holophrases" (single words used to represent a phrase or sentence) can have lots of different meanings. "Milk" could mean "I want more milk" or "I have dropped my milk." These holophrases won't be around for long, though, as your child is getting ready for a language explosion in the next few months.

GROWING INDEPENDENCE: Your child will begin attempting to dress himself. He may find buttons and zippers tricky, so put him in clothes with simple fastenings if you can, and help out if he gets stuck.

✻ Look to you for guidance about how to behave in unfamiliar social situations. If you look happy and offer words of encouragement, they will approach new toys and people with confidence.

✻ Start to engage in pretend play by copying what they have seen you do. Your child may pretend to cook or clean, make coffee, and fix things using real objects.

At 18–24 months children may:

✻ Walk up and down stairs, run, jump, and climb. Your child can get to wherever he wants—there is no stopping him now.

✻ Begin to recognize their reflection in the mirror and identify themselves in pictures.

✻ Have good bowel control. It could be time to think about toilet training. Don't force this issue though— go at your child's pace.

✻ Help dress and undress themselves. (They will still need your help with buttons and zippers.)

✱ Move gradually from playing alongside other children to playing cooperatively with them, taking turns, sharing, and working on play activities together.

✱ Develop their own pretend-play routines rather than copying what they have seen you do. Dolls, action figures, and teddy bears may be put in charge of directing the action. Children will also enjoy scribbling on paper, pouring water and sand, and throwing a ball.

✱ Begin to say how they feel and recognize that other people have emotions that can be different from their own. This will lead on to developing empathy.

✱ Begin using lots of words now to name objects, people, and places they are familiar with. Words may also be combined into two-word sentences such as "Mommy gone" and "More milk." Remember that children understand much more than they can say.

At two to three years children may:

✱ Give their name when asked.

✱ Be able to feed themselves with a spoon and fork.

✱ Enjoy running and chasing games and rough-and-tumble play. Some children may also engage in playfighting with other children.

✱ Encourage other children to join them in a pretend game by saying "Let's pretend we're…." Your child may also use objects to represent something else—an empty cardboard box could be a car, a house, or a pirate ship.

✱ Recognize when someone else is feeling sad or upset, and offer them comfort by hugging them, giving them objects, or getting help. They may also retaliate on behalf of another child.

✱ Begin to understand that other people see the world differently from them. This is the basis for children to develop a "theory of mind," which first emerges at around four years of age. Theory of mind is your child's ability to put himself in someone else's shoes and to recognize that other people have knowledge, ideas, beliefs, and desires that are different from his own.

✱ Be using sentences and occasional made-up words for things they find difficult to say, such as "yo yo" for yogurt. Conversations are focused on the present, and your child's thirst for knowledge about his world may lead him to ask lots of "Why?" questions. Try to answer as many of these as you can, and look at books together to develop your child's inquiring mind.

BETTER BALANCE: From 18 months of age your child will have enough balance to get himself from place to place in any way he chooses, including running, jumping, and riding on scooters and trikes. Wheeled toys can help to develop stability and coordination.

JOINING IN: Moving from parallel play, where children play alongside each other, to cooperative play, where they play together, is one of the milestones of this age and is a sign of growing social skills.

And then there were two…
a new baby

My toddler wants to pick up his new baby sister. Is this safe?

It is positive to see that your toddler wants to help with the new baby, to touch and cuddle her. As he's seen you pick her up, he will almost certainly want to copy you, and may even try to carry her around. This is not safe at all: His strength and balance are not well-developed enough to hold her safely or to support her head as well as she needs. One alternative is to have your toddler put his arms around the baby while you have her fully supported on your lap. This way he gets to feel close to his sister while you keep her held safely.

Your toddler should not be left alone with the new baby for even the shortest period, since he does not have the understanding to treat her safely. This may seem overcautious, especially if you just want to leave the room to get a cup of water or answer the phone, but take your toddler with you every time. It only takes a second for a child full of initiative and curiosity to experiment with whether he can pick up his sister.

Our new baby is very sick. How can we tell our toddler without worrying him too much?

At such an anxious time, it can be hard to know how much or little to share with your toddler. There is no doubt he will know something is wrong and be wondering about it. He may even fear that the baby is sick because he had an unkind thought, such as, "I wish she wasn't born." This sort of worry is natural at his age; his egocentric view of the world means he thinks he has this sort of power. It is up to you to let him know your baby is ill but that it's not because of anything he did or said. He may ask whether the baby will die. This might be very difficult to handle because of your own fears and distress. Be truthful in your answer: If this is a possibility then say so, but

stress that right now, everyone is working hard to make your baby feel better. By being honest with your toddler, you allow him to be a part of the process of caring for his sister.

Explain that lots of people, such as doctors and nurses, will be helping the family and that there will be trips to the hospital and clinic to check the baby. Minimize the impact of medical appointments on your toddler by bringing along plenty to keep him busy. Having a puzzle and coloring books, or a favorite book to read, gives him some choices while he waits. Enlist friends and relatives to come with you to entertain your son or ask them to care for him at home. This allows you to concentrate fully on the doctor's advice during your appointments.

Why has our toddler reverted to babyish behavior since the birth of our new baby?

It is common for the arrival of a new baby to coincide with a setback in your toddler's progress, such as more toileting accidents, demands for a diaper or bottle even though these have been phased out, and more clingy behavior.

One explanation for more baby-like behavior is that your toddler is trying to get the same priority treatment from you as his new sibling. He sees the baby get immediate attention when she's thirsty or

Your toddler has lost his privileged position as your only child—it's no wonder he's out of sorts

ESSENTIAL INFORMATION: TODDLERS

Here comes baby
Preparing for a new arrival

A new baby brings great pleasure and real upheaval—not only for parents but for older children, too. Your toddler's world will change. He'll need to share your attention and may have to wait while the new baby is seen to first. Explaining to him that he'll be sharing his home, and your time and attention with another child can be a challenge which needs thoughtful and sensitive handling.

Your child's feelings: Developmentally, your young child will find it very difficult to see things from someone else's perspective. As far as he is concerned, he is the very center of the universe, and he may not understand why you would want another child. He may even be concerned that you are going to replace him with your new baby! If your toddler is feeling anxious, you may find that he is more clingy and upset, or has more temper tantrums than usual. Continue to manage his behaviour as before: It is important to maintain consistency as this will be reassuring for him.

Pregnancy and delivery: Your child will have a very limited understanding of time, so think carefully about when you are going to tell him that you are having another baby. Too early and you will be answering questions for a very long time; too late and your child will pick up on the fact that something is different and may feel left out and insecure. Linking the birth to a significant event around the time, such as a birthday, can help your child to understand when their sibling will be arriving. Taking your child to prenatal appointments so he can listen to the baby's heartbeat, allowing him to stroke and talk to your belly, and feeling the baby kick will make him feel included, making the pregnancy more real to him.

Many children's books tell the tale of a new baby coming into the family. Reading these stories together will help his understanding and prompt questions about how life is going to be.

If you are having a hospital birth, it can be helpful to explain a little about what will happen as children tend to associate the hospital with sickness, and may worry about you.

Dealing with changes at home: Include your child in preparing your home so he does not feel the baby is pushing him out. For example, he could help with choosing equipment, clothing, and room colors. If you are going to allow your child to help out in this way, make sure that you give him a limited range of options to choose from.

Your child may be excited at the prospect of having someone new to play with and may not understand that, initially, his sibling will be unable to run around and have fun with him, and will actually be a rather noisy addition to the household. Show him photos and videos of himself at that age to help him to be more realistic in his expectations.

WHAT'S IN THERE?: Involve your child in your new baby's life by allowing him to talk to your belly.

ESSENTIAL INFORMATION: TODDLERS

Jealous toddler
A common reaction to a new birth

Your toddler has to cope with a big change—the entrance of a rival for your affection. Not all toddlers are jealous of their new sibling, and most react positively, at least in the early days. At first your toddler is likely to be fascinated by the baby, want to touch and stare at her, be eager to choose a gift, and proudly introduce "his" baby to everyone who visits.

Jealousy emerges: For some toddlers, this initial goodwill turns to jealousy as the excitement of birth gives way to everyday routine, and he realizes he gets less of your attention and that his sister isn't yet the playmate he wanted. Many toddlers think the baby is a temporary visitor and, once she leaves, everything will go back to normal. Discovering the change is permanent can trigger his negative reaction. Having been first in line for your time, now he's often at the end, as the baby's cries are attended to first. It's no wonder he's a little out of sorts.

You may find your toddler shows only a mild reaction, perhaps regressing to wanting his pacifier, increasing his thumb sucking, having worse separation anxiety, or wanting to be by your side rather than play independently. This can be remedied by plenty of loving reassurance that he's still important to you. It is essential that he still have one-on-one time with you every day, even though this can be difficult to achieve. A few minutes of games on the carpet when the baby is in her bouncy-seat and some quiet cuddle time before bed, perhaps sharing a story just like you used to, will reassure him that your feelings for him haven't changed. Where possible, keep to the same outings and activities as before. This reassures him that he's not going to miss out on playgroup or visiting friends because of the new arrival. He'll feel more settled when some things in his life stay the same.

A strong reaction? A small number of toddlers react strongly to the new arrival and show their anger at being displaced through tantrums, trying to hurt the baby, and saying things like "I wish the baby was dead" or "I hate the baby." These reactions can be very distressing as you naturally want him to love his sibling, and you may be shocked at the strength of his emotions. Be reassured that his harsh words are "in the moment" expressions of anger, and he may well be loving toward the baby within minutes of an outburst. No matter whether your toddler is delighted or unhappy about the new arrival, he should not be left alone with the baby. Close supervision is especially important if he is angry or jealous, because he's not able to judge how dangerous it could be if he hit or

MOMMY'S LITTLE HELPER: Passing the diaper or fetching a towel or bottle can make your older child feel useful and important, reducing her jealousy.

pushed the baby or covered her face, and he may cause her serious harm. When it comes to his angry words, avoid lecturing him or showing how upset you are. It is preferable if you acknowledge his emotion and leave it at that, for example saying, "You seem angry with the baby" or "I can tell you're not happy with the baby right now." This is an important sign to him that you still notice and recognize his feelings.

His jealousy can be toned down if you give him the role of your assistant. Give him a doll to care for so he can copy you as you bathe and tend to the baby. Role playing the behavior of adults is a favorite activity for young children and allows him to express his feelings through play rather than directly at his sibling. Work out a plan for times when you have to give the baby lots of attention and can't respond easily to demands from your toddler. If you set up your older child with a snack or game it can give you those precious few minutes to settle or feed the baby, and keep your toddler satisfied too.

ALL TOGETHER NOW: Take the time to play with your toddler when the new baby is present, but not in need of your direct attention.

needs to be changed, and copies to see if you'll come to him as quickly. This is not a conscious plan but is driven by his deep need for your attention.

It's likely, however, that the reason is more complex, since regression is a reaction to stress. He's been the center of attention in your family, essentially the king of the castle, demanding and receiving your attention whenever he asks for it. All of a sudden he's been "dethroned"—pushed out of this position, no longer first for your attention, but having to wait until the baby's needs have been met before he is seen to. This loss of his place as the youngest or only child in the family and of having your sole attention may be expressed through more dependent behavior.

Be reassured that this is a phase in his adjustment to family change and usually goes away as life settles down into a routine. While babyish behavior may be exasperating, chiding him for it isn't helpful. He'll benefit from reassurance in the form of extra cuddles and comforting hugs but try to avoid putting him back into diapers or returning his pacifier, because you'll have to work hard to phase them out again.

Should I accept offers from family to look after my toddler for a few days to give me some time with my new baby?

This sort of offer is very tempting, especially at times when your toddler is misbehaving or demanding and you're lacking in sleep. However, consider what type of message this sends to your older child. It may reinforce his belief that he's being pushed out of the family by the new baby or that he's no longer wanted. Being away from you for long periods, such as a whole day or overnight, is a significant separation for your toddler and likely to result in withdrawn or angry behavior or more clinginess when he gets back. An alternative to long breaks might be to accept offers to care for him more frequently but for shorter periods, such as an hour or two. He can have an exciting time with family friends or relatives, but the time apart won't be so long that he feels anxious and is unsettled on his return. Do make the most of this time by resting yourself.

School starters
out into the world

* **Starting school**
  the next big step

* **The birds and the bees**
  when to address sex

* **Learning difficulties**
  helping them through

* **My child's a genius!**
  the perils of pushy parenting

* **She won't eat her greens**
  food issues tackled

* **The odd one out?**
  making friends

* **Family bonding**
  forging close connections

* **Run, jump, and play**
  keeping them moving

Starting school
the next big step

Q My son complains of stomachaches on school days. Is he just attention-seeking?

Upset stomachs and headaches are often a sign of anxiety, but you may want to rule out any physical causes with a visit to your pediatrician. However, if your son is genuinely worried about school, his stomachache may be very real, even if there is no medical explanation. Talk to him when he feels safe and relaxed (perhaps at storytime) to see if there is anything specific he is worried about. It can help to keep track of when he reports feeling ill to see if there are particular days or activities he is concerned about. Make an appointment to see his teachers and share your concerns with them—they may have ideas about what is going on, too. Let your son know that you are taking him seriously and you are working with the school to make things better for him.

For a small number of children, anxiety about school can develop into a phobia, so it is important to address issues quickly and sensitively to prevent things from escalating.

Q I'm getting reports from school that my son is being disruptive in class. He's fine at home. What can I do?

Starting school brings a whole new set of challenges for children to deal with. They have to follow a set routine for most of the day, learn and follow the school rules, and fit in with everyone else. As they progress through school, the emphasis shifts from learning through play to more academic work, which means that children have to sit down, listen, and focus their attention on a task. Some children find it more difficult to control their behavior and may only be able to concentrate for short periods before needing a break. This can make learning more difficult and lead to feelings of frustration. Others may struggle with certain subjects, such as reading or math, which may result in them being disruptive.

Speak to your son's teacher to find out exactly what is going on. Agreeing some simple, achievable targets with the school can help make it clear what is expected. Your son may feel disheartened about the situation, so make sure he gets plenty of praise and encouragement to boost his self-esteem. A home/school diary can also be used to share good news.

Q My daughter is afraid of her strict teacher. What should I do?

Trying to maintain order in a large class of noisy, excitable children is no easy task. Teachers take control in different ways, and some are bound to be more authoritarian in their approach. This style of classroom management can be difficult for children who are not used to raised voices and stern faces. Young children may also feel that the teacher is targeting them personally rather than addressing the behavior of the whole class, and may be very sensitive to being "scolded" if they have not done anything wrong. Try discussing things with your daughter to help her see that the teacher's behavior is not just directed toward her. If she continues to be upset, arrange to meet with her teacher to explain how she feels. Making her teacher aware of the situation will make her sensitive to your child's reaction. It is unreasonable to expect that your daughter will get along well with all of her teachers.

All children need to learn to cope with change, but some take longer to adjust

ESSENTIAL INFORMATION: SCHOOL STARTERS

Preparing for school
A new beginning

Making the move to school is one of the biggest transitions in your child's life. Some children will be excited by the new opportunities this brings, and others will be worried about leaving the comfort and familiarity of the people they know. Make it clear to your child that he'll be going five days a week, so he doesn't think this is a one-time event! Parents may also feel anxious about how a child will adjust, and sad that he is growing up so fast.

✱ **Get to know your child's school:** Going on at least one visit to his new school, meeting his teacher, and spending time in his classroom will make it much easier for your child to settle in once he starts. With the school's permission, you could even take a photo or two to remind him of where he will be going and who he will meet. Over the summer, practice the route you will take to school. Try a couple of full dress rehearsals so that you and your child can get used to the new morning routine.

✱ **New shoes:** Children enjoy helping to choose new things for school, such as shoes, bags, lunch boxes, and pencils. Stores tend to sell out of popular items, so try not to leave everything to the last few days before school starts. Buying a few things at a time over a longer period will help him get used to the idea of starting school. Remember to label everything clearly with your child's name.

✱ **The big day:** Get things ready the night before, and make sure you both get up in plenty of time. When you get to school, your child may want to stay firmly by your side, or he may see a friend and want to spend a few minutes playing. Stay with him until the bell rings, then give him a hug and a kiss, and say good-bye. Remind him that you will be there to pick him up later, then wave and leave.

✱ **After school:** Greet your child with a big hug and a warm, welcoming smile. Take time to look at the things he has brought home, and put his work on display to show how proud you are.

THE FIRST DAY: When you get to school, boost your child's confidence by talking about the fun she will have and the new friends she will make. Make sure she has all her belongings, then calmly take your leave.

MORNING ROUTINE: Make sure you have plenty of time to help your child get ready in the morning before school when he is still young. Short cuts, such as shoes with Velcro straps instead of laces, may speed up the process.

Physical challenges
Coping with disability

If your child has a physical disability such as cerebral palsy (a condition that affects movement, posture, and coordination), or a hearing or visual impairment, starting school will bring additional challenges. Many more children now attend mainstream as opposed to special schools, which is a positive step forward in many ways. However, this means that some schools may lack experience of supporting children with additional physical needs. Open, honest, and regular communication with the school will help them make the adjustments necessary to ensure that your child is fully integrated into school life, and not just included on the attendance roll.

Team approach: The key to a smooth, successful transition to school is to have all the involved professionals—health, education, and social care—working together with you on a coordinated plan to support your child's needs. Ideally this team of people should begin meeting with you some time in advance of your child's move so that the appropriate support will be in place when he starts, before specific needs arise. If your child has experienced a successful day-care or other preschool placement, talk to the staff from that setting as they may have valuable information to share. Make sure that they are invited to attend these meetings.

Raising awareness: Staff and students will have different experiences of children with special needs. This will affect their expectations of your child and how they behave toward him initially. Your child's classmates will probably be curious and ask questions about your child's difficulties, while some teachers may be anxious about how best to interact. It will take time for

everyone to get to know each other, and this could be a steep learning curve. People will want to do their best to support and include your child. However, a simple lack of understanding may result in well-intentioned but unnecessary or inappropriate attempts to help. At other times, your child may struggle because not enough help is provided. Be clear in communicating your child's needs, and encourage him to speak up when he needs additional help. Write down a list of your child's strengths and weaknesses to share with the school. To be more comprehensive, you may also wish to provide the faculty with a fuller description of your child and his story so far.

School environment: Consideration may need to be given to the content and layout of your child's classroom, as well as other parts of the school he will need to access, such as the playground and science labs. Bear in mind the following questions when you are meeting with faculty:

✱ Can my child get into school safely and easily, or will adaptations such as ramps and lifts be necessary?
✱ Is the classroom easy to access and move around in? Where will my child sit to ensure he can take part in all activities?
✱ How will my child be assisted in moving around school for recess, assemblies, and lunchtime?
✱ Are the signs around school clear, visible, and easy for my child to understand?
✱ Can my child access the play area independently?
✱ In the unlikely event of a fire, how will my child be supported to exit the building quickly and safely? Fire doors fitted with magnetic safety catches (so they close only in the event of a fire) can make life much easier for children with mobility problems.

Curriculum: Discuss with school faculty what support your child needs in the classroom to enable him to join in with his classmates and follow the curriculum. Remember that this is likely to change as the demands of the curriculum change, so make time to schedule regular meetings with his teachers to stay up to date. If your child finds the coursework too difficult, a more individualized education plan may be suggested.

The following issues will need to be explored:

✱ Will a special teacher or counselor be available to provide additional support to my child and his teachers?

✱ Can my child access all the materials he needs to use in the classroom?

✱ What additional teaching resources can be used to help my child?

✱ Will staff be given special training or any specialist equipment my child may need to use?

✱ Will my child need any one-on-one support? If so, will this be rotated to avoid his becoming too dependent on one particular person?

Social life: The quality of your child's social life at school will have a significant impact on his confidence, self-esteem, and happiness. Careful consideration needs to be given to the opportunities he will have for social interaction with his classmates. Morning arrival, recess, and lunchtime are all social hotspots, and your child should be as fully included in these activities as possible. Some schools employ a buddy system, where one of a number of pupils will take a turn spending time with and helping your child. School trips and after-school activities are also important for building bonds. Find out what trips and activities are planned for the term, and speak to your child's teacher about ways in which he can be included.

Children with obvious physical needs can often be overprotected by others, which may limit their opportunities to spend time with their peers. Getting the balance right between safety and independence can be tricky at times. You know your child better than anyone else, so talk to him about what he would like to be involved in and try to make it happen.

SPECIAL HELPER: Some schools provide a dedicated member of staff to look after your child, helping him adjust to his new environment.

BEING PREPARED: Discuss with the school any piece of special equipment your child needs, and make sure they know how it works.

PLAYING AROUND: Whether your child enjoys school or not will to a great extent depend on her interaction with other children.

School holidays

School breaks are both loved and dreaded by parents. You may find yourself counting down the days to the start of school if you don't plan ahead.

✷ Structure and routine: As much as your child may be looking forward to vacation, moving from the structure and routine of school to the freedom and flexibility of one or more weeks at home can be difficult. Help everyone enjoy the break by maintaining your child's familiar routines. As children get older, you may want to allow them to stay up a little later when school is out. If so, agree a time and stick to it.

✷ Things to do: Rather than having to think up activities on the day, it's helpful to draw up a list of fun things to do before the break begins. The weather will play a part, so make sure you have a number of wet and dry options. For example, you could go on a bike ride together, see a movie, go swimming, go bowling, visit a museum, go for a picnic, walk a nature trail, play board games, do arts-and-crafts activities, or bake cookies and cupcakes. School breaks are a prime time for family-friendly entertainment, so look in the local papers and on the internet to see what is going on in your local area. Involve your child in deciding what you will do together each day, but don't overload him with too many choices. Agree the order of things so that everyone knows what is happening. Try to balance indoor and outdoor activities, and arrange play dates if your child has friends who live nearby.

Q Going back to school after a break always seems to cause problems. Is there anything I can do?

The longer the holiday, the more difficult it can be to make the shift back to school routines and work. At the start of a new school year, some children may also feel anxious about changing to a new class and having a new teacher.

It's important to keep things relaxed over school breaks, but try to keep some routines in place—even if things like bedtime may happen a little later. You can also help to keep school on the agenda by talking about friends and activities she enjoys at school. Shopping for new school supplies will also help her to start preparing for the return to school. Toward the end of vacation, you will need to gradually reign in your child's bedtime routine so that her sleep pattern fits with the early-morning start.

Q My son never tells me anything about school. Should I give up?

When your son has been working hard all day at school, the last thing he will feel like doing is going through it all again in detail. Give him some time to relax, then pick up the conversation with him later. It's frustrating to feel that your child is shutting you out but, the more you push him to talk, the less willing he will be to share things with you. Make yourself available to talk when he is ready: Helping out with homework can be a good time. Start with general questions then try focusing on particular classes or activities: "What did you do in science today?" might get you further than "How was school?" Check his bag for notes from school and use these to stimulate conversation about activities and events in school. If you show that you are interested, he will let you know how things are going in his own time.

The birds and the bees
when to address sex

My parents told my son that if he touched his private parts, they would drop off. What should I do?

The difference between generations in handling sexual development can be wide; it is now more clearly understood that curiosity about the body is a normal stage of development, and old anxieties and taboos have been relaxed.

Your first priority is to let your son know that touching himself is not wrong, and will not result in anything bad happening to his body. Explicitly tell him that his penis will not fall off so he is absolutely clear about this. Now may be the opportunity to talk about privacy and when it is okay to touch himself. You could explain that his genitals are sometimes called his private parts because they are a special private area of his body just for him. Go on to emphasize that exploring his body is fine, but is something to do when he's at home, rather than around other people. You could say, "It's okay to touch yourself, but this is something to do in private, in your bedroom." It is up to you how you explain his grandparents' warning. You could say that this is an old myth, but now we know it's not true. Try to avoid saying that your parents told an untruth, since this could get in the way of his future relationship with

them. The only way to avoid a repeat of the situation is to talk to your parents about how you handle this issue, and try to get them to back you up by doing the same. Remind them that your child probably had no idea they found this behavior offensive.

My child asked me what sex was. What should I tell him?

There is wide variation in when children ask specific questions about sex, and also in when parents think it is appropriate to talk about it. However, sometime between ages four and seven, the questions will come, since he's likely to have heard the word in songs or on television and may even have picked up some misinformation from older children. When you speak calmly about this subject and are open in answering his questions, you're teaching him a valuable lesson that sex and love go together and are not secretive or bad.

You'll need to keep it simple, though, so you might say, "Sex is something grown-ups do when they love each other very much. The man and the woman get their bodies very close together and show they love each other by kissing and cuddling. Sometimes when a man and a woman have sex they make a baby start to grow inside the mummy." If you prefer to use the word "make love" then explain clearly that this means the same as "sex" so he doesn't think these are two different things.

You may wonder if talking about sex could make your child so comfortable with the idea that he's more likely to act on it earlier than children who haven't been so well-informed. The opposite is true: Children in families where sex education and discussion is commonplace are less likely to take part in underage sex and, when they do begin sexual relationships, are more apt to take precautions.

Talking about how babies are made gives you the opportunity to pass on your values about relationships and love

ESSENTIAL INFORMATION: SCHOOL STARTERS

"Where do babies come from?"
How to explain to your child

You may be dreading the words, "Where did I come from?" from your inquisitive child. The temptation to answer, "the hospital" (or something equally evasive) could be strong, but you probably know that it'll be up to you to provide education about sex, gender, and reproduction. You may find his interest appears earlier than you expected, perhaps because of a greater openness about the subject in society, and the fact that there are more images of pregnancy and intimacy on television and in magazines than ever before. Avoid the surprise by taking the initiative and tell him about babies without being asked.

Plan ahead: Getting the balance of information right for your child's age and understanding may be your first challenge. Too much detail, and you'll end up confusing him; too little, and his curiosity won't be satisfied. It is a good idea to plan in advance how you'll respond so you are prepared no matter what he asks. Find your own style and words you're comfortable with by reading books and discussing what you'll say with your partner, so you're both ready with a similar response. Whatever you decide to say, find a quiet, private moment to open up the subject. If you're reacting to a question, try to stop and answer as soon as he asks, even if it's embarrassing to you. If this isn't convenient, address the topic at the next opportunity, and avoid talking about the human body or sex as dirty or wrong. Otherwise, your child may get the impression that the subject is secret, bad, or taboo, and be less likely to ask you again.

"Where do babies come from?" This is a typical form of the question your four to five year old is likely to ask. He is ready for some basic

information. Before you start, ask him how he thinks babies are made. This makes you aware of any misconceptions he has, allowing you to correct them. It also gives a guide to his level of understanding from which to start your answer. Your young child may think the baby has always existed, and has just got bigger now. A little older, and he's gained a more advanced concept, knowing the baby has been created and that Daddy was involved, but no realistic idea of exactly what went on. Explain with a simple statement, such as, "Babies are made when an egg from a woman and a sperm from a man are joined together. The baby grows in the woman's tummy for almost a whole year, and then comes out into the world." Your answers will no doubt prompt plenty of other questions about what an egg and sperm look like, how they get inside Mommy, and how the baby gets out. Be ready to reply to all these accurately, but with your child's age in mind. If your explanation is too basic he will ask more questions

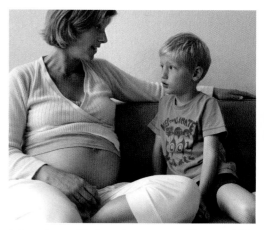

CONFIDENCES: Find a quiet moment with your child to discuss how babies are made.

and, if it's too complicated, he'll look away and may even wander off to do something else. Watch for signs that you're not pitching the information quite right, and adjust your style in response.

Clearly illustrated books can help with these explanations and be shown as you talk. However, asking children to look at the books on their own is not enough—your explanation is required. Expect to come back to the subject at a later date; your child's curiosity will lead them to want to know more.

"Why are boys different from girls?" This is a natural follow-up to finding out how babies are made. At this age, your child will be interested in obvious physical signs of difference rather than internal organs or the longer-term differences that appear at puberty. He will want to know the names for girls' and boys' genitals, and be intrigued as to why there is any need for the difference.

He will probably be satisfied with a simple answer, along the lines of, "Boys have a penis and girls have a vagina. Girls' bodies are made so they can have a baby in their belly, and boys' bodies are made so they can help make the baby, but they don't carry it in their belly."

IMPORTANT LESSONS: Your child may be given some basic explanation of reproduction at school.

How early should I tell my children about good and bad touching and secrets?

You can begin teaching your child about the difference between good and bad touching as early as three years of age, then build on her basic understanding as she grows. She will benefit from being taught that her body belongs to her, and that she can say "no" when she doesn't want to be touched. Have fun explaining and practicing good touching, such as tickles and hugs from Mommy and Daddy. As she reaches four or five, you can talk about when touching is bad, for example if her genitals are touched when she does not want them to be or she's asked to touch the genitals of an adult or a child who is a more grown up than she is. Let her know that she can tell you or other adults, such as her teacher, when she has felt uncomfortable about being touched. Introduce the idea of bad and good secrets; those who abuse children will often tell them to keep it a secret, and threaten them or their family if they tell.

Explain to your child that good secrets are things like not telling Mommy about the birthday present she and Daddy bought, or keeping it a secret that a party is planned so it is a nice surprise. A bad secret is one where she feels uncomfortable or scared rather than excited. If she's not certain about a secret, make sure she knows she should tell an adult—and keep telling until someone listens to her. However, even if you explain all of this clearly, there is only so much your child can do to keep herself safe, so your own vigilance about where she is and who she's with plays a large role in protecting her. Be choosy about who looks after her, notice if she is uncomfortable or upset, and remember—children are much more often abused by people they know than by strangers.

My son asked me what "gay" means, because the children at school say it. Is he too young to know?

It is up to you when you introduce the idea of same-sex relationships. However, the fact that he may be hearing the word "gay" being used to tease or bully means he'll benefit from some education to ensure he does not copy this negative attitude. Your explanation can be straightforward, for example, "Gay means someone who loves a person of the same sex. That could be a boy in love with another boy or a girl in love with a girl." With older children you could expand on the subject and let them know about the meaning of other words such as "lesbian" and "homosexual." This is also a chance to give a lesson about bullying. You could talk about how words can be used to hurt other people, and ask him to imagine how it might feel to be called names. Ensure he gets the message that name-calling is not acceptable because it can make other people feel sad or left out. If you do not feel comfortable speaking about same-sex relationships, perhaps another trusted adult could cover the subject for you. If you feel it is inappropriate to speak about it at all, then concentrate on the name-calling aspect and go into more detail about why this is unacceptable.

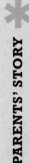

PARENTS' STORY

Caught in the act
what are you doing?

My partner and I recently faced the embarrassment of our six-year-old walking in on us having sex. I am not sure who was more shocked, him or us, and we reacted by yelling at him to get out. After hurriedly getting dressed I went and spoke to him, and it seems he'd heard noises from our room that sounded like a fight and he'd come to help. I reassured him that nothing unkind was happening and explained in basic terms that Mommy and Daddy were being loving, not fighting. It was a real learning experience for me, and we're now more careful about when we make love, try to keep the volume down, and have put a simple lock on the inside of the door to avoid any more surprises. We've now got a privacy rule too—all of us knock before we go into each other's bedrooms.

Q I found my son and a friend from his class naked and giggling in his room. Should I be worried?
Looking at and touching another child's body, including their genitals, is common among children aged four to seven. If the children were around the same age, usually with no more than two years' difference between them, appeared comfortable in their play, and were not acting out or describing explicit sexual behavior, then it should not be cause for concern. This is just another aspect of your child's exploration of his body and the similarities and differences between himself and others. Role-playing moms and dads, teachers and pupils, or doctors and patients is also common at this age. It is worth considering whether to let the parents of the other child know about the play so they, too, can consider how to react. They may hold a different view about whether this is acceptable.

However, if your child seems to know more about sex than usual for his age, acts out clearly sexual behavior, or uses detailed sexual language, then seek advice from your pediatrician.

Q My child used a dreadful word. How should I react?
Sexual swearing is common, usually copied from others when your child gets a sense of their excitement at using words that are shocking and forbidden. Between the ages of four and seven, she is unlikely to know the true meaning of the words or be aware of how offensive they are. Your reaction will be a key factor in whether she realizes her mistake or keeps this up. Try to control your initial response; she'll be watching to see exactly what you do. If you giggle or get angry, she knows she's onto something big!

Try a calm reaction, such as, "Using that word is not okay, please don't say it again," and then distract her attention right away. Remember, the more fuss you make, the more she'll do it again. Make a point of reacting positively when your child uses pleasant and respectful language, and praise her for it to balance the attention she's had for any bad words.

MYTHS AND MISCONCEPTIONS

Is it true that...

✳ **I must use anatomically correct words when I tell my children about sex and reproduction?**
It is recommended that you use the anatomically correct names for children's body parts and explain some harmless nicknames, too. Knowing both allows your child to understand, no matter what terms are being used.

✳ **It's okay to say the stork leaves babies or that they're found in a cabbage patch?**
These stories of how babies arrive are not harmful; they're part of a magical way of thinking that suits your child under age four. Do tell a more accurate story of birth from age four onward, as your child is ready and curious for the facts and may be confused by seeing pregnant women and reconciling this with the stork and cabbage-patch stories.

✳ **He'll bring it up when he's ready, so I should wait until he asks about babies before I introduce the subject?**
This is false. When you open up the subject you can be well prepared, rather than ambushed by a question. Deciding to hold this conversation before you're asked means you can give accurate information before your child hears tall tales from the playground.

Learning difficulties
helping them through

Q My six-year-old son has a developmental delay. Does that mean he will always be behind?

The term "developmental delay" is a confusing one for parents. It implies that skills your child has yet to acquire will eventually arrive—in the same way that a delayed train is annoyingly late, but definitely on its way. Since your son is still very young and has lots of growing and developing to do, it's not possible to say for certain exactly how his skills and abilities will compare to those of his peers in the future. However, the more wide-ranging his difficulties, the less likely it is that he will catch up in all areas. Like all children, as your son gets older he will reach a peak in the development of particular skills. This means that the gap between him and his peers will be wider in some areas than others. All children have strengths and weaknesses, though—so try to focus on what your son can do well, and use that to compensate for his difficulties in other areas, in order to help him achieve his potential.

Q Our daughter has a moderate learning disability. Should we go easy on discipline?

Within their capabilities, all children need to learn how to behave in an appropriate and socially acceptable way. Just because your daughter has a learning disability, there is no reason to treat her any differently. If you fail to set firm and consistent boundaries around your daughter's behavior now, you are likely to have difficulty managing things at home as she gets older. She may try to get away with things at school, too, which could cause more problems. Discuss your concerns with your partner and agree some simple house rules about behavior. To help your daughter understand them, draw the rules out in picture form and display them somewhere visible, such as on the refrigerator. Use plenty of praise and encouragement when she follows a rule ("Great job putting all your toys away!") and use simple consequences for rule-breaking. Don't be surprised if things seem to get a little worse at first. It's normal for children to turn up the volume when parents clamp down on their behavior. If you and your partner are consistent, your daughter will quickly understand what is expected of her. You may also find it helpful to attend an appropriate parenting group, where you could learn other strategies to promote your child's development and manage behavior. Talking with other parents of children with special needs is a great way to get support and share tips. Your pediatrician should have details of local courses.

Q My son has autism, and I have just read about a new therapy on the internet. Should I try it?

The internet is a fantastic resource for parents and puts a wealth of useful information at your fingertips. The downside is that there is a lot of conflicting and confusing advice out there, so you need to be careful not to take everything at face value. As a parent, you will naturally want to try anything that claims to offer help for your child. Most therapies will probably do no harm, and you may see some improvement in certain behaviors, but unfortunately there is no cure for autism at present. Some therapies are better researched and tested, so they will have evidence to show how they work, what patients they work best with, and what kind of changes you might expect. Other approaches rely more on anecdotal evidence from parents, and have less scientific research to back them up. If you know someone who has used the approach you are considering, speak to them about their experience. You could also contact one of

ESSENTIAL INFORMATION: SCHOOL STARTERS

Delay, difficulty, or disability?
Understanding the difference

Many children experience delays in reaching their milestones, and around five percent of children have some form of learning difficulty. If there are concerns about your child's development, health professionals will use terms like "developmental delay" in your child's early years. This does not always mean that your child has a learning disability.

Global developmental delay, learning difficulty, or learning disability? If your child's development is significantly delayed in a number of areas, she may be described as having a "global developmental delay." When she is older and her abilities can be assessed more accurately, this term may be changed to learning disability. A learning disability is a pocket of relative weakness within the child's overall capacity to learn. Some children have relative weaknesses reading written language, writing, understanding spoken language, or putting their ideas into words. Only two to three percent of children have a learning disability, and 80 percent of these are mild. If your child does not meet the criteria, she will be referred to as having learning difficulties. Sometimes these terms are used interchangeably, which is confusing for parents. Ask professionals to clarify what they're saying if you're not sure.

If your child has a learning problem, it may take her longer to learn how to do certain tasks, she will require more support at home and school, and she will perform at a lower level than her peers. She may also experience some difficulties in managing her behavior and emotions. Some children are born with genetic conditions, such as Down's syndrome, that result in some learning disabilities. In most cases, however, the exact cause of a child's difficulties is unknown.

If the difficulties were picked up at a routine doctor's visit, you may already be in contact with specialists who will arrange testing as necessary. If learning problems have become apparent since school started, you could be referred to an educational psychologist. You can also talk to your pediatrician about referral to a specialist, clinical psychologist, nurse specialist, speech and language therapist, or occupational or physiotherapist.

What can I do to help? Your regular strategies at home may need to be adapted to your child's special needs, so attending a parenting group for children with additional needs could be helpful. Break tasks down into small steps to help her learn and give lots of praise, making it clear exactly what you are pleased with. Keep your instructions short and to the point; using pictures can help. Raising a child with learning problems is demanding, but there is lots of support and help out there.

ENCOURAGEMENT: Learning problems can result in low self-esteem and feelings of frustration, so make sure your child has plenty of time to engage in activities that he or she enjoys as well.

ESSENTIAL INFORMATION: SCHOOL STARTERS

Autistic spectrum disorders
A complex condition

An autistic spectrum disorder (ASD) is a neurodevelopmental disability that affects the way your child understands the world and how he relates to others. ASD is an umbrella term that includes autism, high functioning autism, and Asperger's syndrome. Everyone with an ASD has difficulties in three main areas: communication and social interaction, rigid thinking, and behavior. These are known as the "triad of impairments." Children with very low, average, or high intelligence may have an ASD. Boys are three to four times more likely to receive this diagnosis.

What does it mean for my child? Children with an ASD will experience difficulties in understanding the social rules of communication, relating to other people in a meaningful way, being flexible, and using imagination. However, all children are affected differently. For example, some may struggle to develop language, whereas others may have excellent language skills but only want to talk about their particular interest. Some children may also be hyper- (over) or hypo- (under) sensitive in one or more of their senses. Intense interests and routines are also common.

Some of these behaviors are also found in children who do not have an ASD. For example, if your child is very interested in a particular cartoon character, he may have books, toys, themed clothing, sheets, bedroom curtains, and favorite DVDs of them that he watches over and over again. The list of behaviors associated with ASD is very broad, and having a handful of traits does not mean your child is autistic. Children with an ASD have a unique way of looking at the world, which can result in particular strengths, such as the ability to focus on detail and an excellent memory.

A very small number of individuals (known as autistic savants) have exceptional mathematical, memory, artistic, or musical skills. These abilities include calendar memory (for example, calculating the day of the week for any given date in history in seconds), in-depth knowledge of particular subjects, and the ability to draw fantastically detailed scenes from memory alone or to play complex pieces of music after hearing them just once.

How do I get my child assessed? If you think that your child might have an ASD, speak to your pediatrician, who can arrange for referral to a specialist. Assessments are usually conducted by at least two of the following professionals: pediatrician, psychiatrist, speech and language therapist, educational or clinical psychologist, or neurologist.

What causes it? At present the exact causes of ASDs are unknown. Various theories have been

HELPING HAND: A child with an ASD may struggle in a number of areas. However, early intervention and support will make things easier.

proposed, and many experts believe that the wide range of behaviors associated with an ASD may not result from a single cause. A number of recent research studies have concluded that there is absolutely no link between the MMR vaccine and autism, and the original study that established a link has been widely discredited. There is no evidence that single vaccines are safer or as effective. One thing that is known for certain is that parents are not responsible for their child's difficulties with ASD.

What can I do to help? Individuals with an ASD may have a wide range of difficulties, so working closely with professionals from health, education, and social perspectives will result in the best outcome for your child. There is no cure at present. However, early intervention can help you understand the unique ways in which having an ASD affects your child, and will help you promote communication skills, build your child's relationships, and manage difficult behavior. Speak to your pediatrician or one of the national organizations that represent people with ASDs to find out about groups and courses in your area.

CHILD GENIUS: A very few children with autism, known as autistic savants, display amazing abilities such as enhanced musical or mathematical skills.

the national organizations that represents people with autism to see what their views are. If you are changing your child's diet in any way, speak to your pediatrician before you go ahead.

Q My daughter goes to a special school and doesn't get to see her friends much. I'm worried she will be lonely as she gets older.
As special schools move toward accepting a wider variety of students, this is a problem that many parents and their children face. Friends are important for acceptance, support, and security—they generally makes us feel happier and more confident. If your daughter is unable to spend time with her friends outside of school, this will also place extra demands on the family to ensure that she is entertained. At this age the foundations of friendship are built more on shared activities and having similar expectations. One way to address this is to see if there are any after-school clubs or activities that your daughter could attend. If not, see what is available in your area—you may find that other parents from school already have a meeting place. If you find something that other school parents may be interested in, spread the word. Try to be inclusive when you are looking for suitable activities. Lots of clubs now provide for typically developing children and for those with additional needs. If you are unsure, don't be afraid to ask.

Developing links and making friends in your local community is just as important as maintaining your daughter's social network at school.

Q My son used to love looking at books. Why has he lost all interest since he started school?
Starting school means that activities that were once about play and having fun suddenly become linked with school and "work," which can make them less appealing. It may also be that your son is finding learning to read a difficult task, so he is avoiding books at home. Try to make books and reading as much fun as possible. Join a library and help him

choose books he is interested in. Listening to other people read is just as important for your son as trying to recognize and sound out words himself, so aim to get at least one bedtime story in each day. There will be lots of opportunities to read together at other times, too, but try to avoid challenging him to see if he can read new words. Praise his efforts when he does read and correct any mistakes sensitively. If you are concerned that your son may be struggling with his reading, speak to his teacher to see if there is any additional support he may benefit from in school. Learning to read is a complex task so do what you can to take the pressure off and go at his pace.

My son struggles academically, but is included in lessons with the rest of his class. His behavior is getting worse. What can I do?

As your child progresses through school, the demands on him will increase. Work will become more difficult, he will have to sit and concentrate for longer periods, and he will be expected to develop independent learning skills. If your son is now finding certain aspects of his work too challenging, he may be showing this by becoming disruptive in the classroom. Including him in lessons with his peers is good for his self-esteem and confidence—as long as he feels as though he is keeping up with them. All children need to be treated equally, but that does not mean they should all be treated the same. If his needs are not being met, it may be time to think about a more individualized approach to his education. Parts of the curriculum that he finds more difficult can be broken down into smaller, more achievable steps. He may also benefit from some one-on-one support or small group work. It can take time to get additional support in place, so the sooner you act, the better. Speak to his teacher to see what options are available in the school.

What is a 504 and an IEP? Does my daughter need one?

504 and IEP (Individualized Educational Plan) are the two means provided by the federal government to arrange extra classroom accommodations to meet your child's special needs.

A 504 plan is a less formal agreement between school staff, faculty, and parents to help your child succeed. It could involve special seating, limited homework, or receipt of notes before a class presentation. An IEP is a more formal and detailed arrangement that will require that your child be "coded" as having one among a dozen types of learning, behavioral, sensory, or physical differences. This plan will seek to provide your child with the means necessary to learn in the "least restrictive environment" possible. It should set out the short-term targets set for or by the child; the teaching strategies to be used; the provision to be put in place; when the plan is to be reviewed; success and/or exit criteria; and outcomes (to be recorded when the IEP is reviewed)

If your daughter has a physical or a learning disability, she will be evaluated if she meets certain critera. These should include a medical diagnosis, aptitude and achievement tests, teacher

PARENTS' STORY

The earlier the better
getting extra support

When I saw my son getting more and more frustrated with his math homework, I knew exactly how he felt. I always found math really difficult and I didn't want him to go through the same experience. I spoke to his teacher and pushed to get him some extra help at school. At first he was not thrilled with having to do some of his work in a small group away from his friends. However, he gets along well with the support teacher now, and seems far more comfortable working with children who are at a similar level. My advice to any parent whose child is struggling at school is to get help early on—don't wait for things to get better on their own.

Dyspraxia

Around five percent of children are thought to have dyspraxia, which is sometimes known as developmental coordination disorder (DCD). It affects movement, planning, and coordination, which can lead to difficulties with language, perception, and thought. Dyspraxia can make learning more difficult.

What does it mean for my child? Your child may take longer to reach developmental milestones, such as walking and talking. As he gets older, he may find it harder to jump, run, ride a bike, catch or kick a ball, and have difficulty concentrating—particularly on problem-solving toys such as shape sorters and puzzles. Your child may also have a poor sense of time and direction and a tendency to fall, trip, or bump into things due to reduced spatial awareness (which is why this condition used to be called "clumsy child syndrome"). He is also likely to struggle with tasks such as dressing, tying shoelaces, and using a fork. At school, he may avoid joining in with playground games, and his written work may look immature for his age. Little is known about the causes of dyspraxia,

but it is thought to be due to incomplete development of motor neurons (the nerve cells that control muscles) in the brain. As a result, messages are not properly transmitted to the body, which makes it difficult for your child to turn these into actions.

How do I get my child assessed? Your pediatrician can arrange for an assessment if you are concerned. This is usually carried out by a pediatrician, educational or clinical psychologist, speech and language therapist, or physiotherapist.

What can I do to help my child? Dyspraxia cannot be cured, but there is a lot that can be done to improve things for your child. Help will be available from a range of professionals, such as occupational therapists and physiotherapists, to look at how your child manages everyday activities at home, at school, and during play. Skills training can help with the development of literacy, numeracy, spelling, reading, and physical skills. Doing these exercises at home and school will give maximum benefit.

recommendations, physical condition, social and cultural background, and adaptive behavior. Once a diagnosis has been made and your child provided with a 504 or IEP, it will be reviewed periodically to ensure that she is receiving the most appropriate learning aids. IDEA (Individuals with Disabilities Education Act) requires that this evaluation takes place every three years or more frequently if it is warranted, or if the child's parent or teacher requests a re-evaluation.

My son's friends tease him about his difficulties at school. Should I stop him from seeing them?
Children can be cruel to one another at this age, and name-calling is fairly typical behavior. In most cases it will be quickly forgotten, but of course this does not

make it right. If you are concerned that your son is being persistently targeted by his friends because of his learning problems you could always invite them over to play at your house so that you can keep an eye on things. You may find that your son dishes out as much as he takes, particularly when he is on familiar territory, so be prepared to step in and address his behavior, too. When children have additional needs, it is easy to find yourself becoming increasingly protective of them. Keeping your child safe is the main priority, but it is important to strike a balance between protection and independence.

    Like all children, your son needs to learn how to cope with other people and difficult social situations. Overprotective parenting can lead to social withdrawal, so help your son develop the confidence and skills he will need to look after himself as he grows up.

My child's a genius!
the perils of pushy parenting

Q I try to constantly praise my son to make sure his self-esteem is high. Is this the right thing to do?

Getting the balance right with praise can be difficult to achieve. On the one hand, experts recommend that you acknowledge all your child's positive behavior, while on the other hand, studies have found that by the teen years, children who have overinflated self-esteem are more likely engage in risky behaviors such as drunk-driving or driving too fast.

You can't go wrong if you give genuine compliments and let him know exactly what you like about him and his behavior. However, try to avoid going over the top by creating in him a belief that he is better than everyone else or will always win, no matter what he does. This will inevitably backfire when he's faced with times when things don't go his way, perhaps not getting picked for a team at school or failing to get an A on a test. Your child will face disappointments better if you build up his resilience. This means showing that you value his effort over whether he wins. It includes promoting persistence, so if he doesn't achieve an objective, he can decide to work harder and try again or switch his efforts to another goal. For example, if your child doesn't get a role in the school play, encourage him to try out for a different part or work toward being a good singer to support the production. This way your child gains an understanding that he can influence his own life and have a role in solving the challenges presented to him. Resilient children tend to cope better and recover more quickly from difficulties because they are motivated to try but don't expect to automatically achieve everything they want.

Q My child seems to be on the go all the time. How much is too much after-school activity?

It can be hard to resist your child's enthusiasm for after-school pursuits, and it is beneficial to support her interests. Only you and your child can decide exactly how much to do. As a general rule: At age four, simple activities such as play dates with friends are probably enough. At ages five to seven, one or two organized events a week work well and create a good balance with free time, playing with friends, and being with the family.

However, be aware that in her eagerness she may overstretch herself, and it's up to you to step in if there is a negative effect. You know she's doing too much if family mealtimes frequently become an "eat on the run" rush as you dash out to the next activity, or if play or family time is pushed out. Another warning sign is overtiredness—for example, if your child falls into bed exhausted most nights and is hard to wake in the morning for school. If you notice negative effects, help her decide what she wants to keep doing and what to give up. Too many evening activities can affect you, too. If you are feeling harried, becoming resentful, or constantly nagging your child to hurry up to get to the next event then it is time to slow down. Being over-stretched by her extra-curricular interests can result in family tensions that outweigh the value of the activity.

> The greatest influence on your child's self-esteem is your love, affection, praise, and recognition that she's lovable no matter what

ESSENTIAL INFORMATION: SCHOOL STARTERS

Supporting your child's aspirations
Or pushing her too far?

You are your child's biggest fan: You see the best in her, have pride in her achievements, and hope she does well. You are in the best position to ensure she has opportunities to learn and develop through your support of her interests and schoolwork. Research tells us that the greatest influence on a child's academic achievement is the involvement of parents in her education.

✳ **Choice:** Offer your child the opportunity to experience a range of hobbies or interests. Once she's tried each one a couple of times, prompt her to choose the activities she thinks she will enjoy. Some of these may involve learning new skills or even, eventually, lead to a career.

✳ **Diversity:** It's difficult to predict exactly where your child's long-term aptitudes and interests lie, so avoid focusing on only one specific area of development. Getting engaged with several hobbies or sports means that if she tires of one or isn't achieving to her satisfaction, she has others which will maintain her self-esteem and interest.

✳ **Motivation:** Practice sessions that focus on small achievements, rather than being a set length of time, are more encouraging.

✳ **Balance:** All children need free time. If your child is over-scheduled with organized activities, homework, and practice, she'll miss out on what many see as the work of childhood—play. She'll also have fewer opportunities to occupy herself, a key skill she'll need as she gets older.

✳ **Pushing too hard:** Before you go all out to get your child started on extracurricular activities, examine your own motivation. Ask yourself whether you're working in your child's interests or acting out your own aspirations, perhaps hoping she will achieve the dream you once had? It may be that you want her to keep up with a certain set of children or to reinforce some friendships over others. Perhaps she's struggling to make friends and classes may help her meet new children, or you're concerned that too few activities makes it appear that you're not supportive of her. Carefully consider how many extra activities she can handle.

PLAYING ALONG: Do encourage your child to take part in extra hobbies and interests, such as music lessons, but remember it's your child's pleasure in the experience that will keep him motivated.

PRIMA BALLERINA: If your child is gripped by a certain activity, for example ballet lessons, and has a balance of school and family time, then there is no reason to hold her back from doing what she wants.

ESSENTIAL INFORMATION: SCHOOL STARTERS

Is my child really a genius?
Talented and gifted children

"Gifted" and "talented" are the new buzz words for children who are, or show potential to be, high achievers. These are the accepted phrases you'll find used within the education system. Your child fits the category of gifted if she excels in one or more academic subject, such as math or english. The term "talented" is applied if your child shows an aptitude in practical, physical, or creative subjects such as sports, design, music, or the arts. To determine if your child is gifted or talented is not always easy; the opinion of yourself and your child's teachers, as well as high-quality work and test results, are used to reach a conclusion. It is not known how many gifted children there are in the population, but as a rough guide 10–15 percent of children are usually placed in this category. Signs may not become apparent until she is at least six or seven. Be prepared to have your assessment that your child is a genius challenged. She doesn't need to be gifted to do well at school and in life.

✱ Recognition: It is important that your child's abilities are recognized by school staff so that the curriculum can be adapted to keep her engaged and avoid problems of boredom. Sometimes teachers are concerned about identifying special talents, since they worry that concentrating on one child will disadvantage others in the class. However, not to do so can both impede your child's progress and result in classroom management difficulties.
✱ Self-direction: When she's encouraged to identify her own interests and learning preferences, your child will achieve more at school. Self-direction is usually limited to free play for a younger child, but will increase as she moves through the school, as she gains more autonomy to select methods of learning herself.

✱ Balance: Whatever your child's talent or gift, she still needs free time to relax, play, or simply be with you. She may also benefit from low-key activities outside her area of special interest. For example, if she's focusing on an academic topic, then leisure time could include physical or outdoor pursuits. A family walk, bike ride, or swim can be a refreshing change from homework.
✱ Difficulties: School is not always plain sailing for your gifted or talented child. If lessons are not well adapted, she may find the work is too easy, and boredom may set in. This can lead to frustration or misbehavior. You may have to work hard yourself to keep up with her learning so you can support her homework tasks. Whatever your child's talent, she'll benefit from your support. When you praise and reward her effort, you build her self-esteem and identify her as someone who tries hard. This way she won't be so dependent on coming first or winning for her sense of self-worth.

PAYING ATTENTION: Whether your child is gifted or not, she'll benefit from a wide range of activities and close interest from both teachers and you.

Will using our family time for educational visits make my child achieve more?

Involving the whole family in learning can certainly assist in your child's education. Family trips to places of interest and playing educational games have the dual function of shared enjoyable experiences, and improving your child's knowledge. Other methods known to help your child's learning include valuing education yourself, showing an interest in your child's school subjects, investing in time to read with her, lending a hand with homework, and ensuring she's absent from school only when sick.

Introducing formal learning into the home, such as extra homework, requires careful consideration of the costs and benefits. Your child has other important developmental tasks to practice with the family, such as playing, socializing, investing time in religious or cultural pursuits, and being able to relax. These can be lost if too much time is given over to added education. In relation to homework, ideally her teacher will have judged the type and quantity of work she should do to support her learning in school without overloading her. Her assigned homework is therefore often sufficient. If you believe, however, that the assigned work is not stimulating her, then a discussion with her teacher may help you understand their reasoning behind the tasks or guide school staff to give more challenging homework.

When deciding how much education to add, consider whether your child is at risk of seeing home as an extension of school rather than a place of family fun that just happens to include learning.

My child is gifted. Is it worth getting extra tutoring for her?

Historically, out-of-school tutoring has been used for pupils who were falling behind in their studies, and there is evidence of success in this approach. More recently, the focus has turned to giving children a head start by beginning education, often on specific subjects such as math or music, early in their lives or through tutoring to reinforce or advance learning achieved in school. It is difficult to determine whether

Talented but not motivated

It can be frustrating if your child appears to be unconcerned about achieving, though you know that with a little application he'll do great things. Motivating a young child is a delicate business; his learning is highly dependent on enjoyment and interest rather than straining toward a distant goal. If he's disengaged at school, talk to his teachers to make sure he's being given varied work with both playful and practical elements to keep his interest. He may be motivated by rewards for extra effort, such as stars or points for completing a task.

You can support his gift or talent by making learning out of school fun. For example, visit places of historic, sports, or artistic interest. Most museums have interactive exercises and multimedia information designed to engage, entertain, and teach. No matter how you feel, try to avoid nagging, lecturing, or forcing extra study as these rarely improve motivation, and can lead to resentment and resistance from your child.

tutoring will make a difference for your gifted or talented child—for some children enhanced-learning support in school is sufficient, while others enjoy and benefit from tutoring. Your decision needs to take into account how you will balance tutoring with your child's other needs for physical activity, social life, family time, and relaxation. Do seek her opinion about a tutor; this will make the difference between tutoring being a success or a battle. For some children tutoring is seen as a status symbol so do check her reasons if she agrees.

If you decide to have extra lessons, find a well-qualified, reputable tutor with experience of teaching at your child's age and level. Have a trial period and regularly review progress. Decide on what you count as success; for example, you may want lessons that keep her excited about the subject, promote motivation, and result in higher achievements. You could also consider general study-skills tutoring.

She won't eat her greens
food issues tackled

Q My daughter says that she doesn't want to eat meat. Is it OK for her to follow a vegetarian diet?

Your daughter is beginning to make some of her lifestyle choices based on a wider view of the world rather than being driven solely by her own needs and wants. Talk this idea through with her to check out her understanding of what she is giving up. Vegetarian diets can be a healthy way of eating, provided they are sufficiently well thought out. You will need to ensure that your daughter gets enough iron in her diet. Iron is associated with mental and physical development and a lack of iron (anemia) is one of the most commonly reported nutritional problems. As a vegetarian, your daughter will get most of her iron from eggs, cereals, vegetables, and legumes. This type of iron is not as well absorbed by her body as the iron found in meat. However, vitamin C improves absorption, so make sure she gets plenty of fruit. Nuts and peanut butter are a good alternative source of protein, minerals, and vitamins.

Do some research and plan your daughter's diet out with her to show that you understand and support her choice. It may help to set aside a shelf in the kitchen cupboard and fridge for your daughter's food. Agree to a trial period so you can review how things are going. Changing your diet is hard, so if your daughter decides not to keep it up, praise her for standing up for something she believes in and at least giving it a try.

> If you want your child to eat a healthy diet, you need to lead by example

Q My child usually brings at least half of her packed lunch back home. Is she eating enough?

School lunchtimes are usually busy, hurried affairs as children rush to meet up with their friends, get through their lunch as quickly as possible, then make the most of their free time before lessons start again. Your daughter may simply not have enough time to eat everything you have prepared for her.

Alternatively, she may not like all the things in her lunchbox or she may be eating enough for her appetite. If you have no other concerns about her diet and she is eating a reasonable amount of her lunch each day, stay calm and try not to worry too much. At the moment your daughter feels confident enough to bring her uneaten lunch back home, knowing that you will find out but trusting that you will not overreact. If you make too much of this issue, she may start throwing the remains of her lunch away at school, leaving you none the wiser. Pack things that you know your daughter likes to eat, and don't overwhelm her with too much food. Try varying traditional sandwiches with rolls, wraps, bagels, and pasta salads to keep lunch interesting, and make sure she has plenty of healthy snacks for break times—particularly if you are concerned she may be filling up on sweets instead. Most importantly, don't forget to praise her when she eats well.

Q How can I get my son to eat breakfast in the morning?

The saying goes, "Breakfast is the most important meal of the day," and there is some truth in this. When he wakes, your son's body has not had any food for several hours, and breakfast will give him the energy he needs to face the day. Research also shows that children who eat a healthy breakfast are less likely to be overweight, have fewer blood-sugar

What is a healthy diet?
Knowing your foodstuffs

Young children need nutritious food and plenty of water to fuel their activity, growth, and development. Learning how to eat healthily now will get them into good habits for life.

What do children need to eat and why?
The five major food groups are:
* Fruits and vegetables
* Bread, cereal, and potatoes
* Milk and dairy foods
* Meat, fish, eggs, soy, beans, and legumes
* Foods containing sugar and/or fat

A healthy diet will contain more foods from the first two groups, a smaller number from the next two groups, and occasional foods from the last group. Getting this balance right will give your child all the carbohydrates she needs for energy, protein for growth and repair, iron and calcium for healthy blood and strong bones, essential fatty acids for cell growth, fiber to keep her digestive system working well, and plenty of vital vitamins and minerals for optimal development.

Snacks and drinks: Allowing your child to have too many unhealthy snacks and sugary drinks could undo all your good work with the rest of her diet. Banning these foods from your home will make them even more appealing, so it's best to allow your child to have these treats occasionally. You can encourage your child to eat healthy snacks by keeping a well-stocked bowl of fresh or dried fruit and nuts available. Remind your child that she can eat these when she has exhausted her cookie quota for the day! Smoothies are a great way to get children interested in fruit, and you can easily make your own. Give water with meals rather than soda or juice, which leave less room for food and so make children hungry later. Soda and many juices also contain lots of sugar, which creates a spike in blood sugar levels followed by a crash soon afterwards. Sodas and sugary drinks may also contain artificial colors and flavorings which some parents would rather avoid, as they feel that these affect their child's behavior.

Lunchboxes and school dinners: Most schools now have a healthy-eating policy, so make sure that your child's packed lunch and breaktime snacks are consistent with their goals. School meals should now have healthy options on the menu, too—although you can't guarantee that your child will always choose them.

If you want your child to eat a healthy diet, you need to lead by example. Don't expect them to get excited about fruit if every time you get hungry they see you reaching for the chocolate cookies!

FRUIT AND VEG: Encouraging your child to eat a healthy diet will pave the way for good habits and help keep her fit and strong as she gets older.

Little chef
Helping out in the kitchen

If your child does not seem particularly interested in food and mealtimes are a real battle, try buying her a children's cookbook. Her reaction may surprise you. Your child may really enjoy taking charge of her food by trying out new recipes of her choosing and shopping for ingredients. Serving up her creations will also give her a sense of pride, and being in the kitchen means that you will get to spend more quality time together. If you can develop her interest in food and cooking you may even be able to hand over kitchen duties to her full-time in the future!

problems (which increase the risk of developing diabetes), may be more alert and better able to concentrate, are more likely to participate in physical activities, and tend to eat healthier overall. Like many children, your son may not feel like eating when he first wakes, and time pressure of the morning routine probably doesn't allow you to wait around until he is ready. You could try getting your son up earlier, to give his body time to adjust. As an alternative, try making him a packed breakfast the night before. This could include fresh/dried fruit, nuts, a carton of fresh juice, and slices of fruit bread. Some cereals

contain high levels of salt or sugar, so check the nutritional label. Breakfast bars are not always a healthy option, so, if you are going to include these, make sure you read the label first to look out for high levels of fat, salt, or sugar. You could also find out if there is a breakfast club at school; your son will probably be more willing to eat with his friends.

Q My daughter eats everything on her plate except her vegetables. Should I make her?

Vegetables can taste very bitter to younger children, and if they don't develop a liking for them early on, it can be more difficult to get your child into the habit of eating them later. Don't make a battle of this situation. You can't force your daughter to eat her vegetables, and as she gets older you will want her to eat them out of choice. Presentation can help; the shape, size, color, and texture of foods can make them more appealing. Try mashing and seasoning vegetables or finely chopping them. Since your daughter will probably be hearing about healthy eating in school, you could appeal to her increasing knowledge of food and discuss with her why vegetables are an important part of her diet. There are lots of vegetables to choose from, so take your daughter shopping with you and let her try something new. If you have space, you could also consider starting your own vegetable garden. Involve your daughter in deciding what you will grow, planting, caring for your crop, and harvesting. It's amazing what children will eat if they have grown it themselves!

Q Help! My child is getting picky about her food because she says she doesn't want to be fat.

Your daughter is exposed to lots of messages on TV, in magazines, at school, and in society that emphasize the importance of healthy eating and the dangers of junk food. It is a fact that childhood obesity has increased significantly over the last 10 years, and your daughter should be praised for recognizing that she can take positive steps to improve her diet and well-being. However, it is important that you encourage her to take a balanced view and avoid labeling foods as either "good" or "bad"—a practice that can lead to eating problems later. A healthy diet should include some foods that contain the essential fatty acids your daughter needs. If she wishes to cut down on the amount of excessively fatty or sugary foods she eats and replace these with healthier options, this is a positive change that you can embrace as a family.

Talking about other factors that will affect your daughter's body shape (such as physical exercise and the genes she has inherited from her parents) will help her to understand that she will not become overweight simply as a result of what she eats. Focus on developing a healthy lifestyle, and this should reduce your daughter's anxiety about food.

My son only eats half his evening meal because he says he's full, but then wants snacks later. Where do I draw the line?

It is important to understand how much of an issue this really is before you address it head on. If you are worried, it can feel like problems are happening every day and you may forget the times when your son clears his plate without argument. Keep a simple food diary to record what he eats each day—including snacks and drinks as far as possible.

If your son is regularly leaving a large part of his meal, there are several possible explanations. It may be that he doesn't like the food he is given; he may be overwhelmed with portions that are too big for his appetite; he may have eaten too many snacks after school and not be hungry at the right time, and, of course, he may be telling you the truth—that he has eaten enough and is full. A food diary should give you some idea as to which explanation seems most likely. Offer a light snack after school and avoid juice and soda, which will fill him up and can be high in sugar and sweeteners.

At mealtime, serve a sensible portion of food that you know he likes and water to drink. If he has eaten enough of his meal, allow a few snacks later, but keep track of them and set a limit—it's easy to lose track over the course of an evening.

My son insists on having energy drinks when he plays football. Are these really suitable for children?

Energy drinks have become very popular in recent years, and some are endorsed by celebrities, which appeals to children. There are two types of energy drinks available: those that claim to give you a lift if you are feeling tired, and those aimed at the sports market (these are often labeled as isotonic). The energy rush delivered by these drinks comes from their sugar content, which gives them a higher calorie count. The combination of fast- and slow-acting sugars claims to give an instant energy boost plus endurance, so it is easy to see why your son feels these will make him a better player. Some also contain herbs, caffeine, and other stimulants. A young child is not used to the effects of caffeine on his body and may find it unsettling. Caffeine is also a diuretic and will make your son urinate more often, so he will actually lose fluids. If your son is eating a healthy, balanced diet, isotonic sports drinks in moderation should do him no harm—but check the label first. However, if he drinks plenty of water while playing and eats potassium-rich fruits like bananas and oranges at half-time (as many athletes do) he will gain much the same benefits.

PARENTS' STORY

Variety, the spice of life
introducing a guest

For months the only vegetable my daughter would eat was corn. Eventually I decided to introduce a "guest vegetable" alongside her favorite once a week. To get her interested I used vegetables she was familiar with, and others like sweet potatoes, artichokes, and asparagus. The whole family rated each guest out of 10, and the most popular ones were invited back. Making it a game in this way seemed to take the pressure out of the situation and she gradually added new vegetables to her diet.

The odd one out?
making friends

Q **My child keeps coming home crying, telling me he's been left out. What can I do?**

Not knowing whether he'll be welcomed or rejected by friends can be both upsetting and anxiety-provoking, since each day brings uncertainty about what he'll face. While falling out with friends is common at his age, the situation is more serious with repeated exclusions that cause distress. This should be treated as bullying, so let him know you are going to speak with his teacher to work on a plan to help. He may ask you not to do anything, but bullying is unlikely to stop without an intervention from you and his teacher. Your plan with the teacher may involve holding lessons with the whole class on friendship and bullying issues. The teacher could also assist your child to make new friends by pairing

> Friendships started in the early years can be strong enough to last your child into adult life

him up with others for tasks in the classroom. Break-time staff can be alerted so they're watchful of children being left out and step in to help. The children actively excluding your son and their parents may also receive some information about how behavior should change.

Speak regularly with the teacher to find out how these ideas are working, and ask for a daily update of what's going well, or not, with your son. If the situation does not change, then review and adjust strategies with the teacher. When you act to support your son, he learns that telling about bullying helps and is more likely to confide in you if it happens again.

Q **My daughter never gets asked to birthday parties. Does this mean that she's unpopular?**

Seeing your child disappointed or left out can be distressing, but the number of parties she's invited to is only one indicator of friendships. Perhaps, like many girls, she's formed strong bonds with one or two others and so has a smaller circle of playmates to offer invitations. However, if your daughter is upset by this situation, it is worth investigating why it's happening. It may be maturity: There is great variation in the rate of social-skill development in young children. If your child is slightly behind her classmates, she may have difficulties with shyness,

PARENTS' STORY

The sociable child
introvert or extrovert?

I've always been outgoing, often being the one to start up conversations and friendships, so I was surprised when my daughter was the opposite. It was painful to watch her hovering on the outside of an activity not having the confidence to ask if she could take part. I decided to teach her what to do. We rehearsed how to wait for a gap in the action, step forward, look someone in the face and say, "Can I join in?" then wait to see what happened. I made sure she knew that this wouldn't always work. Having a plan seemed to kick start her into action, and although she's not a leader in the games, she's now usually part of them.

ESSENTIAL INFORMATION: SCHOOL STARTERS

Stress-free children's parties
Ensuring a good time for all

Children differ in the sort of party they want, but at ages four to seven it is most likely your child will want to celebrate with a large group of friends. A little older and he may involve two or three "best friends" in a bigger event such as a day trip.

✱ **How to prepare:** To avoid finding the whole class are on his invitation list, ask your child to choose those he sits next to at school and plays with at recess. By six to seven years old, he should be able to come up with a list without much help. Some schools encourage an "invite the whole class" policy to avoid disappointment. However, it is you and your child's decision how many children to ask. If you'd rather not invite everyone, perhaps sharing a birthday cake in school will ensure no one feels left out. On the day, do a safety check of the venue. For example, make sure any outdoor ponds or pools are not accessible. If you're at

home, move breakable items and your child's favorite toys away from party areas. If adults are attending and alcohol is being served, make sure there is a place to keep drinks away from the children's play area, and do limit amounts. Supervising a party can be a busy task so recruit as much help as you can from friends and family.

✱ **Games:** Plan a mix of active and quieter party games; for example, follow a treasure hunt with a more sedate game such as telephone. As a final wind down try a craft. A modern slant on traditional games will make sure no child feels left out; in a game of statues, simply reward the children who stand still the best rather than having the child who moves go "out."

✱ **Emotional overload:** Keep a look out for signs that children are getting upset, such as small disagreements, snatching toys or going quiet. If this happens, get that child to help you with a little task.

TOP LEFT: Younger children will enjoy a shorter party with plenty of planned activities and treats, such as paper hats, to make it feel special.
BOTTOM LEFT: As your child gets older, he may want to invite fewer children but for a longer event, maybe a day out.
RIGHT: The expectations and excitement of a party add to the fun, but can also lead to upset and tantrums as children reach a fever pitch of emotion. Step in quickly if you see things escalating or a child becoming overwhelmed.

Friendship skills
A complex activity

It may seem that making friends just happens, an effortless side effect of your child playing with others and having fun. However, underneath this apparently simple activity, a host of personal and social skills are being tried and tested.

✱ **Give and take:** Your child's ability to share, developed gradually between ages three to five, will stand him in good stead as a friend. Children will prefer to play with him if he can hand over a toy rather than hog it, and if he is willing to follow their play ideas as well as suggest his own. Encourage him to be a good team player by setting up and supervising games or activities involving cooperation and praise him frequently when he gets along well with others. Remember, your child is still working on skills such as cooperating, so things won't go smoothly all the time.

✱ **Creativity:** Friendships have to be started somehow, often through a shared and playful activity. When your child has the imagination to start up a game and spark the interest of others, he creates an opportunity to make and strengthen friendships. Simple ideas work best—perhaps he just shouts out to a group of children, "Let's play pirates," or presents a challenge like, "Who's fastest at running around the swings?" Whatever happens, he's having fun and drawing other children to him.

✱ **Empathy:** Getting along with other children involves your child tuning in to their needs and feelings as well as recognizing and regulating his own. His ability to understand and react to others' emotions has grown from his experience of you being responsive to his feelings. When you soothe him you teach him how good this feels, and the value of doing the same for others. At age four you might see him comforting friends by sitting close

and patting them, or knowing when to call an adult to help out. As he matures, he'll use words to calm his friends, try to problem-solve, and may challenge other children if they've done or said something hurtful. Help him to tune in to his friends by asking him to imagine how they feel and how he'd feel in the same situation.

✱ **Opportunity:** The more time your child spends with a friend, the stronger that friendship is likely to be, as each gets to know the other more fully. Encourage bonds to grow by providing plenty of out-of-school playtime and activities with others. Get to know the parents of your child's friends so you're comfortable for him to visit their houses, and they can let their children come to yours. This way you may find you build your own social networks at the same time as you support his.

✱ **Personality:** Your child's temperament will also influence his friendships. Outgoing, confident children often prefer a larger group of friends, while shy or quiet children tend to be at ease with a small number of playmates with whom they have a closer relationship. There is little value in pushing your child to have more or fewer friends than he wants. However, do take active steps to help friendships grow if your child wants to, but lacks the confidence to do this alone.

✱ **Cementing friendship:** It is common for children around six or seven to strengthen their group identity by setting up a group or club, sometimes giving themselves a name or constructing a den. This is a way to build bonds, but may also create problems. Rivalry can develop between groups, or situations occur where children are anxious about being left out or thrown out. Many schools discourage clubs as a consequence. It is up to you to judge whether your child is engaged in a playful and positive group who share values and enjoy the idea of being a club, or if the group identity is having a negative influence. If your child's school discourages clubs, support their efforts—they're acting out of concern for the children's well-being.

Tips for making friends

✶ Time together: Create frequent opportunities for your child and his new friend to spend time together. Arrange play dates at each other's houses, set up a shared carpool, or take them to the park together.

✶ Work together: Friendship will be strengthened when children have a project or shared goal to achieve. Set tasks or challenges which encourage them to communicate, plan, and work as a team. You could suggest a task such as making a clubhouse in the yard.

✶ Lead and follow: Your child needs to recognize when to lead a play activity and when to follow the ideas of others. Being controlling is often a confidence issue, so build his self-esteem with praise and games at home to reduce his need to dominate.

✶ Understanding: Good friends notice and show sympathy to others' feelings and celebrate or comfort as needed. Be sure your child is tuned in to others' emotions by teaching and talking about feelings at home. You could also role-play different situations, modeling a good response for your child to copy.

✶ Go second: When your child is prepared to let his friend go first some of the time, to share toys, or lose at a game without storming off, he'll be rewarded with firm friendships. Close supervision, rewards for good sportsmanship, and plenty of practice in taking turns at home build these abilities.

✶ Making up: If your child has a fight with his friend, help him to resolve it right away to avoid lingering resentment. A quick explanation and apology is often all that's needed, and playtime can start again.

✶ Make friends yourself: Sociable children tend to have sociable parents, so work on your friendships, too. When you make friends with the parents of your child's friends you'll create more chances for them to play together too.

TEAMWORK: Playing or working together on a shared task to achieve a common goal will help strengthen budding friendships.

HAND IN HAND: Being able to feel empathy for others and sharing emotions, whether happy or sad, are important aspects of friendship skills.

TAKING TURNS: Learning to share and play cooperatively is an important skill for this age, helping your child to make friends.

Party pressure

A quarter of parents report feeling pressure to give expensive party favors. Feeling anxious about keeping up with the latest in organized events can take the pleasure out of planning any party. Put things in perspective by reminding yourself what your child really likes about parties: Having fun and feeling special among people who love and care about him. Ask him what he remembers from the last couple of parties he went to. It was probably a game he played with friends and a joke he shared, rather than the contents of the party bag or the fancy invitations. No matter how much you spend or how elaborate or simple the party venue, it will be the atmosphere you create that makes it a success.

taking over, or talking over others that can make her less appealing as a friend. Help her develop social skills by encouraging her to join organized clubs that promote teamwork. Invite children home to play and supervise closely so you can prompt conversation, and encourage sharing and cooperation.

My child is very shy and won't leave my side to play. How can I get her to be less clingy?

Shyness is part of your child's temperament, just one aspect of what can be seen as an introverted or inward-looking personality. Your child may never be as outgoing or extroverted as you'd like, but being reserved is not necessarily a problem, nor is it a permanent quality. What your child learns in everyday social situations can reinforce or dispel some shyness—for example, if she's pushed forward in social situations and is embarrassed, this will tend to increase her reticence, whereas joining in with a game or conversation successfully will encourage her to be more outgoing. However, at the moment her temperament seems to be getting in the way of her social development and everyday family life.

Do introduce her to new people and places, but don't surprise her by putting her in social situations without warning, since suddenly doing so will increase her anxiety. Instead, explain in advance where you're going, who will be there, and how long you'll stay. Stay near your child at first when you're somewhere new. You are her secure base, and eventually she will move away to explore then return to reassure herself you are still there. Encourage her gently to mix, perhaps standing beside her as she begins to play with another child. Don't sneak away once she appears settled or push her into situations she dislikes—feeling abandoned, lost, or pressured can increase distress. You can put a positive slant on her shyness by saying she's careful who she mixes with. But don't repeat any label too often, or she may start to identify with this characteristic even more. Other people could also expect less of her, giving her fewer chances to socialize.

My son wants to win so much he alienates others. Can I help?

At this age your son's games will grow more competitive, and he'll care about winning and strive to come first. There are advantages to strong motivation; he'll try his hardest to do well. However, if he has a competitive temperament, strong reactions can result in boasting when he does win and sulking or becoming aggressive if he doesn't.

Holding a debrief after a sports event can tune him in to how each player contributes to a game. Ask him to identify what each person, from the coach through to the captain of the team, did toward the end result. This will focus him on cooperation and the value of good teamwork. Help him practice dealing with winning and losing by playing games together. When he wins you can model being a good loser by congratulating him; if he loses, praise him for playing well. If he starts to argue or disrupt the game, ask him firmly to stop and, if he can't contain himself, take a break from the activity to calm down. Don't fall into the trap of "letting" him win all the time to avoid a tantrum, since this doesn't give you a chance to teach him how to handle not coming in first.

Family bonding
forging close connections

Do I have to pay attention right away every time?

When your child says "Look at me," she's presenting you with a golden opportunity to show her she's more important than anything else. Sometimes these moments are not convenient—they come at busy times of day, while you're making a meal or on the phone. However, her need to be noticed is immediate. Ask yourself: Would it really matter if you took a couple of minutes out to notice her achievements?

So, if it is safe, stop what you are doing and see what she wants. Watch and comment with enthusiasm as she demonstrates her skill, whether it's jumping on the trampoline, riding her bike, or showing you what she made in school. Be careful that, if you do say "Just a minute," you mean it, and take a moment

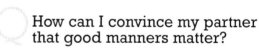

Stopping to listen and respond to your child with interest, warmth, and sincerity shows her how important she is to you

to speak to her as soon as you can. Otherwise you may find your child says this back to you when you ask her to do something. If you get so busy that you don't remember to pay her that attention later, she will use the same tactic to avoid complying with your requests. These small portions of positive attention are the building blocks of her self-esteem.

How can I convince my partner that good manners matter?

Good manners help your child get ahead in life: She will tend to get a better reaction from the people around her if she is pleasant and polite. These skills make others feel respected and valued, and it's rewarding at home when you hear a thank you after you've made a meal or helped with homework.

Whether your partner agrees with you or not, you can still role model and reward good manners. Your own behavior is most influential in teaching your child how to react. When you are in the habit of saying "please" and "thank you" to both children and adults, and speaking respectfully about others, she will pick it up, too. You can speed up her learning by making clear what you expect. Remind her that she must say "please" and "thank you" and praise her when she does so. Other easy ways to make

Family values
avoiding contradictions

My partner and I work different shifts, and we seem to pass in the hall every night as I go out and he comes in. For a while, we had almost daily issues when I'd tell the children one thing, and he'd contradict me without knowing it. It came to a head when he let our six-year-old play a violent video game that I had expressly told him he couldn't use. There were heated words at first, but we calmed down and put our energy into a solution. Both of us love technology, so now we leave each other a daily email or text with any issues or decisions, plus highlights from the children's day. We're finding out more of the little details we were missing before and have less conflict.

Attention and communication
Hearing what your child is saying

You probably find you communicate nonstop with your child, and most of this is a steady stream of instructions—from "Please, eat your breakfast" through "Brush your teeth" to "Put on your coat." Often it's not until the afternoon or evening that you find time for the two-way exchange that demonstrates you're interested in each others' daily lives, thoughts, and opinions. Make these conversations count by finding one-on-one time with your child every day.

* **Pause:** Stop what you are doing, face your child, and give her your undivided attention. Make eye contact, listen, and try not to be distracted.
* **Be clear:** Make it easier for your child to understand how you feel and do as you ask by being clear. For example, asking "Please put your cup in the sink" will get better cooperation than a vague request such as "Please clean up."

* **Listen:** Listen to what your child is saying and notice her body language and expression without interrupting, jumping to conclusions about what she means, or coming up with suggestions.
* **Disagree:** Good debates and discussions, matched to your child's level of understanding, increase your knowledge of each other. When you disagree, express different points of view, and argue without becoming angry or aggressive, you teach your child how to resolve issues respectfully.
* **Routine:** Find a quiet time every evening (just as you tuck her into bed is ideal) to spend five minutes asking for the highlights of her day and give her a chance to bring up any difficulties. Try asking, "What were the best and worst things that happened today?" to get her talking.
* **Long distance:** When relatives or friends live far away, keep relationships strong by using technology to stay in touch.

CHATTERBOX: The more children converse with their parents, the greater their vocabulary. Make one-on-one time with your children, such as going for a walk or a chat at bedtime, to catch up on their day.
AFFECTION: Tell your child you love her—don't assume she knows how much you care. Using physical affection will demonstrate your love.

communication more courteous include going up to a person to speak rather than calling from across the room, and adding "excuse me" or using a person's name when asking a question. Explain that when she comes up to you and says, "I'd like a snack please, Mom," it's more polite than shouting "I want my snack"—and more likely to get your cooperation.

My child confides in her grandmother and not me. How can I get her to tell me what's wrong?

Grandparents can provide a valuable listening ear for grandchildren. At one remove from your generation, her grandmother can offer a safe place for your daughter to sound out ideas and gauge reactions before she talks to you at home.

Even so, it can be hurtful to find your child more willing to talk to someone else than yourself. Perhaps she's concerned she'll upset you, or wonders what your reaction will be. In the past, if you've been too busy, dismissed her worries as trivial, or not believed her when she's told you she's been hurt, she may have learned not to be open with you. Rebuilding this trust will take time. When you stop, listen, and respond to your child by taking seriously what she says, she will gain confidence to open up to you. Create more opportunities for communication, perhaps an evening each week when you spend time one on one. On a daily basis, encourage her to share the highlights and low points of her day. You may also request that her grandmother tell you if something is of major concern, such as bullying, and ask if she'll encourage your daughter to confide in you in general.

I dread celebrations—I'm afraid my family's disputes will spoil things for my son. What can I do?

Sadly, disagreements often happen at times of celebration, when relatives who would usually spend little time together are expected to gather and get along for hours on end. When alcohol is served, this can also be a catalyst for outspoken views and taking things to extremes that might otherwise be avoided. Taking action before the event can reduce the chance

PARENTS' STORY

Embarrassingly honest
teaching values

My four-year-old son is a delight but a constant embarrassment, since he comments loudly on everything he sees. Recently he asked his aunt why she was fat and told his grandma her dress was a horrible color. I realize he's curious and is simply saying what he sees, so I make an apology and encourage him to do so, as well, to get him into the habit, although half the time he looks at me as if to say "What am I apologizing for?" I've also started to talk to him about how people have similarities and differences and give a very basic explanation that our world is interesting because it's full of people of all sorts of sizes, shapes, and beliefs. Hopefully this is the beginning of him understanding my values about accepting and respecting everyone, regardless of how they look.

of tension. If you're aware of sensitive issues, talk things over with relatives beforehand. It's ideal if people are willing to meet in advance, perhaps with a respected family member to act as peacemaker, and resolve specific conflicts. Otherwise ask that, in the interest of everyone's enjoyment, issues are put aside at the event, perhaps reaching an agreement not to bring up subjects that tend to cause an argument. If alcohol tends to make things worse, try suggesting a limit on the amount provided.

As a last resort, if people really can't agree to stay calm, arrange celebrations separately so everyone has a chance to take part. Perhaps having a small family dinner for the occasion, and a larger, more informal gathering a little later will be satisfactory. Having an adults-only celebration will avoid your son observing disputes if they flare up. At cross-generational celebrations, be on hand to distract and remove him if you notice tension growing.

ESSENTIAL INFORMATION: SCHOOL STARTERS

Generations getting along
Involving the whole family

Whether grandparents are involved with your family on a daily basis, through occasional visits, or are present in your memories and values, they play a role in raising your child. They're able to tell your child about past generations, achievements, and the qualities your family share. Events from your own upbringing can be especially fascinating, as your child tries to imagine that you were once her age. When generations get together and tell tales, look at old photographs, and recall the past, it establishes a shared pride and strengthens your child's sense of security and belonging.

* Appreciation: Grandparents may give practical and emotional help such as childcare, parenting advice, and listening to your woes and worries. They may look after your child on a regular basis while you work. These are wonderful opportunities to spend quality time with their grandchildren, but be aware that your appreciation is always welcome. A sense that they are being used as unpaid childcare or taken for granted can build resentment and undermine good family relationships. It may also be important, as the years go by, to check whether grandparents still feel they have the energy and good health to look after their grandchildren. Even the most devoted may eventually have to reduce the input they give.

* Well-meant? Having actively involved grandparents isn't always clear sailing. They may have strong views about your parenting, or you could feel undermined, for example, if your child is given treats and sweets by grandparents when you've said "no." More often than not, however, grandparents offer well-meant and welcome suggestions, and it is up to you to make your mind up as to whether you take their advice. There may be times, however, when you need to ask them change their approach with your child. This is often more successful than you expect if you are calm, assertive, and clear about what this will achieve and how much it will help you.

HAVING FUN TOGETHER: A wonderful treasure trove of stories and history, grandparents are an important part of the family.

GENERATION GAME: Grandparents can teach your child the tricks that amused you during your younger days, and so pass down good memories.

Brothers and sisters
sibling rivalry

 My four-year-old wants to be with her older sister all the time, and follows her around like a puppy.
First of all, it is important to empathize with your older child and acknowledge how annoying it is to have her little sister wanting to spend every waking (and some sleeping) moments with her. At the same time, you will need to make it clear that any mean behavior or cruelty from your older child is not acceptable. Sharing a similar experience from your own childhood can help her to see the situation from both sides. Being the older sibling can be a heavy burden if you expect her to "know better," so it is best to avoid this approach. Also best avoided is expecting her to care for her little sister for you.

Have some simple rules that protect private space and possessions, and help your younger child to abide by these. Make sure that there are opportunities for both of your daughters to have play dates with other children, perhaps one at home and one at a friend's house, to ensure further separateness. There may be some games that you can encourage the two girls to play together that capitalize on the age difference, such as school or family. Unless you really have to intervene, stay out of their interactions as much as possible.

How can I be equally fair to both my children?
When it comes to material things, give according to your child's need and interest and keep a mental tally to ensure you are giving equally. Make sure that you are even-handed when you give your children candy, but give each child the choice of when to eat them. Trying to be scrupulously fair can be unachievable. If you are trying to give your children exactly the same, you are likely to come unstuck at some point. Some would say that you are not preparing them for

life, which is frequently unfair. So perhaps learning the value of equality may be a useful lesson. Give your time to each child individually and equally, so that they do not have to fight with each other for it. And most importantly, give your love equally.

Even when you have achieved all this equality, someone will still complain that it's not fair. Sometimes it seems that it isn't the outcome that matters, rather the insistence on justice and the reaction it receives from you.

PARENTS' STORY

✳ Favoritism
a misguided approach

I was not aware of it, but I was favoring my youngest daughter because she is so different from me. My eldest, Sally, reminds me so much of myself, a good girl, who always does what she is told and never shows any defiance. In my experience this has not always been a successful approach to life and I guess I wanted her to be a bit more feisty, like her younger sister.

It did not take long for me to realize what I was doing and to see how misguided I was being. Sally began to resent her little sister and was probably taking out her anger at me on her sibling. I can see that I was in danger of setting up a flaw in their relationship that could have lasted them into adulthood, and all I really want is for them to be good sisters to each other and happy in their lives.

To resolve this, I've tried to give Sally extra-special praise for her compliant nature and treat defiance more firmly.

Fighting between siblings
A constant battle or beneficial?

Eighty percent of us have brothers and sisters. Within this common and familiar relationship runs the whole gamut of human emotions, from murderous hatred to fawning adoration and, in between, considerable ambivalence. All of these emotional responses cause parents a great deal of worry and present them with distressing management challenges. In fact, research looking at children's reactions to seeing their baby brother or sister upset shows that it is normal for children to show a range of emotions from being upset themselves, to not being affected at all, to being delighted at the baby's distress, with some even trying to make them more upset! The bottom line is that rivalry and conflict between brothers and sisters is normal and inevitable.

Practice for later life: Sibling rivalry is a perfect opportunity for children to practice conflict resolution. Given that they live together, some resolution has to be found: They cannot walk away from this situation. In an argument, each child needs to be able to state his case and stand his ground. He needs to learn to say how he feels and what he wants. Finally, he must negotiate terms of ceasefire or surrender, and an end to the conflict. Your son or daughter is learning an important lesson about how to understand, manipulate and dominate, comfort and appease another person. It is better, therefore, for parents to intervene as little as possible, and allow these skills to be developed and honed in this relatively safe environment.

Factors affecting conflict: The closer in age siblings are, the more likely there is to be keen competition between them and an increased risk of conflict. Same-sex siblings tend to fight more.

The younger the siblings are, the more likely it is that they will come to blows. Sometimes the rage and frustration can be overwhelming, especially for a toddler who does not have the verbal ability to hold his own against an older sibling. But it can be equally galling for an older sibling who is expected to treat his destructive younger sibling with special tolerance.

All getting along? To prevent situations from reaching boiling point, there are important measures that parents can take to promote sibling harmony. It is important to be fair; not to make your children compete for your time and attention; not to favor one over the other; to model harmonious, respectful relationships with your partner, your own family and brothers and sisters; not to "guilt trip" one, often the oldest, about fighting with his sibling; and, very importantly, to make a big show of your approval

FIGHTING AND MAKING UP: Younger children are more likely to fight, especially if they are the same sex or similar in age. However, battles, although frequent, will probably be short-lived at this age.

when they are cooperating and playing nicely together. Parents will need to set rules about hitting and hurting each other and about breaking property. They also need to enforce these rules. They can make it clear that they understand each child's position and sympathize with their dilemmas, but that they do not approve of aggressive or destructive behavior.

Last resorts: When it gets extreme, and warnings have been given but the rules have still been broken, parents will need to intervene. At this point, you still have an opportunity to encourage some non-violent resolution, such as taking turns. If all else fails, the best course of action is to keep calm, remove the source of conflict, and apply normal consequences for unacceptable behavior. These consequences could include being sent to sit on a "time-out step" or having the toy or object they are fighting over removed for ten minutes or so. Make sure that any consequences are immediate and brief, since at this age children have little self-control. Next time, the warring parties may be more likely to find their own resolution.

CONFLICT RESOLUTION: Although it is best to allow your children to find solutions to their own squabbles, you may have to step in occasionally to model good behavior or apply consequences.

What should I do about tattling?

You can find yourself caught in a dilemma with tattling between siblings: Obviously you do not want to encourage it, but there are times when you need to hear what has happened, especially if one of your children has been hurt. Most tale-telling is best played down and generally discouraged. Encourage your children to resolve the issue themselves, and remember to pay attention and give praise to any signs that they are resolving their conflict. Make it very clear that you are not interested in who did what to whom.

However, if one child is uncharacteristically letting you know about some serious misdemeanor of his brother's or sister's, you probably cannot ignore him. Rather than just stepping in and sorting out the situation yourself, it may be a good idea to think through with him about how he might in future resolve the situation without telling on his sibling.

My children always fight about who is going in the front seat of the car. Is there anything I can do?

If airbag safety and carseat laws allow it, use this as an opportunity to get them to learn some problem-solving skills. First of all, address the issue at a time when they are both in a good mood and not when they are about to go on a car ride. Make it into a game or a story, so that they enjoy the process. You could tell a story about two other children who always fought over something.

First get them to name the problem: two children, one front seat. Then get them to suggest possible solutions. Come up with some crazy solutions as well as realistic ones, so that you can laugh to lighten the mood. Allow fighting to be one of the possible solutions. Don't come up with the answers yourself, but encourage them to use their imaginations, maybe prompting them from other experiences they have had of finding solutions. The next step is to think with them what the consequences of each of their solutions might be. Think about what might happen if they are hitting and fighting over the seat, as well as the consequences of their other possibilities, such

Respect: Do unto others…

What is respect and how do you teach it to a young child? It's a difficult concept but easy to demonstrate. If you treat your children with respect, they will be more likely to treat each other in the same way. A child who is criticized and belittled by his parents will taunt and sneer at his brothers and sisters. The way in which you talk to and talk about your own family and your partner will influence the way your child deals with his. Simply saying "please" and "thank you," being patient and kind, showing consideration for others' feelings and tolerance for their shortcomings—this will all set the tone for day-to-day interactions in your home.

Reminding an older sibling about what she was like at the age her younger sibling is now is a helpful way to get her to put herself in someone else's shoes. Getting her to think about how she would like to be treated in that situation may soften her approach.

Property rights are an important lesson to teach early on. Sibling conflict often emanates from squabbles over ownership of toys. Learning to share is challenging and will be helped by feeling secure in the ownership of an object. Teach your child to respect other people's property and to ask permission before using it.

as taking turns or flipping a coin. Finally, get them to decide which solution might have the most positive consequences and the least negative ones. Give the chosen solution a try and consider with them whether they have made a good choice.

My children are always squabbling. I've run out of ideas for keeping peace. Any tips?

When your children are old enough to be able to talk about problems and solutions, try having a weekly family meeting. Set aside a regular time and get the whole family together. Encourage everyone to contribute to setting the agenda and to thinking positively about resolving the difficulties. Have a couple of simple rules, such as only one person can talk at a time, and everyone must stay calm and speak kindly about each other. You might want to have a "talking stick" that gets passed from one family member to the next, and only the person holding the stick can talk. Discourage blaming and "bad mouthing" each other, and encourage problem-solving and constructive solutions. You can address all sorts of issues, from household chores and family treats to sibling squabbles. Taking turns is also a powerful rule to follow. It is worth keeping your own tally for whose turn it is next, as this can become a battle in itself. Taking turns to choose allows some flexibility and the possibility of a pact being made between siblings. Time alone with a parent is another valuable commodity often battled over. If you make sure each child gets time alone with you as well as time to play with his own friends without the other being present, this may ease the pressure on the time they spend together. Time, all on their own, is also worth establishing and protecting. Being fair is what it is all about, but this does not mean things have to be absolutely equal—your children are not identical. Give each child time and opportunity to do things that they like and are good at.

Run, jump, and play
keeping them moving

I'm always in the car taking my son to his after-school activities. I don't feel the whole family is getting much exercise from this.

It may feel like you're just the family taxi driver, but this is an important role in keeping your child active. While driving to an activity is not strictly family exercise, you could make the most of the journey by asking what each activity entails and find out what he likes best. Of course, if it's possible to walk together to the activity, that would count as family exercise as well as time to talk. Even if you're just the driver, you can still get involved in your child's activities by staying to watch a lesson or practicing at home with him afterward. Whether you have goal-shooting practice in the yard, help him learn lines for his part in a play, or practice tumbles and balance for his gym class, you're doing your part.

Our doctor said that our son is overweight for his age. Isn't this just baby fat that he'll grow out of?

It doesn't always feel good to be given this sort of news, and sometimes being told what's best for you and your family can initiate the opposite effect—active resistance. It may help to ask yourself what the motivation is of the person who is offering advice: Doctors do not wish to annoy or upset you and are well aware of how sensitive the issue can be.

It is their responsibility, however, to challenge your belief in "baby fat," since the majority of children do not grow out of it without being introduced to a healthier lifestyle. In effect you are being told that you are the best person to solve this problem. Not to do so risks long-term health problems for your son and, sadly, he may be targeted by bullies, which can affect his self-esteem. If you can, set aside your emotions and put your energy instead into making changes in

the activity levels and diet of your whole family. This way you'll all reap the benefits, and your son won't feel like he's being singled out.

How can I motivate my child when I hate to be active myself?

A small shift in how you think about exercise can work wonders on your motivation. When you label physical activity as "play," as your child probably does, then you gain a different set of expectations and emotions. You may have associated exercise in the past with effort, boredom, or strain, whereas the label "play" could bring up thoughts of fun, family times, and being light-hearted, all of which make

PARENTS' STORY

Couch potatoes
a wake-up call

We have always been a family of couch potatoes. Flopping down in front of the TV was our main form of relaxation. Our wake-up call came when our daughter had to do an exercise for her math homework, adding up, hour by hour, what we did over the course of one weekend. It was embarrassing exactly how much of our life revolved around the TV, and it was obvious that she was missing out on other things.

We still love our TV, but now we make regular trips to the local playground and, once a week, we go bowling as a family. We eat our meals at the table, too, since we weren't appreciating our food when we watched TV and ate at the same time. If that math exercise happened now, I know we'd come out looking better.

ESSENTIAL INFORMATION: SCHOOL STARTERS

Everyday active play for families
Some suggestions

Making a commitment to active play couldn't come at a better time, since the benefits to health and child development are now well known. Getting active together can build family bonds, improve your child's confidence, and teach her about both teamwork and playing by the rules.

* Daily dose: Studies predict that if every family took part in just 15 minutes of active play per day, then childhood obesity could be halved. Your family doesn't need to go on a five-mile walk or have a full game of football to get the benefit of exercise. Try playing Frisbee, hula hoops, or skipping in the yard, take a walk to a local pond to feed the ducks, exercise the dog, go down the street to mail a letter, or have a dancing competition indoors, and you'll fit in your 15 minutes of activity easily.

* Ages and stages: If you're trying to suit children of different ages, it's easier if you avoid team sports and try for activities in which each child can go at their own pace. Swimming, trampolining, and cycling fit the bill and can be organized for the whole family together. Games in the yard or park such as treasure hunts, obstacle courses, and throwing competitions can be made fair for a young child by giving them an advantage such as standing closer or starting ahead of the rest, which means everyone can join in.

* Organized activities and clubs: Bump up motivation and a sense of mutual achievement by taking part in an activity with a group of children and adults. Commitment to other players makes it harder to opt out of sessions when your energy levels are low. Try out a few different sports or teams to find the ones that suit your family. Martial arts, swimming clubs, dance classes, and drama groups often take children from age five onward.

Remember—however welcoming a club is, at first your family may feel like the outsiders compared to long-standing members. This will soon change as you get to know each other and enjoy working toward similar goals.

* Get out: Give your family a mood-boosting moment by playing outdoors. Studies show that being in any sort of natural environment such as a garden or park can improve health and lift the spirits. Make the most of warm days by getting out the baby pool or sandbox, join in with a water fight, have a picnic in the park, or venture into the countryside. Let yourselves go by splashing in puddles and give your child a giggle by getting muddy together. Don't let wet or cold days stop you—bundle up your child and take to the outdoors.

✱ **Balance:** Being active is important for your whole family, but can get out of balance if you have one child who's truly talented or passionate about their sport. If one person's interests dominate at the expense of others and you don't want to limit their enthusiasm, creative solutions are needed. It may be possible to allow your sports fanatic to keep up his practice as much as ever but perhaps you don't join in or stay to watch every time. This will clear some time to take other children to different activities or to follow your own interests. A change of venue for the sport can help: Lessons for one child at a multi-use community center may allow others in the family to pursue different activities in the same building at the same time. If these solutions aren't possible, perhaps other relatives can take your child or watch him once a week, or you might consider an arrangement with other families at the community center. If all else fails, figure out whether there are non-essential sessions your child can miss to create space for others in the family to pursue their favored activities.

LEFT: Getting outdoors for a fun activity, such as a game of soccer, is good for you and your children.
ABOVE: Swimming is an excellent form of exercise, and one enjoyed by most children. Find your nearest community center with a pool and dive in.

it more likely you'll want to join in. Test out your perceptions with an experiment to see if you find active play enjoyable. For a week, engage in some energetic play every day, and monitor your mood afterward. Try playing tag or ball games outside with your child, or join in dancing or hide-and-seek in the house. See if you rate yourself as having improved or lowered your level of happiness or satisfaction each time. It's likely, no matter how unwilling you were, you'll be energized and positive afterward, and both you and your child will be motivated to do more.

Q Does running around before bed help my child sleep?

It's great to see children playing out and running around, but physical activity immediately before bedtime can make it harder to settle down to sleep. Do bring your child inside about an hour before you expect him to be in bed, and start his regular bedtime routine. This way he can wind down from the excitement of his bike ride, game of tag, or other game, and be ready to sleep on time.

Q I'm reluctant to let my child play outside in case she is abducted. Am I being overcautious?

Any harm to a child is truly terrible, and while child abductions are very rare, their devastating impact appears to have contributed to parents being more sensitive to risks than in previous generations.

Only you can decide how to keep your child safe, but playing outdoors, exploring the natural environment, and trying new things are important to her development. It is worth carefully considering how you can increase your confidence that it's safe to play outside. Begin by making sure outdoor space is free of dangers. Remove broken glass or plant pots, repair old play equipment, and lock away garden implements to make it safe. Get supervision organized to your satisfaction. It is recommended that children up to age eight be supervised by an adult or mature older child even when playing in a group.

ESSENTIAL INFORMATION: SCHOOL STARTERS

Resisting the sedentary lifestyle
Making positive changes

Encouraging a healthy lifestyle is the best antidote to the sedentary life. This involves the whole family eating a balanced diet and making physical activity a routine part of your week. Achieving this might seem like a sea change in your lifestyle or require only minor adjustments.

✷ **Why bother?** Understanding why a change needs to be made is known to increase the chance of any adjustment being sustained. Your child probably won't be too interested that a healthy lifestyle should reduce her risk of disease in the future. However she may like to know she could have more energy to run, jump, and climb, and that she'll get extra time with you for family activities. Engage her interest by explaining what happens to her body when she gets active. She may be fascinated by children's anatomy books, which show how her heart and muscles work and why she needs good food to give her energy.

✷ **Family favorites:** Ask each family member to name their favorite sport or play activity, and add something they'd like to try which they don't do at the moment. If your child struggles to come up with new ideas, help out by listing some examples. Scheduling plenty of what your family enjoys increases their motivation to get active.

✷ **Seek solutions:** Even a minor change in family lifestyle will need effort to get the logistics right. Solve problems before they arise by asking yourself what's going to hold your family back from being active? Are there going to be practical problems such as getting to and from the activity, will the cost be prohibitive, can you enroll in trial sessions or is a commitment required right away? Consider how each activity will fit around other priorities in your life, such as finding time for children's homework and friendships or making sure you can still catch your favorite TV shows. When you recognize these barriers and actively try to find solutions you're more likely to succeed.

✷ **Make a plan:** Setting clear, small goals for your family can give you a motivation boost when you achieve each one. Make a plan stating what your family is going to do, write it in positive language, and be specific. For example, you might say, "We will always walk to neighborhood shops," rather than, "We won't drive as much." Be realistic, and set goals you can achieve. If you give your child the task of winning a swimming trophy, she may not appreciate just taking part in the race.

✷ **Lead by example:** Don't expect your child to get active if you don't do it yourself. When you make changes to your eating habits, exercise levels, and time spent outdoors as a whole family, you'll have a much greater chance of success.

OUT AND ABOUT: Spending time outdoors together as a family can be fun and provide great exercise.

The biggest boost to your confidence will come when you watch over your child yourself. If another parent is supervising, check their views on safety: Don't assume these are the same as your own.

One of the biggest dangers your child faces outdoors is road traffic, because she's not yet able to judge speed and distance accurately. Teach her road safety, stay close to her as she plays, and set clear rules, such as, "You can play in our yard, but not outside the gate or on the road." Keep in mind that achieving the delicate balance of protecting your child while teaching her independence will keep you on your toes for years to come.

Q I've heard that there is a link between television and an unhealthy lifestyle. What are your recommendations?

Your child's television viewing patterns are probably already well established. However, as her free time becomes increasingly filled with homework and after-school activities, take the opportunity to review her viewing habits. Experts recommend children have no more than two hours per day of screen time; this includes computer, television, and gaming time. Sticking to this limit will enable your child to have a balanced diet of play including time for physical activity and socializing.

Your child may already be pestering you for a TV in her bedroom, and statistics tell us that many of her peers will already have one. However, there is little to be gained by going along with this. Having a television in her room can mean your child spends more time alone just at the age when talking, playing, and being with others is the keystone to her development. It'll also be harder to keep track of what she's watching and for how long.

Another side effect of a bedroom television is that your child doesn't have to share; reducing squabbles in this way denies her vital practice in turn-taking and resolving disputes. If your child has a television in her bedroom, it may be tempting to allow her to doze off while watching. This actually delays her falling asleep, since television programs require her to try to keep her eyes open rather than closed and motivate her to struggle to stay awake rather than fall asleep. A link can also be created between television watching and sleep, meaning your child may find it hard to fall asleep without it in future. It's preferable not to start this practice, but if it's already happening, act now to swap the television for a bedtime story from you. She may resist the change, but stick with it—you'll have more quality time together, and she won't be dependent on the television to go to sleep.

The lack of balance between the energy your child consumes in food, and the amount of physical activity she takes is the cause of obesity. Television doesn't make your child overweight, but it does contribute to this energy imbalance by its sedentary nature. If your child regularly spends hours each day in passive pursuits, then she will have too little time for the active play and physical sports which are essential for maintaining a healthy weight. Get the balance right by ensuring her free time involves a mix of physical, social, and passive activities. Limit television time if you need to, and be ready for some resistance at first.

Q What's the best way to introduce extra activities?

To begin, take it slow and just add one activity a week, then build from there. This will allow everyone to get used to the change. Making more effort to get active doesn't mean going to extremes, such as banning all computer games or cutting out every snack or treat. Radical change can backfire if your child resists or becomes resentful. Get the balance right between active and sedentary play by ensuring neither takes over his schedule.

Any change in behavior or attitude is more successful if those around you support your decision. Get your relatives, neighbors, and your child's friends involved by explaining what you hope to gain from sitting less, playing more, and eating well. Encourage them to notice positive changes as their interest will help him recognize what he's achieved. After a few months of healthy lifestyle change, review your progress. You may be pleasantly surprised!

Grade-schoolers
their lives expand

* **Why doesn't she like school?**
  phobia, loneliness, bullying

* **Firm friends**
  peer pressure and falling out

* **Extra effort**
  struggling with learning

* **Staying connected**
  spending time together

* **How can I get them to help?**
  chores, housework, motivation

* **Distressing times**
  coping with death and depression

* **Screen time**
  how much is too much?

Why doesn't she like school?
phobia, loneliness, bullying

Q My daughter forwarded a cruel email about a classmate on to her friends. Is that cyberbullying?

Yes it is. It is easy to be caught up in someone else's bullying activity and to feel pressured to be part of the joke without realizing the harm it can do.

The important thing here is that she felt uncomfortable about what she did and told you about it. Because you don't have face-to-face contact with your victim online and the whole interaction can remain anonymous, sometimes rules of acceptable behavior are broken before you realize what you have done. It is worth stressing the message that the rules of behavior online are just the same as they are offline, and get your child to think how she would have felt to have seen something like that written about her. Encourage your daughter to continue talking to you about what she is involved in online. Reinforce the message that by forwarding something unpleasant you become part of the bullying. Emails, text messages, and activities in chat rooms can be traced, and site administrators can ban people. If you are unhappy with what your child is involved in, contact the website administrator, internet service provider, or mobile phone service provider.

Q I feel like confronting the bully's mother because no one is doing anything about it. Can I?

If your child is being bullied and people don't seem to be taking it seriously, it is easy to get angry and frustrated. You are probably not at your most effective when you are in this frame of mind, so do not try to take matters into your own hands. Remember that your goal is to stop the bullying and to show your child how to be calm, assertive, and effective. Go back to the teacher and make it clear that the bullying has not gone away and that

it is distressing your child. Ask the teacher what is being done about moving the bully farther from your child's desk, how other teachers are keeping an eye on things outside the classroom, and what is being done to change the bully's behavior. Perhaps bullying and its impact can be discussed in class. Find out how your child can be helped to tell an adult when a bullying incident happens, without incurring further intimidation for "tattling" to the teachers. Once you and the school have agreed how you will work together to combat the bullying, ask for a review appointment in a couple of weeks to check on progress.

If you still feel that you are not being taken seriously, go and see the headmaster or the school counselor. Take a list of all the incidents that have happened. Ask to see the school's anti-bullying policy and ask what actions the school will take to protect your child. Follow up your meeting with a written account of what was agreed. If all else fails, speak to the school board: They have to ensure that school policy is adhered to.

Q I try to ask my child if he is being bullied, but he just closes up. Should I push further?

Try just chatting about your day and his day on a regular basis. Choose your timing—don't pounce on him the minute he comes out of school, but perhaps in the car on the way home or at bedtime when he is relaxed. Try not to grill him but, rather, have a general chat about work time and playtime, what he did and what others did.

If he does talk about things that have upset him at school, your reaction is crucial to whether he tells you any more or decides the information is too hot to handle. Stay calm and try not to overreact. Once he has found a way of talking to you about the bullying, you can think of effective ways in which he can tell the teacher. He may think that it is his fault and feel ashamed to tell, or he may worry that there will be further bullying. Help him practice the best way to tell his teacher or school counselor. Think about who is the most approachable.

Once you've got him talking, you can start to think of ways in which he can deal with the bullies: How to walk away with his head held high as if he doesn't care, or deliver a witty response or a dismissive laugh. It takes courage to sound braver than you feel, so help him rehearse and reward his efforts and bravery. Safety must always be paramount, so don't encourage him to take any risks, but remember the confidence-boosting kick he can get from dealing with an incident himself and coming out on top.

What is meant by school refusal and school phobia?

It often starts with a tummyache on Sunday night and can develop into an aversion to going to school that affects on your child's education and emotional well-being. School refusal and school phobia describe a range of reactions—from mild apprehension to crippling anxiety—about going to school.

There are a range of factors that may be relevant to school phobia that have to do with the individual child, home and family, or the school and community. Your child may be a generally anxious child who has always struggled to separate from you. Or she may have had an illness resulting in absence and then find returning to school problematic. She may be struggling with the schoolwork but is unable to articulate this or appropriately seek help on her own.

It takes courage to sound braver than you feel, so rehearse with your child and reward his efforts

Something may have happened at home to precipitate this anxiety, such as marital difficulties, parental illness, or other family stresses. School factors may very well include bullying, or it may be that your child is having difficulties with a particular teacher. She may not have made friends in this school and be dreading days of loneliness. She may be struggling academically in all areas and see school as a gruelling catalog of failure. Finally, there may be some aspect of the community surrounding the school that is frightening her, such as unpleasant encounters with children from neighboring schools.

My child seems afraid to go to school. What is going through her mind?

There is a particular way of thinking that characterizes anxieties such as school phobia. It may be apparent to you that your child is overestimating the perceived threat of attending school and underestimating her ability to deal with it. She may say things like, "I know the teacher doesn't like me because she always shouts," or, "I'll be the last one chosen in PE." You can gently challenge her thinking by asking questions to show her that there are other ways to see the situation, and that her thoughts are not facts. You could ask how many times the teacher has shouted, or whether being last to be picked happens to other children, too, and whether there is anything you and she can do about it (for example, practice catching and throwing a ball together).

One of the most effective ways of challenging your child's negative perception of the "danger" present in going to school is to get her to experience it in tiny, manageable steps. Sometimes school phobia involves a complex combination of child, home, and school issues and requires further help from a therapist. Common clinical practice is to advise that a school-resistant child MUST go to school, even if that means delivering the child directly to the school counselor who can help to wean her back into the classroom. Every day that a school-resistant child misses school makes returning the next day harder for all.

ESSENTIAL INFORMATION: GRADE-SCHOOLERS

Bullying
A remarkably common problem

Bullying is often a factor behind a child's reluctance to go to school or even to leave home. Unfortunately, with so much digital connectivity, children are not even safe from bullying in their own homes now that mobile phones and the internet provide more insidious means for intimidation and persecution.

Who does it happen to? Bullying is remarkably common in primary school, and most children will have some experience of it, even if it's only witnessing it happen to someone else. It is a major factor in school refusal, with all its associated educational and emotional damage, and also leads to loneliness, loss of confidence, low self-esteem, anger, and a sense of helplessness that is strongly related to the development of depression. Sometimes adults are confused about the difference between an disagreement or distancing between friends and the victimization that is characteristic of bullying. Bullying behavior can include unpleasant teasing, threats, spreading rumors, and socially isolating someone. It can also be physical aggression, such as pushing and shoving in crowds. It quite frequently involves extortion of personal property under threat, and can include taunting about disability, race, or gender.

Bullies are often feared and admired by other children. They are perceived as strong and they get satisfaction from hurting and humiliating their victims. However, bullies are often victims already, and frequently learn to bully by being bullied themselves. No child is immune from being a victim, but certain factors increase and decrease their risk. Having friends protects children from bullying. Being alone at playtimes at school, being shy and anxious, and less popular all seem to set a child up as a bullying risk. Surveys show that

children rarely tell anyone that they are being bullied. Parents should therefore look out for unexplained injuries, ripped or damaged clothing, loss or damage of personal property and money, mood swings, and sleep problems.

Helping your child: The best way your child can protect himself against a bully is to always tell an adult when he is being threatened, to hold his head high and act as if he is confident, and to stay close to friends, and play in a group rather than alone. Please advise your child not to fight back when bullying happens. If he attempts to fight back, he is likely to be overpowered and his reaction will give even more satisfaction to the bully.

Learning to be strong inside can be hard for many children, and you can help with this. You can build your child's emotional strength so he is less likely to be bullied or, if bullying happens, the effects will be less. Remind your child of his good points so his self-esteem is raised. Any activity that gives your child a taste of success and the opportunity to have a few friends such as swimming classes or Cub Scouts and Brownies or Boy Scouts and Girl Scouts are all good ideas. Martial arts classes may be a good idea for confidence boosting—although the idea is not to teach him how to fight, just how to feel confident, square his shoulders, think positive thoughts, and walk tall.

If the problem continues, you could enlist the help of your child's school. The class teacher, school counselor, or other members of staff can help you work out ways to support your child. Most schools have an anti-bullying policy that tells you what the school will do to tackle this issue. This should spell out how the school will work with victims and how they will help the bully to act with kindness. Really effective policies are those that pupils, parents, and teachers have developed together. As well as building anti-bullying subject matter into the curriculum, schools can help by investing in playground improvements, establishing buddy systems, and possibly even offering formal assertiveness training.

Loneliness and making friends: Being lonely at school is a miserable experience. Being able to make and keep friends is an important protective factor against school phobia and bullying. Being part of a circle of friends makes it much less likely that your child will be bullied. In fact having a close friend in these middle-childhood years is important for good psychological health in adulthood. Friendships are about liking the same activities, helping each other out, being able to take turns in a game, and learning how to share and compromise with ease. Friends like and admire each other and share a sense of loyalty and commitment. They do argue, but they are better able to make up than children who are not special friends.

If your child has the skills to make friends, she is more likely to appear confident, making her happier about herself and about being at school—and less of a target for bullies. These are skills that can be learned through play with cousins or neighbors; friendships are often built on proximity. They are also about sharing similar interests, so you can encourage your child to join a class, club, or a sports team. Encouraging your child to invite friends over to play can also build friendships. If she is struggling to make friends, practice with her—act out together how she might approach others and ask to join in their games. Also enlist the help of her teacher to have your child paired with others in the class to form bonds by working together.

LEFT OUT: Social exclusion, or being left out of activities, is a fairly common form of bullying.

STAYING STRONG: If your child is being bullied, martial arts can give her a sense of confidence.

IN THE TEAM: Clubs and activities that take place away from school may offer your child a new set of friends.

Minor disagreement or bullying?

Your child has probably developed a fierce loyalty to her close friends. Her bond with her best friends means she'll be ready to defend them if they're in conflict with other children or in trouble at school. This loyalty has a flip side, since she'll be hurt when it comes to the day-to-day disagreements that are common at this age. Falling in and out of friendships often occurs over minor issues such as not getting invited to play or mild negative comments. Your child may come home in a state of anger or distress. However, if you go into overdrive to mediate or take action to help her make new friends you could be wasting your time. It's often the case that, by the next day, all will be smoothed over and the friendship will be back to normal as if nothing has happened. Your best strategy, if your child comes home feeling rejected, is to listen to her woes and console her, but wait and see what happens before you step in.

It can be very difficult at this age to determine whether your child is simply falling out with her friends or being bullied. If she is repeatedly left out, physically or verbally attacked either by individuals or groups, and feels hurt and distressed, this should be treated as bullying.

LOYALTY: Although your child probably has a group of close friends *(left)*, fallings out and disagreements are frequent at this age.
CHAT: Don't discourage your child from speaking to friends after school *(right)*; this is one of the methods of building a close-knit social network.

Q My child goes to school very reluctantly. How can I get her to like it better?

This sounds like a situation that requires a meeting with your child's teacher and a concerted effort on a number of fronts to improve her motivation and enjoyment of school.

Discuss ways in which the school can enhance her position in the class by giving her a special job, such as taking the attendance record to the office or feeding the hamster. Check whether she has particular areas of difficulty academically, and arrange to focus on doing some practice at home for which she can be rewarded in school. Find out if the school can set up some sort of group work or buddy system to encourage friendship-building in the class and playground. If she is finding recess and lunchtime particular lonely, perhaps she can come in to play with a friend or do a task together to help the teacher out. You could follow this up by arranging for the new friend to come over after school one day.

Find out what her strengths are and work to them. If she is good at reading but a shy child, see if she can help out with the younger children, or be the narrator in the class play. Try to identify something that she is really interested in and work out a way that she can access this through school. Plan fun things to do after school as a reward for going in every day. Talk about the good things that happen at school or even the things that were all right or the boring things but comment that it is not all bad and few children really love school!

Firm friends
peer pressure and falling out

Q **She was top of the class. Why has my bright daughter stopped trying at school?**

There are many possible reasons your daughter's performance has changed; exploring these with her will help you pinpoint the problem. The issue may be peer relationships: Perhaps her academic success makes others look bad, or she's constantly held up as a good example—a "teacher's pet"—which can cause resentment. The desire to belong to a group of friends is strong, and your daughter may feel it is worth dropping her grades in order to fit in and be liked.

Alternatively, she may have found a peer group that encourages rebellion, and tasted the social pay-off for becoming a rule breaker and neglecting her studies. Talk with her about your concerns and try to re-ignite her interest in studying by providing incentives for effort. Help her strengthen friendships with others who share her love of learning, and make sure she has time for fun and frivolous activities to balance her academic work and serious side.

Q **My daughter and her friends were caught stealing from a store. Can she be trusted again?**

Don't despair—this doesn't necessarily mean your daughter will continue into a life of crime. Shoplifting is often carried out as a dare, rewarded by the adrenaline rush after the event and the bond of a guilty secret between friends. Tackle the issue without flying off the handle. Try to involve the parents of your daughter's friends to give a strong message to all involved. Your child should never benefit from stealing, so stolen items need to be returned to the store along with an apology. This face-to-face encounter will emphasize the serious nature of her actions and form the basis to rebuild trust.

Q **My son's best friend is the worst-behaved boy in his class. Can I get him to choose a nicer pal?**

Children are often drawn to friends we wouldn't choose for them as parents. However, most friendships are based on shared interests or attitudes that create a positive bond. Rather than assuming the worst, get to know this friend when he visits your home to play and try to discover his positive qualities alongside his difficulties. Recognize that your son could be at risk of getting caught up in troubles but, equally, he may influence this friend to be better behaved instead. However, if you notice a negative influence, for example your son becoming disrespectful or adopting disagreeable behavior, you can weaken the friendship by reducing the amount of time the two of them spend together and actively invite different children to play. In school, try asking teachers to pair your son with others for classroom

PARENTS' STORY

Collecting
the latest craze

Like most boys in his class, my son loves to be in on the latest thing, from baseball cards to crazy bones. Collecting can get a bit out of hand with pressure to keep up with friends and anxiety about completing a set. I've found it helps to set a limit of one collection at a time and encourage my son to complete that collection before going on to another. He uses his pocket money to buy more cards then swaps with friends, which gives him a little more flexibility. I put in some extra supervision to prevent swapping from descending into one-upmanship.

ESSENTIAL INFORMATION: GRADE-SCHOOLERS

How children play at this age
An evolving pastime

Friendships are becoming more important to your child as his interest grows to include not just playing and having fun, but also why his friends think and act the way they do. You will still be his strongest influence, but he will care about how his friends view him, his home, and his family.

New technology: Your child's play will be evolving along with the technology he uses. He will organize to meet friends through texting and instant messaging so getting together can be more spontaneous. His indoor play, alone or with friends, may revolve around a games console or computer rather than a box of Lego and board games, although he won't have wholly let go of these traditional activities. His competitive spirit will probably come through no matter what game he plays. Helping him get the balance of indoor and outdoor, physical and quiet play that he needs may be your role. Playing isn't just for your child.

When you participate, either by watching or by playing with him, and especially if he's teaching you the latest game, you're getting to know his changing interests and friends.

Difference between sexes: Both boys and girls tend to develop a few close friendships, but your son is likely to prefer playing in a large group and enjoy teams and competitions. In contrast, girls will often have less boisterous play and may spend their time in smaller groups with one or two best friends. Your son, when asked what he thinks of girls, is quite likely to say "yuck" and make a face. He will play primarily with children of the same gender. He may be teased if he plays with girls, and it's much less common that he'll do so.

By comparison, your daughter at this age is more willing and comfortable to join in with the boys, although she too, will most often be with her female friends.

ONE OF THE BOYS: At this age, boys are likely to stick together, away from the girls.

ME AND YOU: Girls tend to spend their time in smaller groups with one or two closer friends.

PEACEFUL SCENE: As well as outdoor, physical play, help your child enjoy quiet activities.

tasks. Avoid an outright ban on contact, since the rebellion of staying in touch can simply cement the friendship.

How can I give him the confidence to say "no"?

Increase your child's resistance to peer pressure by building his confidence to say "no" to hurtful or harmful suggestions. Children with strong self-esteem are less likely to worry about losing a friend or two through not going along with risky ideas. They'll be confident that their decision not to take part will be accepted or that other friends will come along. However, be realistic: Your child will give in to peer pressure sometimes. When this happens, talk openly about what worries you, and use the opportunity to discuss the outcome of your child's decision, and what they could do differently next time.

My son says he will go barefoot if he doesn't get Nike sneakers. Why is he being so unreasonable?

This is entirely reasonable to your son: Being in the "right" clothes can seem immensely important as he strives to be accepted and even become one of the "cool" kids. If he's determined to have the Nikes, you may decide he has to save his pocket money to buy them. Unfortunately, owning the brand probably won't give him the status he desires, but this is a lesson he may need to learn through experience. For a different perspective, help him to separate the person from their appearance by talking over the qualities he likes in his friends; try to draw out the conclusion that it is their personality, humor, or kindness that appeals, rather than what they're wearing.

My daughter seems to be a tomboy. Should I discourage it?

The label "tomboy" usually goes to the girls who are seen as adventurous, play with toys and games more closely associated with boys, and are not particularly concerned about their appearance. Far from being seen as negative, young tomboys are popular and viewed as good leaders. However, as girls move into adolescence, being a tomboy is less well accepted by peers. By this stage, your child will be making her own decisions about how she fits in, so it is probably inadvisable to attempt to discourage this behavior. Tomboy behavior appears to come from both biological and social factors. Research has found that if your daughter is exposed to higher levels of testosterone in the womb, then she will display more "masculine" interests and activities as a young child. You will influence her behavior, too: If you praise and provide opportunities for her varied pursuits, she'll feel comfortable with this aspect of her identity.

Why does my daughter want a bra when she doesn't need one?

Showing the physical signs of puberty can be a status symbol for girls, and their first bra marks this change. While we may want our children to enjoy the relative innocence of their childhood, they seem determined to leave it behind as soon as possible. There is little reason to say no to this request, whether your daughter physically needs a bra or not. She may value your help to choose new underwear, so take this as an opportunity for parent-child quality time, and guide her on age-appropriate designs. At all costs, resist the temptation to joke about her shape or size—this can be devastating to a girl sensitive about her changing body.

My child wants to imitate her new friend's vegetarianism. Is this simply a passing fad?

Friends often copy each other, from the way they dress to the music they prefer. This mirroring is stronger in the early phase of a friendship. It is a way to strengthen the bond between children rather than a sign of pressure to conform. The intensity of the need to match each other should wear off as the relationship becomes firmer. In the meantime, as long as requests are not too outrageous, you might as well go along with them. The only caution comes if you feel your daughter is a slave to her friends' whims. Then you may need to help her develop other, more balanced, relationships.

Extra effort
struggling with learning

Q My son has learning difficulties and is fine at school but wears me out at home. What can I do?

Schools are run on predictable routines and timetables, which help your son feel contained, supported, and safe in this environment. As much as he enjoys this consistency, he will want to let off steam after following school rules all day, and may need some help to organize his activities at home. Write a list of all the fun things he enjoys, then either find or make a picture to illustrate each one. After he has had a little time to unwind after school, sit down with him and put together an activity schedule for the evening using the pictures. Allow him to choose the activities he wants to do, but try to include a mixture of things he can do with you (for example, cooking or playing a board game) and those he can do on his own (for example, drawing or watching a DVD). Mix the activities up so that he has a slightly different choice each day to prevent him from getting bored, and make sure you only offer him activities that you can deliver! Stick the pictures up somewhere visible and accessible in the order he chooses, and let him know when it is time to move on to the next activity. Add in pictures for routine tasks such as taking a bath and brushing his teeth, and he should have plenty to keep him occupied all evening.

Q My child has reading and writing difficulties and always forgets her homework. Can I help?

In their rush to get out of class when the bell rings, most children are able to juggle packing away their things, chatting with friends, and thinking about where they are going next while sparing half an ear to listen to the teacher give out homework instructions. For your daughter, remembering more than one thing at a time is likely to be somewhat

more difficult than it is for her friends, and instructions will be quickly forgotten unless she writes them down. If she does not already use a homework planner, buy her something with enough space to write a brief note about each piece of work she has to do. Speak to your daughter's teachers and ask if they can put homework instructions up on the board so she can copy them down—something that the whole class will probably benefit from!

Your daughter may need extra time to do this, so ask her teacher about giving homework instructions five to 10 minutes before the end of the class, rather than as the bell goes. Realistically, she may still come out of school with nothing more than a brief scribbled note which she hopes will be enough to jog her memory about what he is supposed to do. Get her into the habit of using her planner effectively: Go through it together and talk about what she did in class and make sure that she has a good understanding of the homework task.

Q My son's teacher has told him to do what homework he can, but he still gets frustrated. Is there anything we can do?

Being presented with a sheet of homework which both your son and his teacher know he will not be able to complete is bound to raise his anxiety levels and is setting him up to fail. Allowing your son to only complete what he feels capable of shows some consideration for his needs, but handing in half-finished homework will make your son's difficulties even more obvious. This strategy may also result in your son gradually turning in less and less homework, and provides little motivation for him to learn. Speak to his teacher to see if he would be willing to give your son just the questions he can complete, to avoid him feeling overwhelmed by the

Visual activity schedules

Visual activity schedules are a simple, flexible, and very effective way to support children's learning and promote independence—particularly for those with additional needs. An activity schedule is basically a sequence of pictures (with or without words) which breaks down a routine into a few simple steps. For example, it may illustrate your morning routine, starting with getting out of bed and finishing with getting on the bus to school. There are thousands of pictures available on the internet, or you can use photos of your child performing each step. Laminate pictures if you can; they will not last long otherwise! Pictures are usually stuck on to a board with Velcro so that after each step is completed, your child can remove that picture and look to see what comes next. Another method is to have them in sequence on a key ring so he can flip through them easily. Once your child understands how his board works, you can use activity schedules to help him learn new skills and routines, and plan out his day so he can

see what he will be doing. For children who struggle to understand time, an hourglass can be used to show how long each activity will last. Best of all: Activity schedules are portable, so you can take them anywhere.

size of the task. If he feels able to finish the whole of his math homework, this will give him a far greater sense of achievement and boost his confidence. Make sure you give your son plenty of support and encouragement at home—you could even consider arranging some additional tutoring. Working for shorter periods then taking a break is likely to be more successful than sitting your son at the table until he has finished everything. When he has mastered a subject, speak to his teacher about gradually increasing the volume of work. A small success is better than a large failure, so go at his pace.

Q How can I improve my daughter's short attention span?

Having to keep nagging your daughter to do things at home is frustrating for you, makes your daughter more aware of her difficulties, and may cause friction between you both. If she is getting into trouble at school, this will also undermine her self-esteem.

However, there are a few simple strategies that you can use at home to build your daughter's skills and confidence in her ability to stay on task. When you give her an instruction, make sure you are in the same room and she is giving you her undivided attention, rather than having one eye on the TV! Give her one simple instruction at a time and back it up with something visual. This could be a picture or a real object. For example, if you want her to put her shoes away, take her to them. Ask her to repeat out loud what you have asked her to do to help her hold your instruction in her memory. Be sure she understands, and give her a gentle reminder if she has not started the task within a few minutes. Give her plenty of praise as soon as she finishes. As her skills improve you can give longer instructions.

Ask where your daughter sits in school: Being at the front will make it easier for the teacher to focus her attention and give her extra support without making it obvious to the rest of her class.

ADHD
Attention deficit hyperactivity disorder

Children with a diagnosis of attention deficit hyperactivity disorder (ADHD) have difficulties in three core areas: inattention, overactivity, and impulsiveness. Usually these are found together. However, some children are primarily overactive and impulsive, whereas others struggle more with attention and concentration. Children with attention/concentration difficulties were previously referred to as having attention deficit disorder (ADD), but this term is no longer in use. ADHD affects your child's thinking skills, emotions, and behavior. Cognitively, your child may be very distractible, have a short attention span, find it difficult to plan and organize himself, and struggle to see the consequences of his behavior. Emotionally, he may be excitable, lack impulse control, and have a low tolerance threshold when things don't go his way. Behavior is characterized by persistently high levels of activity, restlessness, and risk-taking. Estimates vary, but ADHD is thought to affect three to nine percent of children and young people, with more boys than girls receiving the diagnosis.

What does it mean for my child? Children with ADHD have difficulty filtering unimportant information from important information. Their attentional "net" is too broad most times (but other times can become so focused that it's hard to break out of an activity such as video play). This means that he will often be criticized or reprimanded for "not paying attention" or "not keeping up with the class." His hands will fidget and his body may be in constant motion. He likely has difficulties planning ahead, getting organized, and completing (even brief) tasks once begun. Lack of impulse control means that he may shout out answers at school, have difficulty taking turns, and be more likely to

engage in potentially risky activities such as skateboarding down that very steep road with no helmet or pads.

These difficulties mean that your child may find it harder to conform to expectations and follow social, home, and school rules regarding his behavior. Making and keeping friends can also be a problem if he moves quickly from activity to activity and fails to take turns in games. A lack of understanding regarding the nature of difficulties associated with ADHD may result in children being labeled as "bad." This can undermine children's self-esteem and lead to feelings of failure, frustration, and sadness. However, children with ADHD have many strengths, too. They are often creative problem-solvers, have good long-term memory, are enthusiastic, and can be very creative.

What causes it? All children differ in terms of their attentional skills, activity level, and impulsiveness. Only those with the most severe difficulties, impacting significantly on their own well-being and ability to function at home and school, will receive a diagnosis. The exact causes of ADHD are unknown, but several possible explanations have been suggested. Genetic factors may play a part, since parents and siblings of a child with ADHD are four to five times more likely to receive a diagnosis themselves. However, no direct genetic link has been established, which suggests that it is the interaction between inherited temperament and environment that may lead to some children developing ADHD.

Difficulties during pregnancy have also been proposed as a possible cause. Risk factors such as maternal smoking or alcohol use, problems in the womb, and low birth weight are also present in many children without ADHD though. Again it is the interaction of these issues with other factors that may be important. Other explanations have focused on possible differences in brain functioning. Messages in the brain are carried by chemicals called neurotransmitters, which switch on or turn off communication pathways. Differences in how the brain uses the neurotransmitters dopamine, noradrenaline, and adrenaline in the areas responsible for controlling attention, inhibiting behavior, and planning and organizing have been argued to account for the core difficulties of ADHD.

What can I do to help? The behaviors associated with ADHD can affect many areas of your child's life, so it is important to share information and work together with other people involved in his care, particularly school staff. As a first-line treatment, you may be invited to attend a parenting program. This does not mean that professionals are blaming you for causing your child's difficulties or that you are a "bad" parent. An appropriate parenting program will equip you with up-to-date knowledge and the most effective strategies. In addition, your child may be offered individual psychological support and/or a place in a group therapy. These groups aim to help him get along better with his peers and develop problem-solving skills, behavioral self-control, and listening skills.

If your child has very significant difficulties or if problems persist over time, medication may be an option. Depending on his needs he may be offered methylphenidate, atomoxetine, or dexamphetamine. These drugs are thought to work by acting on those parts of the brain where key neurotransmitters are not thought to be functioning effectively.

Support groups for parents of children with ADHD can also be a useful source of information, advice and access to social and leisure opportunities for your child.

How do I get my child tested? Talk to your doctor, who can arrange for you to see a specialist. Tests may be conducted by a pediatrician, child psychiatrist, clinical psychologist, or other appropriately qualified healthcare professional. Some areas have specialist ADHD teams that offer assessment, diagnosis, and support services to families.

FULL OF ENERGY: Children with ADHD are often restless, overactive, and lacking in impulse control.

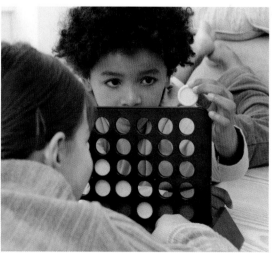

PAYING ATTENTION: A child with ADHD may struggle to sit still and focus on a task that others find simple.

My son gets teased about his learning difficulties and often acts out. What can I do to help him?

Being picked on about such a sensitive issue is bound to upset your son, which will only make it more difficult for him to stay in control of his feelings. If he shows genuine remorse after these incidents, he probably has some insight into the fact that he did not handle things in the best way. This is not just your son's problem, though. If he is being persistently targeted by other pupils, this bullying needs to be reported to his teacher and dealt with. Focus more on helping him develop calm and confident ways of dealing with these situations rather than lecturing him about right from wrong. Your son will be more motivated to change his behavior if he feels supported and understood than if he feels blamed.

At home, pick your time to discuss how his day went. It may help for him to make a drawing about any incidents on paper to show you what happened. Help him to reflect on how he handled the situation, what he did well, and how he might like to do things differently next time. He might find it difficult to think through the consequences of his actions, so write or draw what he might say and do and what is likely to happen. This will give him something to refer back to and learn from. Encourage your son to stand up for himself without being aggressive, and to talk to a teacher if he is being bullied.

You could also ask his school about social-skills training groups—this will give him the opportunity to practice his skills in a safe environment and build his confidence with his peers in school. Your local area might have groups or courses such as these.

Your son will be more motivated to change his behavior if he feels understood, not blamed

My child has ADHD. Before trying medication, are there other strategies I can look at?

If your child's distress and dysfunction associated with ADHD are manageable, there are many sound alternatives to try in advance of medication:

Cognitive behavioral therapy can help your child change the language in his thinking in order to make better choices. This is especially useful when his impulsive behaviors cause problems and he really wants to better control his body to succeed.

Many parents believe dietary changes, nutritional supplements, and vitamins can help. The scientific support for these claims is mixed. Be sure to check with your PCP or pediatrician before trying any of these, particularly if your child is on medication for any other reason (for example, asthma or epilepsy).

Behavior management programs in the home and at school can help by creating clear, concrete incentives to help your child stay on task.

Classroom changes can also be important, and may offer special seating, more breaks for physical activity, and "chunking" work into smaller pieces.

Because the impulsivity associated with ADHD can have devastating effects on a child's peer relationships, especially from age 10 and on, video feedback is a very successful tool with which to help a child see his faux pas and learn alternatives.

My child is dyslexic and says that when she tries to read, the words appear blurry.

This may be a problem with her eyesight, therefore it's smart to rule this out with a visit to an optician or opthamologist. Some children with dyslexia report that words on a page appear "fuzzy" or seem to dance around. This may be because people with dyslexia tend to see all the words on a page as a mass, as if they're trying to read them all at once, rather than being able to pick out individual words in a row, to read from left to right. Transparent color overlays help some children focus better. Different children respond to different colors, so try a few to see which works best for your child.

MYTHS AND MISCONCEPTIONS

Is it true that...

✳ Children who are hyperactive or have behavioral problems should not have soda?

Yes and no. Some sodas have very high sugar levels and caffeine, and may contain artificial additives, which will lead to an immediate energy rush followed by a blood-sugar crash. For some children with high activity levels, this may escalate some of their behaviors. Not all sodas contain these products, but many parents find it easier to just avoid them completely.

✳ There is no point in reading to my child now that he can read by himself?

Definitely not true! It takes years of practice to become an accomplished reader, and listening to you will really help your child improve his skills. If your child struggles with reading, writing, or spelling, reading with him is one of the most helpful things you can do. Learning aside, reading is also a great way to spend some quality time together.

✳ Using pictures with my child will make her lazy with her language?

Quite the opposite. Pictures will help your child to better understand what is expected of her and to express her own needs, wants, and feelings. Reducing her frustration in this way means that your child will be more motivated to communicate using spoken language alongside any visual supports she may have.

Dyslexia
A language-based difficulty

Children with dyslexia have significant problems with reading, writing, and spelling. This condition is often referred to as a specific learning disability, which can be a confusing term as most children with dyslexia are as intelligent as their classmates. It is estimated that five to 10 percent of the population is affected by dyslexia to some degree, with more boys receiving the diagnosis than girls. However, some experts argue that girls may be better at hiding their difficulties by relying more on their verbal skills. Boys, on the other hand, are more likely to be disruptive in school as a result of their learning problems, and so are more likely to be assessed and identified.

What does it mean for my child? Before starting school, your child may have had difficulties in developing clear speech, found it difficult to understand the connection between rhyming words such as "cat" and "mat," and had some coordination problems. In her first years at school, she may have had difficulty in learning the alphabet and multiplication tables, struggled to read more than a few simple words, found it hard to tell left from right, and had problems remembering common sequences such as days of the week and months of the year. Without the right support, she may become frustrated due to lack of progress and feelings of failure, which could result in behavioral problems or in her becoming increasingly quiet and withdrawn.

Research has shown that people with dyslexia make more use of the right hemisphere of the brain, which is involved in creative thinking. As a result, your child may have good verbal and social skills, be able to think laterally and solve complex problems by making unexpected connections, have good visual skills, and be able to see the "big picture."

What causes it? Children are born with an innate ability to learn spoken language. However, reading and writing are relatively new behaviors in terms of human evolution, and require children to master a complex set of skills. Phonological processing theory argues that, in order to read, children must first learn the sounds (phonemes) associated with the shape of written letters (graphemes). These building blocks can then be fitted together to build whole words. Children with dyslexia are known to struggle with breaking words down into their different sounds. However, some experts argue that this is a symptom of dyslexia rather than the main cause.

It has also been suggested that, in the early stages of speech development, children with dyslexia are significantly slower and make more mistakes when repeating words—for example, when singing nursery rhymes with you. These articulation difficulties lead to problems in understanding the sounds of similar words, which leads to difficulties in developing an awareness of the written appearance of these words. Research evidence shows that children who develop the skills of recognizing the sound and visual similarities of words at an early age become good readers, and those who struggle go on to develop reading difficulties.

What can I do to help my child? In school, your child may require a degree of one-on-one or small-group teaching. How much will depend on the severity of your child's difficulties. Both at home and at school, your child will benefit most from approaches that are:
* **Multisensory:** Encourage your child to use as many senses as possible when learning, for example looking at a letter, saying its name and sound, and writing it in the air all at the same time.

✳ Structured: Help your child learn in small steps, building on what she has already mastered. Don't overload her, and take care to only introduce new challenges once she feels confident with what she has learned so far.

✳ Reinforcing: Your child will need more help and practice to learn the basic skills of reading and writing, and will benefit from regular review with lots of praise and encouragement.

Set aside 10–15 minutes each day when you can sit down and read with her. Paired reading is a great way to support your child in developing her skills. Ask her to choose the book you will read—books that are about subjects she is interested in will be far more motivating for her. Sit side by side so you can both see the text and begin reading together. Make sure you adjust your pace to match your child's. When she is ready to read alone, she should signal for you to be silent. If she struggles to read a word, give her a few seconds then tell her what the word is. Be patient—stay calm, cool, and collected—particularly if it is a word you know she has read dozens of times before. Let her read the word correctly, praise her for it, then move on. Afterward, talk with your child about what you have read and answer any questions she may have. Research shows that children who do paired reading with their parents show improvements at three times the speed of other children.

Many children with dyslexia feel more comfortable using a computer to write and learn, and it may be possible for your child to do part of her schoolwork in this way. Word-processing programs use spell-check and auto-correct features that will help her identify mistakes with her writing. There are also lots of fun and engaging websites and educational software packages that she can use to support her learning.

How do I get my child assessed? If your child shows an unexplained difficulty in reading, despite having the necessary intelligence and verbal skills, speak to her teacher about a dyslexia screening test or assessment. Assessments should be carried out by trained specialists—this will usually be a teacher with expertise in working with children with dyslexia, an educational psychologist, or a neurologist.

TECHNOLOGICAL AIDS: Your child may be able to do some of her school work on a computer, which can help if she struggles to write.

LOTS OF PRACTICE: Your child may find it difficult to form letters, so be prepared to help her go over them again and again when she's learning.

BOOKWORM: Extra help with reading will be needed, since your child will probably find it hard. Sit side by side and read a book he enjoys together.

Staying connected
spending time together

Q Our son is bored with our ideas for things we could do together. How can we get him interested?

Satisfying your son's inquiring mind is the key to keeping him interested in doing things with you. When you're out together, take advantage of his natural curiosity by creating family challenges. In the countryside or local park, you can set "seeking" tasks, such as identifying five different kinds of tree or three types of birds. Time trials work well and run off energy, so see who can be fastest to run back to the car or around the edge of the playing field. On special outings, target places of interest to him such as historic sites or particular museums. You'll find there are often trails or activity sheets to complete as you explore. As friends are becoming a more important part of his life encourage him to invite someone along. He'll enjoy the company, and you'll still share time with him. At home he'll probably want to satisfy his competitive spirit by playing games with you, such as two-player video games and board games. He might enjoy making a meal or washing the car with you, or researching possible holiday destinations on the internet.

Q My daughter has become defiant. I don't want to spend time with her. What can I do?

It's easy to get caught up in a negative pattern like this. What starts as a few clashes can build up until you and your child have fewer and fewer good times together. With disagreements dominating your lives, each of you may find it hard to see the positive in the other.

As the adult in the relationship, it is up to you to break this pattern. Make a conscious effort to identify things about your daughter that you like or are helpful. Look for the smallest virtue—perhaps she gets up on time, eats her breakfast when you ask, or hangs up her coat as she comes in. Begin to praise and comment on her good qualities, soften your expression as you speak to her, and show her some physical affection. This may seem forced at first, but making yourself notice and acknowledge her good points is the precursor to feeling genuinely warm toward her. At the beginning she may be suspicious of this behavior, even asking you what you're after. Don't be discouraged; this means she's noticed that things have changed. This may be a long process, since you are each undoing months of conflict, but when you are relentless in pursuing the positive, she'll find it hard not to warm up, too.

PARENTS' STORY

Getting along
sharing a bedroom

My two sons share a bedroom but have very different styles. One likes everything neat, while the other spreads his stuff out everywhere. They get on each others' nerves all the time. In the end I swapped their bunk beds for twin beds to divide the room more easily, and made each responsible for their own half. Each has chosen the decorations and posters for his part of the room, and this has given them more pride in their space. They've agreed set times to put on their own music or an audiobook, and how to politely ask each other to turn the volume down. It doesn't always work, but there are fewer fiery moments. Despite the challenges, room-sharing seems to be teaching them to be more considerate of each other, and they're getting plenty of practice in negotiating.

ESSENTIAL INFORMATION: GRADE-SCHOOLERS

Showing an interest
Get more from mealtimes

Your child may be more independent, have his friends for companionship, and no longer rely on you the way he did, but you are still the person he'll turn to first to share his achievements or disasters. Like many families you may be "time poor," with adults juggling work or studying and trying to get to the gym each week while school, sports, clubs, and friendships keep your child on the go. However, even on a busy day, it will be the short periods of high-quality communication that help keep your family connected.

Eating together: Where does your family do most of its talking? For many it will be at the dinner table while you enjoy your food. Meals are your opportunity to catch up, share the day's events, and gauge the emotional temperature of your family. This daily dose of communication allows you to pick up on moods, either positive or troubling, notice achievements, or soothe tensions as they arise, all helping to strengthen your bonds.

Get the most from mealtimes

✳ Be flexible about timing to try to get as many family members at the table as you can.

✳ Start the conversation and use open-ended questions to get people talking.

✳ Make mealtimes distraction free. You will be able to concentrate on each others' conversation if the television, mobile phones, and handheld games consoles are turned off.

✳ Cook together. Preparing and sharing food together is one way you can express the care you have for your family.

✳ No pressure. Minimize mealtime stress by staying calm and avoiding nagging or pleading if your child is fussy or slow with his food.

✳ No time? If you simply can't get to eat together, find other connection points in the day. Good talking times can be found when your child is just in from school having a snack before he heads out to play, or when he's winding down and you're tucking him in at night.

HAPPY EATING: Keep mealtimes calm and stress free by discussing the day's events, while trying not to nag your child about table manners or berate her for a previous misdemeanor.
JUNIOR CHEF: Getting your child to help you with meal preparation or just spending time together baking increases opportunities to catch up, teaches your child valuable life skills, and takes some pressure off of you.

Q I'm a slave to my child but hardly get to talk to her. How can I get some time to relax?

It is definitely time for your child to start helping herself rather than requiring you to run around after her. Support her transition from helpless to helpful by giving her some clear guidelines. Explain that, as she's getting more grown-up, you are prepared to give her some responsibilities for herself. Put this way it can seem like a privilege to do more, rather than a result of your frustration.

Start small, by asking that she get her own drinks, make herself simple snacks such as toast or a sandwich, and pack her own school bag each morning. Make sure all the tasks are achievable—you may need to rearrange the kitchen a little so she can reach the plates and food items she needs. If she's going to make hot drinks or food, teach her to do this safely. She'll probably continue the habit of asking you for things for a while, but a polite reminder of her new skills and responsibilities should get her helping herself.

With your new-found free time, consider what you'd like to do with your daughter and enjoy the extra family time you have available.

Having a good argument

It can be a positive learning experience for your child to see you have a good argument. You model negotiation and problem-solving skills for him during a "successful" disagreement, in which you are reasonable, calm, and find a solution together. It is not good for him, however, if arguments involve shouting, put-downs or bad language, dredging up the past, or hurting each other physically or in any other way. This creates anxiety and affects his sense of safety and security.

If arguments are a problem for your child or yourself, seek help to improve your relationships. Find a local therapist or speak to your doctor about other local resources.

Support your child's transition from helpless to helpful by giving her clear guidelines

Q My child won't attend family meetings. Should we try again?

This must have been disappointing. However, your daughter is in a rapid phase of development and may have a different view if you try again. Encourage her by putting forward only positive topics for the first few meetings—for example, ideas for planning an upcoming celebration, or redecorating a room of the house. Gradually introduce more challenging subjects, such as chores or curfew, once meetings are established. Do hold the meeting even if your daughter does not attend; each time you meet, you demonstrate your willingness to involve her in family decisions. Eventually, she will be ready to take part.

When family meetings are dominated by crises or misbehavior, they can be punishing for everyone, and your child may opt out by not coming to them at all or refusing to speak. If you need to manage misbehavior, try to do this between yourself and your child in private.

Q My son and I are both stubborn. How can I prevent arguments?

There are definite advantages in your child's stubbornness; an ability to pursue his goals with confidence and persistence goes with the territory. However, as you have found, being stubborn often means being unwilling to compromise, and the possibility of winning an argument keeps you both in conflict. Try a different challenge: Instead of seeking the buzz of victory, try daring each other to find a solution. Slow down the argument so you have time to listen, consider each others' needs, and come up with ideas. Give yourselves a score out of 10 for each

Family meetings

Hundreds of decisions are being made in your family every day—what to have for dinner, who can come to play, where to go on a weekend outing, and many more. As your child matures he may want to play a greater role in this process and voice his preferences. Try having family meetings: a somewhat formal gathering of the whole family as an opportunity to discuss large and small issues, take everyone's point of view into account, and make decisions together.

✽ Family meetings work best when they happen regularly and become a habit or tradition. Once a month, for about half an hour to an hour might be enough for your family, or more frequently if you have plenty to talk about.

✽ Set a time for the meeting and find a place where everyone can sit together, perhaps around the dining table. Turn off distractions such as the TV and computer so you can all concentrate. It may be tempting to have your meeting during a meal but it can be difficult to try to eat and concentrate on a serious subject at the same time.

disagreement—higher points meaning you've come up with more ways to compromise. Lastly, consider whether there is a reason you feel you must "win." Question whether this is how you want to be as a parent, and find the negotiator in yourself if you can.

What might be a good way to structure our family meetings?

Make a list of topics to talk about: Start by asking each person to name one thing they want to have a decision on. Try to get a balance of positive issues with one or two negatives to resolve. For example, a typical list might be: How often are sleepovers allowed? Should we go bowling or to a movie this weekend? For more privacy, should there be a lock on the bathroom and bedroom doors? No one is cleaning the cat-litter box—whose job is it?

Discuss topics one by one, and ask each family member if they have an opinion on it. Listen carefully: You are trying to reach a consensus or a compromise. For example, if three out of four of you want to go bowling then you have a majority view and will probably opt to go bowling. On the privacy issue, there may be mixed views and safety to consider, so a compromise could be to have locks on the bathroom and "Knock before entering" signs on bedroom doors.

There may be times when you exercise the right to make the final decision in family meetings. You have the responsibility to ensure that decisions are reasonable and achievable so, on certain topics, let your child know you will have the deciding vote. For example, she might argue for three exotic holidays a year while you know the budget stretches to just one trip. If so, tell her the range of choice she has; set out the price range, and possibly the option of two short trips or one longer one, and then start the debate.

Finish off your meeting with a round of positive comments. You could invite each person to tell a joke or relate the best thing that happened to them in the past week. These small examples of sharing will end the meeting on an upbeat note.

How can I get them to help?
chores, housework, motivation

Q **My son keeps saying everyone at school gets more freedom than him. Am I really as out of step with other parents as he says?**

Your child is using a common and powerful negotiating tool, that of making comparisons with other parents and children. This can be very helpful, as it is prompting you to consider the freedoms you give him and check whether you are being reasonable. However, don't make your decisions based on just his report. Check out what is acceptable for his age by talking with other parents directly, be guided by developmental information in books, and think through the values and standards you are applying. Once you've gathered this information, decide whether you are prepared to loosen the limits or stick with them. Remember—no matter what you decide, you are in a process of fostering his independence, so freedoms need to be reviewed regularly and adjusted to allow him to make more choices for himself.

Less directive, more reflective

As your child matures, your own parenting style is adjusting along with her growing independence. You will be less likely to tell her what to do and more often be offering advice and support as she comes to her own conclusions. Your child will learn through her own experience and rarely accept that she can learn from yours. While it can be hard to stand by and not interfere, there will be times when it's safe to let her make her own mistakes. If things do end in tears make sure you're ready with a sympathetic attitude and no "I told you so" to be heard.

Q **My partner says I am too hard on the children. I think he's too soft. Who's right?**

Very different parenting approaches can be frustrating for both of you, and may mean your child plays you against each other. There is no single correct parenting style. However, consider what your child is learning from each of you. Is he finding he must be manipulative to get what he wants or that it's okay for adults to disregard and contradict each other? Whatever he learns he may apply in his own relationships outside the home. Consider what you want to teach him. For example, you may wish to show him that adults are respectful of each others' decisions and that he can have a say in what happens through negotiating rather than by finding a way around the rules. As you loosen control and include your child in decision making, he'll learn his views are valued. Similarly, if your partner finds it hard to judge when to give in or stand firm, help him out by talking together about what you'll do. When you model respect for each other and the ability to compromise, your son will follow in your footsteps.

Q **My child's bedroom is a bombsite. How can I get her to clean it up?**

Your child's bedroom is her special space in the home, somewhere to express her personality and have her privacy. It can also be a gigantic mess. Before you take action about the state of your child's room, think about whether this is your problem. If it's not, then simply close her bedroom door and accept she has chosen to live this way. You may, however, feel she needs to learn neater habits or address health or cleanliness hazards, such as spoiled food or toys to trip over. If so, blitz the bedroom with a big tidy up. Do this together with your child, or she'll feel her

ESSENTIAL INFORMATION: JGRADE-SCHOOLERS

Negotiating with your child
How to have a successful debate

Your child is increasingly keen to express her needs and views and, on occasion, stand her ground. The better her ability to communicate and negotiate, the more effective her transition to independence.

✱ **Successful negotiation:** What's the issue? Clearly define the point you are debating. If it's a later bedtime ask your child to be specific about how much later she wants to stay up and on which nights of the week.

✱ **Grounds for debate:** Encourage your child to give you her reasoning: Find out why this would be a good thing for her. Perhaps she's had a birthday and expects bedtime to be adjusted, wants to watch a late TV show, or has friends who stay up and feels her bedtime is babyish.

✱ **Pros and cons:** Try to generate as many positive and negative outcomes of the idea as you can. Be as silly or serious as you like. For later bedtimes you might come up with the downside of being overtired, sleeping in and missing breakfast, or keeping others awake with late night noise. On the upside, perhaps she'll be able to join in with friends at school chatting about the TV show, have more one-to-one time with you after siblings have gone to bed, or feel grown up because you trust her to stay up later.

✱ **Think it over:** Carefully consider each option, try to see your child's point of view and help her to see yours. You might cut out some options quite quickly. For example, if the TV show she wants to watch is inappropriate for her age, then take this out of the debate. Once you have your final list of reasons for and against, weigh them up together. Some reasons will be strong, such as having one-to-one time with you, while others, such as having more free time, could be weaker.

✱ **Reach a compromise:** Agree what you're going to do. Be clear about what is allowed and what is not. For example, you may agree your child will stay up on a Friday and Saturday night for an extra hour, with the proviso that she will go to bed when asked, without complaining.

✱ **Review:** Set a trial period, perhaps two or three weeks, to see if the decision is working out. Keep track of the up and down sides of the idea. At the end of the trial period decide whether to continue, adjust, or stop the agreement.

✱ **When not to negotiate:** On points of safety, health, and values you may decide not to debate an issue. For example, if your child is asking to try alcohol, to go out late at night, or play violent video games classified above her age range, do listen, but go on to state clearly why this is not acceptable.

NOT SLEEPY: Discussing an issue with your child, such as negotiating a later bedtime, is good practice for him and increases his independence.

Chores: Benefits for everyone

Chores are tasks around the home that benefit everyone in the family—for example, setting the table or putting away clothes. Chores should not be confused with your child's everyday responsibilities such as getting his cereal in the morning and packing his school bag. Both chores and responsibilities are important to your child's development. Learning to look after himself and carry out domestic tasks are part of the life skills he needs to become an independent adult.

What do you expect? Your child has plenty of demands on his time. When he's at home he needs opportunities to do his homework, play with friends, and relax, as well as helping around the house. There is no set or correct number of chores to give at each age, so it is up to you to make sure he is not overwhelmed with tasks. Gauge what he can do depending on his school, sports, and other obligations. Start small, perhaps with a 10-minute commitment every day, as it is more effective to build up from there than find he's snowed under and have to back down. Make sure he is ready for the tasks he takes on.

While he'll be able to complete simple jobs such as tidying his room or putting his dirty clothes in the laundry basket, he may need some help learning more complex tasks. Build his competence and confidence by teaching him to use household appliances—for example, how to work the vacuum attachments or microwave. An ideal way to teach is to complete the chores together until he gets the hang of them.

privacy has been violated. Next, agree some rules, such as, "The floor will be cleared of toys each night," and, "Put dirty clothes in the laundry basket daily." Lastly, notice and praise your child for any acts of tidiness and, of course, set a good example yourself and keep your own bedroom tidy.

I constantly remind my daughter to do her chores, yet she does nothing. What can I do?

For you and your daughter, it seems an unhelpful cycle of "you ask and she resists" has developed. In this situation the focus has moved from the chore itself to a battle of wills between the two of you.

    She may feel your constant reminders mean you don't trust her, while her lack of effort builds your frustration. Break the cycle by avoiding the urge

to nag: You know it doesn't work. Instead, find out from your child what gets in the way of her completing her tasks and ask her, if she was in your shoes, how she'd solve the problem. Children can be surprisingly insightful about what would motivate them. You may explore hidden reasons for her behavior—perhaps her favorite show is on at the time she is supposed to clear the table, or she hates the smell of the cat food she has to dish out. Find solutions together, such as changing the timing of tasks or feeding the animals together so you do the part of the job she can't handle. Take the burden of reminding her off your shoulders by using a kitchen timer or a poster to jog her memory. If these don't work agree, to fire off a single reminder yourself, such as a text, to get her going. Bump up her motivation by changing the reward for her chores. Perhaps she's lost interest in the original incentives you offered. A different privilege, such as choosing the Friday-night takeout meal or movie, or a small monetary reward may get her started. If she doesn't help out despite all this effort, then some consequences, such as missing out on rewards and privileges, will need to be used.

Can I take back money earned from chores if my child misbehaves later?

Offering money as a reward for jobs done is a good incentive and gives you the option of withholding small sums if tasks don't get completed. However, it is unwise to take back the money your child has earned through chores for unrelated misbehavior. If you do this, then you teach him that, no matter how hard he works, he may not be rewarded. He'll recognize this is unfair, and may give up on his chores as a consequence. Do make chore money separate from regular pocket money. This way you can use pocket money as a reward for good behavior and hold it back it for misbehavior without affecting your child's incentive for doing his chores.

My children hardly help out at all right now. How can I get them started with housework?

Give a clear reason why chores need to be shared—perhaps explain that when everyone helps at home then there will be more time to have fun together. Give a specific example of something you'll do as a family if chores are shared, or your children may not be convinced.

Create a list of jobs that need to be done each day, and encourage your child to say which ones she'd prefer. She'll be more likely to do her chores if she has helped to make the list and chosen her own tasks. When chores are linked to her personal interests, you'll get better cooperation too. For example, if she's begged for a pet, then her task could involve the animal's care. If she takes pride in her personal space, then encourage her to choose vacuuming her bedroom as one of her

jobs. Your sports-obsessed child may be willing to sort the laundry into whites and colors if this helps get her uniform washed first.

For you, the incentive to complete a task may be the satisfaction of a job well done or seeing tidiness after chaos. However, your child has probably not yet developed this sense of personal fulfilment, and external rewards are needed to keep her going. Spend some time with your child making a list of rewards from which she can choose; but do put limits on cost or time commitment so you don't have to say "no" to too many fanciful or expensive suggestions. Activities and privileges tend to work well—for example, earning a later bedtime on weekends, an extra family outing, or her choice of Sunday lunch. A sticker chart showing she's completed her chores can be motivating, and small monetary rewards are useful, since you'll be able to teach your child about spending and saving as she earns. However, even the most prized reward loses its appeal after a while. Changing rewards regularly keeps your child's motivation up. Write out a job roster, to show who will do each chore on each day. This helps your child see that tasks are being allocated fairly, and everyone is playing his or her part. Rosters act as a reminder of what is needed, and you can check off each item as it's completed. The tally also helps you allocate rewards for jobs done.

Your aim is to teach your child to take a small share in running the household, so identifying one or two brief daily tasks works well and helps establish a routine. Choose the tasks you give your child with care, since her concentration and ability to recognize and manage risks are not fully developed yet.

Children who regularly help around the home are more likely to be prepared for their adult life

Distressing times coping with death and depression

How can I tell if my daughter is depressed and what can I do?

It can be difficult to know how seriously to take your child's ups and downs. Get too involved when there is no need, and you interfere with her learning to handle difficult feelings; stay away when it's serious and she may feel abandoned. Depression can show through a variety of behaviors and emotions, such as an increase in sadness or irritability and loss of interest in things such as friendships, hobbies, sports, or schoolwork. Physical complaints like stomachache, tiredness, or headache can also be an indicator of emotional difficulties. If you notice some or all of these signs for two weeks or more, seek help from a health professional, who may recommend specialist help. Your support at home plays a major part in your child's recovery. Set aside extra time to talk together, and, when she shares her worries, take them seriously even if they seem out of proportion. Give your child support to do things she has enjoyed in the past. For example, run her a bubble bath, spend time cuddled up watching a funny TV show together, or have a favorite friend or relative drop in for just a few minutes to encourage her to socialize. These small pleasures can gradually lift her mood.

Draw your child's attention to her successes. For example, comments such as, "Did you notice how you finished that puzzle so quickly today" help her think in the positive. Support your child to stick to her usual routine: Regular everyday tasks divide the day into small manageable periods, whereas unstructured time can seem impossible to get through. Going to school, although difficult, usually works well to keep up her learning and friendships.

Keep monitoring her behavior and emotions, and go to your doctor if things do not improve.

How do I choose a therapist?

Make your choice of therapy and therapist carefully. Ask for recommendations from your doctor or through friends, and check the credentials of the therapist you choose.

Ask what training the therapist has undertaken. Some professional titles are not regulated, meaning they can be used with little or no training, so do check the qualifications of the therapist you choose. Check that the therapist is licensed to practice. Like anyone working with children, your therapist should have an up-to-date criminal records check. Therapists should also be registered with the professional body responsible for their work. Ask for details of the approach they will use, how effective it is, and how long therapy is expected to take. Discuss the limits of confidentiality. Therapists will not share the content of your child's therapy with you but

Death of a pet
talking about big issues

When our beloved cat, Bubbles, died recently I wasn't prepared for how hard my little girl Chloe would take it. She was distraught. The only way to take the edge off her feelings was to treat Bubbles to a proper burial. We wrapped her up carefully in a towel and found a box for her, buried her in the yard, and I helped Chloe plant a little bush over the top to mark the spot. We talked about where the animal's spirit has gone and the joy she brought into our lives. Even though it was sad, it got us talking about some big issues, such as the cycle of life and death, which I wouldn't otherwise have thought to bring up.

Dealing with death

When there is a death in, or close to, your family, you may be coping with your own grief as well as trying to help your child with hers. Finding comfort for yourself and being able to attend to your child is paramount. Your child will need to have some explanation when a person dies. She'll understand that death is final and that she will never see the person again. Her thinking is quite concrete at this age, and she'll probably want to see the coffin or urn and the cemetery.

Straightforward and honest communication is welcomed. Say, for example, "Grandpa is dead" rather than "We've lost Grandpa" or "Grandpa is at rest." If you use euphemisms for death, such as, "He went to sleep," your child may be reluctant to go to sleep herself in case she dies, too. Include your child in mourning the loss. Trying to protect her by not telling her about the death or keeping her away from the funeral can make dying very mysterious and frightening.

Your child may ask over and over again about death and dying as she tries to make sense of her feelings and fears. This can be distressing for you as

you deal with your own pain. Share the load with your partner or other relatives who can help by going over the subject with her. This may be a time to talk through your spiritual beliefs—for example, it can be reassuring for her to think about people's spirits going to a place such as heaven after death. She may let her feelings out through drawings of the person who has died and pictures of heaven or similar places. This is not morbid, but a way for her to express her loss.

you should expect them to tell you if your child is at risk of harming herself or others.

Whatever therapy your child receives, your support at home will be vital to its success. Read up on the difficulty your child is experiencing so you are aware of what she's going through and anything that might help or hinder her recovery. Obtain specific advice from her therapist as to how you can support her. This may involve changes in how you relate to each other or specific homework with your child to back up what she's doing in therapy. Ask how much she wishes siblings or relatives to know about the difficulty and respect as far as possible her right to keep things confidential. Avoid grilling her about her therapy sessions. Pressure to tell you about them can give her a feeling that they're not private, and she may disclose less to her therapist as a result.

Q My child keeps asking me if I'm going to die. Might it be because her aunt passed away?

Loss of a loved one can raise anxieties for your child about your mortality. Do bring up this topic yourself if you think your child is too anxious to ask. Avoid denying the problem: Her fears about your mortality are first and foremost about her own well-being. Much as we want to reassure our kids (and ourselves) that we'll be around for a very long time, no one has a crystal ball. Thus, the first best answer to your daughter's fears is, "Sweetie, we will make sure that you are always well taken care of, no matter what." If she persists asking about your mortality, best to get at the feeling that she's expressing ("You sound pretty scared that I won't be there for you") before tackling the harsh realities of death. When your child is

ESSENTIAL INFORMATION: GRADE-SCHOOLERS

Therapies for children
The various options

There is a wide range of therapies available, and it can be difficult to judge which one will be best suited to your child and her difficulty. When you're looking at types of therapy, do check that there is clear evidence, preferably from academic research as well as case studies, that each is effective. Take note of whether the particular approach is recommended for your child's difficulty. Some, for example, family therapy, are helpful for eating disorders, whereas cognitive behavioral therapy is suggested for depression. There are guidelines available to assist you in selecting an approach. Whichever therapy you choose, the trusting relationship between your child and her therapist will play a central role in the healing process.

Parenting programs: Also known as parent training, these are attended by parents, caregivers, and sometimes grandparents, and are recommended if your child has difficulties with behavior and hyperactivity. They are based on the idea that you are in the best position to help your child by guiding and encouraging positive behavior. Parenting programs are often offered in groups, usually over eight to 12 weeks, during which you will be taught a range of strategies to build up your relationship with your child and manage misbehavior. Parenting programs are based on social learning theory, have been well researched, and are most effective when all sessions are attended and you complete homework tasks. If your child has serious difficulties with attention, then medication may also be used as part of a treatment plan.

Cognitive behavioral therapy (CBT): This is a widely used approach for difficulties including repetitive habits, depression, and anxiety.

CBT helps your child understand how her thoughts affect her feelings and behavior. She will be guided to challenge and replace negative or unhelpful patterns of thought. CBT is usually brief, around six sessions of an hour each, and can be individual or group. Common topics for group CBT would be coping with anger and improving social skills. CBT is well researched and does reduce the duration of your child's difficulty. It is often offered as the first line of treatment.

Non-directive supportive therapy: Also known as client-centerd therapy or counseling, this is commonly used with children who have mild difficulties. It involves the therapist providing an opportunity for your child to express and explore thoughts and feelings with a warm, empathic, and non-judgmental listener. The aim is to enable your child to become self-aware. The number of meetings varies considerably and is negotiated between therapist, child, and parent.

Interpersonal psychotherapy (IPT): IPT focuses on your child's relationships, aiming to improve her ability to manage disagreements, loss, and change. Your child will meet individually with a therapist for sessions, usually of an hour's duration. IPT is time-limited, lasting for 16 to 20 sessions, and is helpful with a range of difficulties such as eating disorders and depression.

Psychodynamic therapies: This form of psychotherapy includes a wide variety of approaches based on the premise that your child will benefit by gaining an understanding of both her conscious and unconscious experience. The psychodynamic therapist will listen to your child's thoughts, and may comment on or interpret their meaning. The evidence for the effectiveness of psychodynamic approaches with children is limited, although some studies have found it to be beneficial. Psychodynamic therapy is usually of long duration: 30 or more sessions may be needed, depending on progress and the type of therapy used.

Common psychodynamic therapies with children

✱ Play therapy: This allows your child to act out and resolve issues and emotions through play. It is usually offered to children between three and 11 years old and involves sessions once a week with a therapist in a well-equipped playroom. Your child will be invited to play with anything in the room. The therapist will not lead or suggest but may comment on the play. Play therapy may be as short as 12 weeks or take more than a year.

✱ Psychodrama and Drama therapy: Both of these approaches use performance arts such as role play, storytelling, and games to enable your child to express and understand her feelings. Sessions are usually in groups, and each may last for an hour or more.

In psychodrama your child will often take the part of herself during the exercises, whereas in drama therapy she will act a role, perhaps playing someone with difficulties similar to hers.

✱ Art therapy: Art therapy involves the expression of thoughts, feelings, and events through visual arts, such as painting, drawing, and sculpting. Art is used as an alternative to verbal communication for children unable to express their experience in words, or who do not have the developmental ability to do so clearly. One aim of this therapy is to raise your child's suppressed emotions.

✱ Family therapy: Your child's difficulties will be seen in the context of family issues and relationships rather than as her problem alone. This usually involves family members meeting in a group with the therapist although, occasionally, therapy is with each person individually. You will be guided to explore tensions or clashes, your role and your child's role in the family. Alternative ways of relating to and supporting each other will be considered. Family therapy can be effective in 14–15 sessions, but may take longer, depending on progress. It is often offered as a treatment for eating disorders.

PSYCHODYNAMIC: Play and drama therapy are common psychodynamic approaches for children. They allow your child to act out her emotions, as she may find it hard to express feelings in words.
FIGHTING: Very rough and consistently aggressive behavior should be addressed *(bottom left)*. Therapy is an excellent method of helping your child learn to express himself calmly.
POTENTIAL SIGNS: If your child seems extremely sad and withdrawn all the time, you may want to consider therapy.

When do mood swings require therapy?

Just under one in 10 children will experience a psychological problem in their early years. The most common difficulties are behavior problems, fear and anxiety issues, and repetitive habits. The trigger for a psychological problem is often a combination of vulnerability in your child and a stressful event in her life. Perhaps she has a sensitive or shy personality or there is a family history of difficulties that make her more at risk of developing problems herself. She may be suffering from bullying or be reacting to the death of a loved one. None of these experiences mean she will automatically have a psychological difficulty but, for some children, they can be a trigger.

Strong emotions: Your young child will experience a wide range of moods and behaviors that are an entirely normal reaction to everyday life. Events such as falling out with friends, achieving a personal goal, or moving to a new house will trigger strong emotions such as sadness, elation, or frustration. However, keep a watchful eye on your child if you notice she has become sad, appears worried, has difficulty sleeping, or has habits that get in the way of relationships and everyday life. If these persist over a period of a few weeks, find a quiet time to let her know you are concerned, ask for her perspective, and seek advice from your doctor.

Where to get help: Your pediatrician is the first route into help for your child. Both you and she should go to see the doctor together if possible. Be ready to describe how long the problem has been going on, how it affects family life, and any triggers you're aware of. If your doctor thinks your child has mild difficulties, he may recommend a period of two to four weeks of "watchful waiting." Most childhood distress improves without any therapy, but it can recur; this period allows you to monitor your child to see if the problem persists. If her difficulty continues, your doctor will usually refer you to specialist services for some talk therapy. Medication is helpful in only a few situations.

involved in ceremonies like funerals and memorials, they take part in the grieving process and can show their feelings just as you do. A small number of children do not resolve their grief without help. If initial distress is maintained, or a child has emotional difficulties that interfere with her life, therapy, usually involving the family, is recommended.

Q I think my child is having night terrors. What are the signs?

During a night terror your child may thrash around and call out for help in his sleep. They tend to occur around the same time every night, usually before midnight if your child goes to bed around 7:00 pm. This is more frightening for you than for your child, who will often have no memory of the event. It will not help to wake him, and he will usually settle down within 10 minutes. Because sleepwalking can occur, its important to take precautions to avoid your child falling or leaving the house. A gate at the stairs or a deadbolt on the front door may be sufficient. Night terrors are not a sign of psychological distress or upsetting life events. They are a physical fear reaction caused by arousal of the central nervous system. Most children grow out of them by adolescence, but you can step in to reduce them if they are frequent and disruptive.

The solution to this problem begins with finding out exactly when the terror happens each night. Stay awake to observe, and make a note of the exact time he starts to have the night terror each night for a week so that you can see the pattern clearly. The next step is to wake your child about 15 minutes before his night terror would usually start, and keep him awake for 15 minutes. This may not be easy when your child is in a deep sleep, but it is necessary in order to break the pattern. If this is not effective within a week, seek help from your pediatrician.

Screen time
how much is too much?

Q What can I do to manage video gaming safely with my two sons?

Help your boys to choose age-appropriate games and websites by taking into account each individual child's temperament and developmental stage in your decision-making. An energetic, fiery child may well get over-excited and a little aggressive after playing a war game, so you will need to be cautious about what you allow him to play and for how long.

Give yourself the opportunity to be involved in choices about games and websites by making sure that both boys ask permission from you to play, to go online, and to download material. Set time limits and stick to them. Play games together, learn together, and keep an eye on solitary gaming activity. It is not necessarily bad: You wouldn't stop a child from reading alone for hours on end if he was into a really good book and you had no concerns about his social development. But make sure that the games console is kept in a communal area so that you can keep an eye on what each boy is playing and how it might be affecting him.

Nearly all games now have age classifications stated on the packaging, so check these before you buy. There are helpful online information sites for parents about safe gaming, and the industry is building in safety measures such as parental control on gaming platforms. However, you do need some knowledge in order to use these effectively; you cannot rely on the industry to keep your children safe.

Q What are your views on the influence TV has on children?

Some people are worried about television enforcing certain stereotypes and prejudices in society. However, there is no evidence to support the argument that the more TV children watch, the more likely they are to conform to gender stereotypes.

The portrayal of more positive roles on television for certain groups such as disabled people and ethnic minorities may actually have a positive impact on children's views. They also may have a more positive impact on adult's views, and it may be via the adult that the child's view is formed rather than directly through the influence of television. Children are more likely to be influenced by TV portrayals that are similar to the environment that they live in. The clear message is the crucial role parents play in mediating the effects television may have on their children. Parents can limit the time children spend watching, they should monitor and control their choice of shows, and, most significantly, recognize that their own behavior and attitudes are more influential on their children at this age than television will ever be.

Ensuring e-safety

* Install software that blocks access to inappropriate material.
* Monitor internet use and websites visited.
* Set rules about behavior online: no personal information; no-go websites; no illegal downloading; limits to time spent online; behave as you would offline.
* Explain why you are concerned, and that it is your responsibility to keep your children safe; use an offline analogy, like learning to ride a bike.
* Encourage discussion about internet content, contact, and conduct.
* Support your children in making judgments about the reliability of online content.
* Encourage your child to take some responsibility for his own e-safety.
* Share time together on the internet.

ESSENTIAL INFORMATION: GRADE-SCHOOLERS

Video gaming
Risky or beneficial?

Think nine-year-old boys, and a video game isn't far behind! As with internet use, there may be risks (for example, many games feature adult content) but there may also be advantages. Perhaps more than any other screen-related activity, gaming technology is developing so rapidly that parents and researchers cannot keep up. This means that, in many cases, we just do not know what their effects on children might be.

Benefits of gaming: There is evidence of improvements in decision-making and attention in six-year-olds who have had some training on a computer screen. However, caution must be taken when drawing comfort from this research—although changes may be demonstrated immediately following the training, we do not know if this continues in the long term, nor whether it transfers from the gaming situation to real life.

Educationally, using video games to teach your child will certainly increase his motivation, but the overall success will depend on your child, his teacher, and the subject being taught. For children with special educational needs, developments have been made in using video games to teach skills. For example, a game involving Thomas the Tank Engine has been used to teach emotional recognition skills to children on the autistic spectrum. Using video gaming following painful procedures in hospital has been shown to reduce the amount of pain-relieving medication needed.

Playing together with friends and family on video games, from the most basic puzzles and races to the interactive and physically active sporting and musical games, is highly social and great fun. Children are also learning about turn taking, negotiating, winning, and losing.

What do we know about the risks? One of the main areas of concern is the amount of time children spend gaming. Although it may not be appropriate to say that a child is truly addicted, gaming can certainly be a problem requiring significant change if he is playing every day for long stretches of time, instead of doing homework, physical activity, socializing, and sleeping, and if his mood is directly affected by whether he is gaming or not. Hours playing solitary games from a young age may have a detrimental impact on language and social-skills development and, indeed, on learning to control behavior and emotions. Parents should ensure that their child is playing a suitable game for his age by checking the age ratings on the box.

It is up to parents to decide how much time your children spend playing video games. You could have a rule that gaming is only allowed after meals, chores, completion of homework, and enough physical activity.

MODERATION: Playing video games should be fine as long as you impose a time limit.

How can I protect my child from stranger danger?

We hear about predatory adults who go onto children's networking sites, posing as children, to access their targets. Those characteristics that might make a child vulnerable to this kind of approach in everyday life will also make him vulnerable online.

However, we must keep a sense of proportion—although the negative potential is evident, the reality of actual harm is very low. Children aged between eight to 10 are unlikely to be interested in such risky behavior, and can be managed with sensible advice and close monitoring. Ensure that they use public chat rooms that are well moderated and that they learn to look out for signs that someone is not who they say they are. Establish as common practice the rule that no personal information is given out, including email addresses.

My 10-year-old is really into online gaming in a kind of imaginary world. Will this do him any harm?

The new world of online gaming offers extraordinary opportunities for players to take on new personalities, referred to as avatars, in three-dimensional virtual worlds and to play interactively with known and unknown others via the internet. This means your son enters a fantasy universe with a self-created identity, builds homes, communities, and worlds, and enacts battles and adventures with friends and possibly strangers. At 10, he may not be able to fully differentiate between fact and fantasy, and he may also not be able to make sound judgments about the people he meets in his virtual world. He may also encounter material online that is inappropriate for his age.

On the other hand, he may benefit hugely from creating this new identity and being part of enacting colorful adventures. As his parent, you must judge from what you know about his character and his maturity and decide to set some limits upon his behavior. If he will comply with your safety requirements and share some of his world with you, so that you can stay involved and informed,

you may feel good about letting him proceed. You might consider joining the game yourself—this way, you will probably be able to monitor his interactions more effectively.

Is it true that watching TV might make my child violent?

There is a commonly held belief that television is bad for children. Television watching is blamed for, among many other social ills, childhood obesity, passive absorption of mindless programming, creating an endless desire for material goods, perpetuating social stereotyping, and encouraging violent behavior.

Since the explosion of television ownership and viewing in the 1950s, much research has been done on the feared influence TV has had on growing brains and bodies. To date this research remains complex and inconclusive. It is often misunderstood, overly simplified, and misrepresented to support the prevailing zeitgeist. What we can safely conclude is that television can have an effect on the social behavior of children, but this will depend very much on the particular child and factors such as his age, gender, social background, and on the preexisting level of behavior being affected (ie academic achievement or aggressive behavior).

Some research studies suggest that watching violent programs in already-aggressive boys is associated with increases in aggressive behavior. However, there may be other factors influencing aggressive boys that will have more of an influence on their behavior, such as the environment in which they live or their interactions with others. Interestingly, watching informative programs at age five was related to improved school grades later on for boys, while watching violent programs at age five was related to poor school grades later on for girls only.

As long as you limit the amount of time your child spends watching TV—not more than two hours of screen time a day is recommended—and ensure that you stick to age-appropriate programs, television probably will not have any bad effects on your child.

ESSENTIAL INFORMATION: GRADE-SCHOOLERS

The internet
Advantages and disadvantages

Almost all children ages eight to 17 use the internet. Now is your opportunity to influence your child's online behavior while he is young and likely to comply. This gives you an opportunity to get things right in preparation for years of internet use, so that you can maximize the benefits and reduce and manage the risks.

Risks: There are four main categories of risk: What your child might find on the internet; who he will meet; how he and others behave; and, finally, how he understands what he encounters. When it comes to the content found on the internet there is no doubt that this technology has increased the likelihood that children will come across sexually explicit material. The impact of what he sees may be influenced by your child's background, age, cognitive, social, and physical development. However, there is growing evidence that pornography can have a very negative impact on children, ranging from distress to the development of distorted belief systems.

In order to prevent this from happening in your home, you can put parental controls in place that block unsuitable material. It is worth checking that similar controls are in place on computers at his friends' homes. Most parents will be relieved to know that you are just as concerned and proactive as they are. Should precautions fail and your child stumbles across sexually explicit material, he may react in a range of ways, from shock, to curiosity, to amusement or disgust. It is worth having a general conversation about unsuitable images and offering advice and support that suits your child's personality and temperament—reassuring to one who might be upset by such things, calming and serious to another who might be excited and titillated by such lewdness. You as a parent will

have to judge your tone and emphasis and guard against making a big deal that may encourage the seeking out of such images.

Cyberbullying: This has all the damaging features of offline bullying, but with the extra elements of anonymity and the invasiveness of the internet into the safe haven of home. Part of the malevolent power of cyberbullies is their ability to distort and abuse personal information. This represents one element of a greater risk associated with posting personal information on the internet.

Although you may have told your child not to give out details about himself, he may not hesitate when communicating on a social-networking site with someone he believes to be a friend. In a large survey of 8–17-year-olds, nearly half admitted to giving out personal information to people they meet on the internet. If verbal reminders from you get overlooked, it might be worth assigning your son

NETWORKS: One of the great benefits of the internet is that it connects people across the world.

the task of making a big, bright sign above the computer to remind himself and his siblings NEVER to give out personal details, with all the gruesome visual imagery he can muster.

Another considerable risk to young children is the opportunity that the internet affords for commercial advertising and potential exploitation. Side by side, sitting at the computer, you can help him cast a critical eye over what is really available, and the need for caution and a bit more research before purchasing things online. It is also worth quoting real-life examples from friends and family of being ripped off.

Enormous potential benefits: The internet offers wonderful opportunities for learning and developing cognitive skills via fun, interactive sites that engage children in ways that formal education cannot always do. For children who are struggling to engage in school, this can be a lifeline. Online communities represent all manner of interests, affording children the opportunity to participate in ways not available to them offline. In particular, the global nature of the internet can connect children across the world in social, cultural, ecological, political, and ethnic groups.

RISK MANAGEMENT: Sitting with your child while he browses allows you to control what he accesses online.

Q My two children fight constantly over the computer. Should I ban it completely?

Learning to use and share a computer is an important lesson for children. You can use time on the computer as a reward to be earned for behaving according to the rules you have set for its proper use. Time on the computer can then also become a sanction to be removed for rule-breaking. Banning things completely denies you this very powerful incentive and denies your children the opportunity to gain all the benefits that computers can offer.

Q What can I do to ensure internet safety?

As with any other new activity that your children engage in, the internet requires the same balance of parental response: interest, rules, monitoring, and safety measures. You need to know what you are dealing with, put safety measures in place as much as possible, keep an eye on your children's internet activity, and teach them responsible e-safety measures as well.

Most crucially for parents of internet-savvy children is the need to be informed and skilled to use the technology with confidence. If you have to rely on your child for technical assistance, you are at a disadvantage as the responsible adult, and this can undermine your own and your child's sense of security. Set some clear and simple rules about how much time each child is allowed to spend on the computer, when in the day that should be (after homework is completed might be a good idea), and spell out the behavior you expect to see from them toward each other, in relation to you, and toward the computer. You might put up a list of do's and don'ts that include some details about handovers such as: When your time is up, you have five minutes to finish what you're doing and hand over the controls; Wait until your brother/sister has finished his/her turn, including the extra five minutes, to take the controls that are given to you; Treat each other and the computer with respect (no food or drinks nearby); Speak quietly and calmly.

Preteens
the middle years

* **Making the transition**
  starting middle school

* **Tactics for tests**
  how can I help at exam time?

* **She's starting puberty!**
  changing bodies, first dates

* **Lazybones or workaholic?**
  your child's personality

* **What's the fallout?**
  divorce and blended families

* **Their time online**
  safe internet use

* **Wannabe?**
  clothes, make-up, older behavior

Making the transition
starting middle school

Q My daughter refuses to dress nicely for school. I don't want her to get into trouble. What can I do?

Your daughter is trying to fit in with her peers and be part of a group that probably all dresses in a similar way. The school will be used to students bending the rules to put their own individual stamp on the regulation uniform, and, if you insist that your daughter adhere strictly to the dress code, you risk making life difficult for her socially. You may even find that your daughter takes matters in to her own hands and adjusts her outfit each day when she is out of your sight. The key word here is compromise: Work together on finding a solution that you are both happy with. Look at what other students are wearing and try to find the middle ground between the "correct" attire and your daughter's must-have fashion requests.

Fitting in, developing her own sense of identity, and having friends are very important for your daughter at this age, so be prepared to be a little flexible to help her achieve this. If she feels a part of things socially she is likely to be happier at school and perform better academically. Respecting your daughter's point of view and negotiating also means that your daughter will be more likely to approach you with other issues in the future.

It can be hard work for parents to keep up with the friendship roster, since positions at the top and bottom change regularly

Q My daughter has the chance to go on a trip with school but doesn't want to. Should I insist that she go?

Forcing your daughter to go on this trip is likely to make her feel even more anxious and put a strain on your relationship. Instead, talk to her to find out if she is interested in going on the trip in principle and, if so, exactly what she is worried about that you may be able to help with. If she is concerned about travel or sleeping arrangements, the trip organizer should have transportation and accommodation details and be able to let her know who she will be sharing with. Chances are that your child will not be the only student struggling with these issues, so speak to her teacher or the trip chaperone to find out what else they can do to help. Work on a plan with her to give her some simple strategies to cope with her homesickness and let her know that it's perfectly normal to feel this way. She could take one or two photographs and something comforting from home to give her something to focus on when she feels upset. Find out what the school policy is on calling home; this is often discouraged except in case of an emergency. If your daughter does not feel ready to tackle this trip, there are bound to be other opportunities in the future, so help her to get ready for the next one. In the meantime, encourage her to have sleepovers with friends and family to develop confidence in being away from home.

Q My son has become quiet and withdrawn since he started middle school. What can I do?

Starting middle school brings a huge number of changes, and your son may still be adjusting to these new demands. Even if he prefers to work things out on his own, he will still appreciate the fact that you are

Non-public schools
Considering your child's needs

The choice to consider a private, magnet, or charter school can be stressful. Depending on who you talk to, you will probably hear mixed reviews of them all. Consider the following points but, above all else, try to keep in mind which school will best meet the needs of your child.

School environment

✱ Most schools will have an open house for prospective students; make sure you visit those you are interested in.

✱ Don't be put off by less-than-attractive buildings. The outsides may not be pretty, but as long as they are safe, well-resourced, and cared for, it's what goes on inside that matters.

✱ Are there up-to-date displays of student work in classrooms and hallways? If so, this shows the school is proud of its students' achievements.

✱ What subjects are available for your child to study? Are there honors classes available? If your child needs extra help or has a particular talent, how will they be supported?

✱ Does the faculty seem approachable and interested in your child? Try to speak to the headteacher, since he or she will set the tone for the school. Does the faculty seem inspirational and committed?

✱ Visiting on a typical day and driving past at the beginning or end of school will help you get a picture of students' general behavior.

Official sources

✱ Your state's Department of Education will have plenty of information about all schools licensed within the state.

✱ If your child has a particular interest or skill, some schools will be better equipped to develop

this, so check prospectuses and websites for details of any specialist teaching.

✱ Academic statistics and test scores can be a useful guide, but remember that many students thrive in schools that don't rank highly overall.

✱ School inspection reports are freely available, and give a good overview of a school's strengths and weaknesses. Check when the report was written, though, as the information may be somewhat out of date.

Admissions policy Your child may be offered a place at one or more desirable schools, though perhaps not your (or your child's) first choice. All schools have their own admission policy and a limited number of places so, if you are thinking of applying to a particular school, find out how your child fits their criteria and investigate admissions procedures as early as possible. Listen to your child's point of view and involve him in the process as much as possible.

RESEARCH: Read prospectuses and check the school website for any particular interests.

ESSENTIAL INFORMATION: PRETEENS

Middle-school stresses
A new set of challenges

Moving up to a bigger school can be a stressful time, both for you and your child. New places, new teachers, new friends, new subjects, more work and, just when it feels like you should be providing more help for your child, he is desperately trying to prove how independent he is!

✻ Little fish… big pond: Your child's new school will probably feel like a vast maze of corridors and endless classrooms. In reality, he will quickly learn to navigate his way around with ease and will find that each year tends to keep to their own territory outside. Some schools start their new students a day or two before the rest of the school, which will give your child a chance to roam around and look lost without feeling intimidated by the older students. See if you can pick up a school map when you visit or on the school's website. If your child is able to find his way around, it will give him a real confidence boost and probably make him more popular with his new classmates too.

✻ Dress to impress: Your child's new school will probably provide you with a long list of clothing or uniform requirements and essential equipment. Certain items will be very popular in the stores, so it's best to make a start on this as soon as possible. Keep in mind that schools often sell uniform clothing at cost, and may also have some second-hand items. Having the right PE outfit, the trendy school bag, and a pencil case full of favorite pens will help your child feel prepared. Being able to lend a pen to a classmate in need is also a great way to make new friends.

✻ Workload and homework: Your child will have new subjects to master, lots of books to keep track of, more homework, and a very busy timetable. If he is good at organizing himself, this should not

pose a problem. However, if he is used to relying on you to pack his school bag and tell him what subjects he has each day, he could be in for a shock. Take a copy of his class schedule for yourself and suggest he put one up in his bedroom somewhere visible—not buried behind his latest poster. Schoolbooks that are brought home seem to mysteriously disappear the night they are needed. Providing your child with a shelf for school books and homework should help avoid the need for to turn your home upside down looking for them.

Homework will steadily increase as your child goes through school and is an essential part of his education. Make sure he has a quiet place to work and allow him to tackle things in his own way. Some children need a short break after school, whereas others prefer to get their homework done right away. Some schools also have supervised study

HOMEWORK: Your child will have more work to deal with, so set him up with a quiet place to do it.
BUILD ESTEEM: Encourage your child to be confident about answering questions in class.

groups after school. If your child has a planner or homework notebook, look at it with him regularly to make sure he is writing things down and keeping track of his workload. You may still have to prompt him to complete his work if you want to avoid the Sunday-evening panic.

✶ Friend or foe? Even though your child will probably know some of the students at his school, he may be feeling anxious about getting along with the older students. The older kids at middle schools all seem to share the same horror stories about vicious bullies who will beat him up, steal his new things, and flush his head down the toilet. It is no wonder that your child may shrink with fear when he first sees a crowd of towering teenagers standing at the school entrance. The reality is that the older pupils will probably show very little interest in your child, and there will be lots of new classmates to make friends with. Middle school will provide your child with the opportunity to try out new activities and joining a lunchtime or after-school club is a great way to meet others with the same interests.

ALL IN ONE PLACE: Make packing his school bag easier by providing him with a place to store his books.

SHY: Encourage your child to join after-school clubs to meet others if he is worried about making friends.

aware he is not his usual self. Try saying something like, "You seem really quiet lately—is there anything you want to talk about?" so the choice to talk is his. Pick your moment carefully to introduce these conversations. Short car journeys work well, since your child may find it easier to talk sitting side by side rather than facing you and, if he doesn't want to talk, he knows he will be able to escape soon.

A sympathetic ear, a hug, and a few words of encouragement to remind him of his strengths and achievements may be all he needs to get over this hurdle. If there are any signs that your son is being bullied or there are real issues about schoolwork or other aspects of school life, help him come up with solutions to his problems and speak to his teachers or principal if necessary. He may feel happier talking to someone else in confidence about certain issues, so check with the school to see if they offer peer-mentoring or access to a counselor. Agree a time to review how things are going, and keep checking in with him so knows he can call on you for extra support if he needs to.

Should I let my daughter walk to school with her new friends rather than drop her off?

Sooner or later most children reach the point where having their parents drop them off and pick them up from school is seriously uncool and socially embarrassing. Giving up this role is bound to be stressful for you at first and requires you to place a lot of trust and responsibility in your daughter's hands, but there is a lot you can do to make sure she is safe, and your daughter will value her increasing independence. Since these are new friends, get to know them a little by having your daughter invite them over. Travel the route with your daughter that she will be taking to school. If she is catching the bus, find out where she'll get it, and if she is walking, make sure that she sticks to main routes rather than shortcuts and that she crosses at crosswalks. If your daughter is allowed a cell phone in school, you could ask her to text or call you until you both get used to this new routine. You should also agree what your daughter will do when things don't go according to plan. For example, what if the bus doesn't arrive or her friends aren't in school on a particular day? Once you are confident that she understands the risks and knows how to manage them safely, have a trial run and then a longer period of a week or so. Remember—this is a big step for your daughter too, so give her plenty of praise if she sticks to the plan. On days when the weather is bad, you will probably find your services are called on once more!

Q My daughter says she hates school and wants to go to the same one as her best friend. Should I move her?

Being separated from friends in this way can be very upsetting, but there may well be other reasons why your daughter is so unhappy at the moment. Moving schools may seem like a very attractive option which will solve all her problems, but in reality it may not be the best solution. Be sympathetic to your daughter's feelings but help her think about alternatives, without simply dismissing her request. Sit down together and draw up a list of her problems and worries. Ask your daughter to rate how important each issue is, on a scale from 0 to 10. Starting with her most important issues, go through each item on the list and write down any ideas that might help to improve things. Encourage your daughter to think about the consequences, strengths, and weaknesses of each option. For example, if she was to move schools, what would she do if there were lots of things she didn't like about her new one and how would she feel if her friendship ended? Agree what you will both do to work on her problems and involve school staff if necessary.

Chances are, once your daughter has settled into school and made a few new friends, she will feel differently about wanting to move. However, if the situation does not improve by the end of the year, you may need to consider this option, before your daughter begins avoiding school or staying home ''sick'' to get out of an uncomfortable situation.

Q My athletic son doesn't seem interested in joining any of the school teams. Why might this be?

Cheering on your child from the sidelines as they win (or lose) with their team is a proud parenting moment. Sometimes children show less interest in sports once they move up to middle school for various reasons. In order to join a team at his new school, your son will probably have to go through a selection process by putting going for team tryouts. He may be avoiding sports because he is anxious about competing for a place against people he doesn't know, and worried they may show him up with their superior skills. Alternatively, it may be that your son is just not interested in playing sports right now and wants to pursue other interests in his free time. The influence of his friends will play a part in how he chooses to spend his time. With the current focus on healthy living in schools, he may have plenty of opportunities to take part in sports

PARENTS' STORY

Moving on up
a friendly breakthrough

When my son started at middle school, I was really worried about how he would adjust. He moved up from a very small primary school just around the corner from our home to a huge school that is a 20-minute bus ride away. For the first few weeks we had lots of tears and temper tantrums in the morning, and sometimes after school, too. I tried not to interfere too much, just hoping that things would settle down. The breakthrough came when he started talking about a new friend he had made on the bus. They started to meet up outside of school, and my son seemed much happier.

Once he had that one new friend things really picked up—the tears stopped, and he started to get involved in school much more.

activities through his normal curriculum. Once he feels more settled in his new school, he may decide to try out for a team, or his talents may be spotted along the way. In the meantime, look for opportunities to support his other interests, such as music, arts, or drama. If there is little available at school to interest your son, you could suggest other options for him to engage in physical exercise, such as martial arts or gymnastics. Try checking at your local community centre to see if they offer classes.

I thought my son was doing OK at school but his last report card was terrible. How do I get him back on track?

There could be several reasons for your son's drifting academic performance. He may be finding the work too difficult, or he may be spending too much time enjoying the social side of school and not putting enough effort into his studies. Your son may also have other worries that are making it difficult for him to concentrate on schoolwork.

Alternatively, his performance might be related to his current peer group. If your son is being drawn toward the "cool to know nothing" crowd at school, he may not want to risk his place by flexing his intellect. Talk to your son about your concerns and try to identify the reasons for his less-than-glowing report card. Be sensitive, since he might be surprised by his teacher's comments too—try to pick out some positives. If there are problems at school or elsewhere, agree what you will both do to address them. If it is a question of motivation and effort, help your son to organize his study time, but balance this out with plenty of leisure opportunities across the week. You could also offer him incentives to keep his grades up.

My son finds it difficult to make new friends. I'm worried it will affect his progress in school.

The size, structure, and demands of middle school make it almost impossible for children to maintain the same group of friends he once had. Having one or

---

Build them up
Creating confidence

As your child enters this new and important phase in her life, she may be starting to think about her own identity. She will be increasingly self-conscious about her looks, abilities, and social standing with her peers and will be starting to think about what she wants to achieve and where she fits in the world. This may leave her feeling unsure of herself. If she feels confident about who she is, adjusting to middle school will be easier. Praise your child for what she can do well, and use quality time to find out about her day. Try to share in her world, remind your child that no one gets everything right all the time, listen attentively when she is talking to you, and encourage her developing independence and free thinking.

---

two familiar faces around should help reduce any feelings of insecurity and anxiety your son may have, even if they are not his best friends. Friendships at this age are based primarily on shared interests and experiences, so you may find that your son makes a completely new group of friends before too long. Also, don't be surprised if children in whom your son had very little interest in his old school now get talked about in the same breath as his other friends. It can be hard work for parents to keep up with the friendship roster, since positions at the top and bottom change regularly!

If your son finds it difficult to make new friends, encourage him to talk to as many of his new classmates as possible. It's probably worth reminding him to ask their names (and to give them his) to immediately strengthen any connections he makes. It also means that you can ask about his classmates at home. You can support your son's developing friendships by asking if he would like to invite classmates over after school or at weekends. Remind him that he will still get to see his old friends sometimes, too.

Tactics for tests
how can I help at exam time?

Q My child studies for hours on end. Should I put a limit on this and make her do something else?

Achieving at school is clearly important to your daughter, and her motivation should be encouraged. However, her enthusiastic approach to studying is not necessarily the most effective. Pushing herself too hard may backfire and result in poorer performance on a test day. Memories need time to consolidate, so taking regular breaks is not only important for your daughter's well-being, it will improve her learning too. If academic success is important to her, dragging her away from her work is likely to raise anxiety levels and cause friction between you. Instead, you could try suggesting some alternative study strategies, such as looking at websites together or working through previous test papers, or you could offer to quiz her on the material. This will give you more control over the time she is spending on her preparation, and give you an opportunity to discuss the strategies she is currently using.

If your daughter is not approaching her work in the most effective way, this may also be contributing to her long spells of studying. Encourage her to take a 10-minute break out of her room every 40 minutes, offer healthy snacks to keep her energy levels up, and make sure she winds down properly at night.

Q Why does my son always put off studying until the last minute?

There are a number of reasons why your son may be putting off his studies in this way. It may be that he lacks confidence in his abilities and is anxious about taking tests. He may find studying a dull and boring activity compared with all the other ways he could be spending his time. Or it may be that he feels he has a good knowledge of the material and is relaxed about taking tests. However, if he is trying to cram the night before, this seems unlikely. Research shows that boys generally tend to use riskier study strategies than girls. Leaving studying until the last minute may have worked for your son in the past but, as he progresses through school, this strategy will become less and less effective. Learning good study habits now will have long-term benefits. Help your son to organize his time so that he does some preparation with you in advance to help build his confidence. Try listing the topics he has to master and getting him to rate how confident he feels about each of them. Help your son organize his timetable so that he alternates between studying topics he feels confident about and those he knows less well. If he puts off all the difficult stuff until the last minute, he is likely to end his study session feeling as though he knows less than when he started. For the most part, studying really is a dull and boring activity so make sure your son works in short bursts, with plenty of regular breaks. Offering small rewards along the way will also help to keep him motivated.

Q My studious son falls to pieces in tests and exams. How can I help him remember the material?

It must be terribly frustrating and disappointing for your son to put so much hard work and effort into his preparation and then not be able to reap the rewards at the end. He's not alone, though—many actors, singers, and athletes also suffer from performance anxiety, which makes it difficult to recall information that has been learned and stored away for the big occasion. As part of your son's preparation, it may be helpful to go over some simple relaxation strategies with him. He could try using controlled breathing to calm himself before the test starts, and again if he feels himself getting anxious. Practice this with your son: breathe in through your nose while slowly

ESSENTIAL INFORMATION: PRETEENS

Healthy homework habits
Aiding their study skills

Helping your child develop healthy homework habits will support their day-to-day learning and give them the study skills they need to cope with tests and exams. Research shows that parents spend up to six hours a week helping their children with homework and this is time well spent as there is a lot you can do to make sure they achieve their potential.

* Ask about subject meetings for parents so you can learn about the methods being used with your child. Avoid the temptation to show him how you were taught as this will only confuse him.

* Set up a dedicated homework area with all the materials your child will need. Sitting in the same place each day to complete homework will help him switch into study mode.

* Working in front of the TV is generally not a good idea but some children may find listening to music helpful.

* Check your child's homework diary each day so you can help him plan out when he will do each piece and how long he can spend on it.

* Agree a time for doing homework with your child. Give him a break after school and let him eat something first. Don't leave homework until the end of the evening, though, as he will be winding down for sleep and unlikely to perform at his best.

* Ask your child to explain his homework to you and how it fits with his lesson that day. This can be a great way of finding out other information about how he is getting on at school.

* Support your child in his task and try not to take over—particularly if he is struggling. It can be very frustrating when you know he can do something but try to stay calm, patient, and positive about his efforts. Build on his learning by helping him to work things out for himself rather than just telling him the answer.

* Be positive about tackling homework with your child. If he sees your face drop when he hands you his math homework he is unlikely to feel confident himself!

* If your child rejects your offer of help but seems to be struggling, praise him for taking an independent approach to learning, let him know that you are available should he want your help, and offer to check his work afterwards. If he has made a few mistakes, point out what he did well first of all and don't insist that he corrects everything as the school need to be aware of your child's strengths and weaknesses.

* If your child is consistently struggling with his homework, arrange to speak to his teacher about it. Many schools now offer homework clubs with teaching staff on hand to give additional advice and guidance.

HELPING OUT: Getting your child to explain his homework to you will make it clearer for him.

ESSENTIAL INFORMATION: PRETEENS

Study strategies
Realistic methods to help your child

How your child approaches studying is just as important as how long she spends going over the material. Before she buries her head in a book, sit down together and draw out a timetable to help organize her time. If she has several subjects she needs to cover, set some realistic target dates for each, so she can monitor her progress. Once work is underway, staying motivated is likely to be the biggest challenge. Plenty of praise and encouragement goes a long way, but building in extra rewards such as playing on video games, watching TV, or spending time with friends will give her an extra boost when her motivation is flagging. You could also offer a larger reward for when it's all over. Regular breaks, a healthy diet, plenty of sleep, and exercise are also vital when your child is studying.

Strategies for learning and remembering: Every child has an individual learning style that works best for her. Some learn by simply reading over the topic repeatedly, while others may need to write notes and draw diagrams. Although your child's school may recommend particular study strategies, it is worthwhile to look at a wide range of options with her so she can try out alternatives and see what works for her.

Rehearsal and repetition: Repetition is the most commonly used strategy for learning, and involves going over the same material a number of times to help transfer the information into memory. Repetition can be made more effective by encouraging your child to group items together

OWN WAY: Encourage your child to find the tactics that best suit him or her: some will like you to help, others prefer to work alone.

ENCOURAGE: Your child is likely to lose motivation at some point. Have some rewards in mind to help keep him on track.

MIND MAPS: Using charts and diagrams to draw out what he knows about a subject may really help your child to remember.

into categories—this is known as chunking. Younger children may need a little help to use this strategy effectively. Rehearsing the material out loud or mentally (similar to learning lines for a school play) will also improve learning.

Notes and diagrams: Writing notes to summarize material and drawing idea webs or mind maps to show how things link together makes your child's learning a more active and effective process. Redrafting and shortening notes each time she goes over the material will help her to hang her knowledge on key headings. Encourage her to aim for no more than one page of notes and one diagram per topic at the end of her studies.

Elaboration: Information can also be learned by using mental images to link material together— the more unusual the image, the more likely the information will be remembered. Mnemonics are another example of elaboration. For example, the phrase Every Good Boy Does Fine can be used to help your child remember the names of the lines on a musical staff—EGBDF. Younger children are unlikely to adopt elaboration strategies spontaneously, but can easily make good use of them with your help.

Multimedia: Your child will probably use textbooks, handouts, and her own written work for most of her study activities. However, making use of other media will make her learning much stronger. The internet provides access to lots of additional sources of information, and revision websites often contain educational games and fun quizzes to test her knowledge. TV programs can also be useful, and your child may find them more interesting than learning only from textbooks. Visiting museums, historic houses, and other relevant places of interest will help bring subjects to life and give them meaning. The wider the range of memories your child has about a topic, the more effective her learning is likely to be.

counting to five in your head, then out through your mouth, repeating the word RELAX in your mind. When he is feeling more relaxed, encourage him to take a few minutes to read through the test and to start with one or two questions he can answer easily. This will boost his confidence and help him start recalling all that he has learned.

A high fear of failure will make him even more anxious and, therefore, less likely to do well, so help him approach tests in a calm, realistic, and organized way. Help with his revision, let him know that you will be happy if he does his best, and organize a fun activity to do with your son when the test is over— whatever the outcome.

Q My daughter attends lots of after-school clubs but doesn't have much time for homework. How can we create a balance?

Taking part in extracurricular activities is important for children's social, emotional, and physical development, and your daughter should be encouraged to pursue her interests. However, if she is struggling to find time for her regular schoolwork, she may have taken on too much.

Helping your daughter to find a sensible work/life balance will enable her to achieve her potential at school and enjoy her other activities without having to worry about the work she has piling up at home. Sit down with her and draw out a weekly timetable showing all her clubs and classes. This should make it clear where the problem spots are across the week. Rather than setting aside a large chunk of time for schoolwork, try to plan in regular slots across the week. This will enable your daughter to respond better to homework deadlines and break up her schedule at exam time. She might be able to move some activities around, but it may not be possible to fit everything in, and you will have to help her prioritize.

At exam time, some activities may need to go on hold for a week or two to allow for extra study time. Make sure you discuss this with her in advance and draw out a new timetable to reflect it.

She's starting puberty!
changing bodies, first dates

Q **Is it too early for my son to be dating?**

Your son's first date probably won't seem like one to you. At this age, dating often means just being around each other, usually with other friends in a group. This works well as a means for your child to enter the world of dating without all the pressure to be alone, maintain a conversation, and spend too much hard-earned pocket money on going out.

This is a new venture for your son so your support is essential. Do take it seriously: Encourage him to bring his friend home and accept his choice even if you're not convinced this is the right person for him. Show an interest by asking about his friend, but try to avoid too much interrogation, or he may feel pressured and stop offering you information. You will need to decide how much privacy you give him. If he and his friend want to spend time in his room, you may feel more comfortable if the door is open and there is agreement that you'll be nearby. This may be a good time to have a private chat about what you expect of him in terms of sexual behavior. While this could be an embarrassing conversation, it is worth having to make sure he's aware of your values and standards.

As he starts to date, be ready to act as a comforter when he breaks up. Take his heartache seriously: These early experiences can be very painful. It may be hard on you too, seeing him distressed.

Be your child's guide as she adjusts to puberty's many physical and emotional changes

Q **My son has his first crush. He won't tell me who it is. How seriously should I take it?**

Your child's first crush can be both intense and painful to you watching from the outside and may take up plenty of his time. One study has found that high school students spend five to eight hours per week thinking about possible romantic partners. Whatever the emotional fallout, crushes are common because they act as practice sessions when it comes to love. Your child's love interest is probably unattainable, such as a movie star, musician, favorite teacher, or older teenager, so he can indulge in strong emotions without getting up close and personal. It is also normal for many teenagers to have crushes on people of the same sex, as they explore that side of their own sexuality from a distance, too.

These intense relationships give your child a chance to bring up the subject of romance with his friends. When he discusses what a relationship might be like, how he would act, and levels of intimacy he's comfortable with, he is developing his personal values and acceptable behaviors. This preoccupation may seem trivial at times. However, if you think back to the highs and lows of your own adolescent romances, you might find this angst more understandable. When his crush ends, your child will appreciate some time to talk as well as space to be alone and melancholy if he wishes. His feelings will pass, and another person will become his focus, but this may seem impossible to him right now.

Having a crush may mean your son loses some interest in studies and socializing. If this persists to the point of affecting his grades or emotional well-being, or if his need to be near his crush invades their personal space and private life, for example through following them or over-the-top gifts, he's

MYTHS AND MISCONCEPTIONS

Is it true that...

All preteens and teenagers are at a crisis point, and major conflict with parents is the norm?

This is not true. Minor conflict and disapproval is common between parents and children at this stage of development. However, more than half of teens and preteens report few or no intense disputes. The family unit remains a strong source of support and values for the majority of children throughout childhood and adolescence.

Friends become more important than family as children reach adolescence?

This is not entirely true: Both you and your child's peers exert a strong influence upon her. The quality of your relationship with your child affects how much attention she pays to your point of view. A positive connection between you means greater influence on her choices and actions. Reassuringly, children do wish parents would speak with them more frequently, and 75 percent would like to be able to discuss sex and contraception with parents.

Children's physical development is getting ahead of their emotional development?

This is correct. Statistics show the age of puberty has fallen over the course of the last century, but children's social and emotional maturity has seemingly not kept pace with their physical development. This means children appear more physically mature but are not necessarily able to manage the complex emotional and relationship demands that go along with this.

What to expect during puberty
Physical changes

As puberty begins, your child's body undergoes the physical changes necessary to take her from childhood to adulthood. It is the hormone testosterone, produced by the testes, that kicks off puberty for boys, and for girls it is estrogen, produced by the ovaries, that gets things going. These hormones, also known as chemical messengers, start and stop bodily changes.

Puberty usually starts for girls between the ages of nine and 13 and, for boys, from 10 to 15. The exact timing for your child will depend on genetics; a child's age at the onset of puberty is often similar to that of his or her parent of the same sex.

Educate your child on what to expect during puberty. When she knows what comes next she'll be more ready and able to adapt to her changing body. This may involve a long heart-to-heart at first followed up by frequent short conversations as questions come up for her.

Ensure your discussions on the subject are in private, and leave her with books about how puberty affects both boys and girls so that she can find more details at her leisure. Frequently mothers talk this through with daughters and fathers with sons. However, there is no hard and fast rule: Give your child the choice of whether she speaks to one of you or both at times.

On the outside

* **Penis and testicles:** Your son will notice his testicles and penis grow. This could start as early as age 10 to 11 but, for most, will be around 13 to 14.
* **Breasts and body shape:** The first sign of puberty in your daughter is likely to be breast development, beginning with the creation of "breast buds" as her nipples swell, followed by gradual growth of breast tissue, filling out around age 12 to 13 for most girls. Her hips will also widen as her body becomes more womanly and less boyish.
* **Height:** With puberty comes a growth spurt. Your child's rate of growth, averaging around 2–2¼ inches (5–6 cm) a year so far, will accelerate for your daughter to about 3½ inches (9 cm) a year, with the peak of her growth around age 12. Your son's spurt will probably be a little later. He'll gain about 4 inches (10 cm) in height a year, most noticeably between the ages of 14 and 15, but starting as young as 12 or 13 for some.
* **Hair:** Pubic, followed by underarm, hair will start to grow for both boys and girls. Your son will also develop facial and chest hair, and you might find him frequently examining himself in the mirror for fuzz on his upper lip.
* **Voice:** Your son's voice will deepen around age 14 to 15 as testosterone lengthens and thickens his vocal cords. This may be a gradual process, or he may at times have his usual, higher voice, and then, perhaps comically to you but possibly to his embarrassment, his tone will suddenly deepen. Eventually this deeper voice will be a permanent feature. He will also notice an Adam's apple as his vocal cords tilt, showing up as a lump on his throat. Your daughters' voice will also deepen a little, usually later, roughly between ages 15 and 16.
* **Sweat:** Your child's sweat glands will become more active and skin can be affected by acne. Pimples are usually a little worse for boys than girls and are caused when sebum, an oil that works to keep skin soft and supple, is overproduced and blocks pores. Keeping skin clean helps reduce the occurrence of pimples, and good personal hygiene is a must in general, because all that sweat can create body odor if soap is not used regularly. You may need to remind your child about this.

On the inside

✱ The ability to reproduce: Alongside the visible signs of puberty, your child's body is becoming ready to reproduce. Your daughter is likely to reach maturity in this area first, with menstruation (also known as her period or "time of the month"), beginning when she is between the ages of nine and 17, with most girls starting at age 13 to 14. Menstruating is the sign that the lining of her uterus is able to sustain a fetus. It may also mean her ovaries are releasing eggs, but periods can occur, at least at first, without eggs being produced. Your daughter will cope more easily with her first periods if she is well prepared about what to expect, familiar with how to use and dispose of pads or tampons, and knows how to maintain personal hygiene.

Your son will begin to produce mature sperm sometime between the ages of 11 and 17; most boys have reached this stage by age 15. This means his sperm will be able to fertilise an egg and create a baby. He will handle these changes more confidently if you've explained in advance about erections, ejaculation, and wet dreams.

Even though you may feel your child isn't ready for sexual relationships yet, both your son and daughter need to be educated, or reminded, about contraception and the meaning of intimacy in relationships.

When to worry: There is considerable variation in the timing of pubescent development. It will happen in its own time, whether your child wishes it to be sooner or later. However, for a very small number of children there may be a medical issue which affects the timing of puberty. If your child is not showing any signs of puberty, such as the beginnings of breast or testicle development, by the age of 14, seek a medical opinion from your pediatrician.

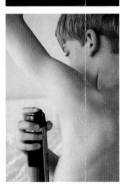

EDUCATE: It is very important that you explain the physical and emotional changes of puberty to your child. If he or she knows what to expect, it will make this time easier.

MOUSTACHE: Your son will start to grow facial hair, starting with a light covering on the upper lip. **KEEPING CLEAN:** Help your child with personal hygiene by providing deodorant. **FIRST BRA:** Buying new underwear will help her feel comfortable with her changing body.

Embarrassment
Struggling to be grown-up

Right now you might be the most embarrassing thing in your child's life. Whether you're trying to kiss her good-bye in public or remind her to dress warm, you're likely to get a look of disdain as she ducks away to avoid being seen with you.

This is all about her struggle to appear more grown-up. Signs of her dependency on you, such as being dropped off at the school gate, undermine the self-reliant image she's trying to portray. The answer isn't to stop helping, but to respect her embarrassment by going along with her. For example, drop her off around the corner from school and keep your kisses and concern for the privacy of home. She doesn't love you any less, but she will appreciate your discretion.

reached a worrying level of intensity. If you are concerned about the power of your child's emotions, talk with your doctor, school nurse, or school counselor for additional help. Youth hotlines can also offer advice and support to you and your child.

Q My daughter developed early, but she shows off her new body. Should I make her cover up?

Your daughter's newly developed body can signal a change in status in her peer group. If her friends value her as a source of knowledge about puberty, she may gain importance with them. This can help her to be proud of her body rather than shy. She may also attract the "wrong" kind of attention from boys or young men, which may be a powerful motivator to show off. It is known that girls who mature early are more likely to mix with an older group of friends and get involved with them in riskier behavior, such as drinking and sexual activity, than girls reaching puberty later. Simply because she is physically mature won't mean she's automatically able to handle the relationships and peer pressure issues

of her older friends. Be open with her about your worries and work on building trust as well as negotiating limits. Monitor her friendships more closely than you would otherwise, encourage her to meet with friends in your home so that you can get to know them, and ensure she has a curfew and freedoms appropriate to her own emotional maturity rather than those of the older group.

Q My daughter is hiding stained clothes and sanitary pads. Is she just unhygienic?

The start of her periods can be a confusing time for your daughter as she adjusts to crossing a physical and psychological threshold toward maturity. She must also get a handle on the practical aspects of menstruating. It is not unusual for pads and soiled underwear to be stuffed at the back of drawers or hidden under the bed. Perhaps your child feels embarrassed about carrying them out into the public areas of the house or putting them in with the household trash. She may be anxious to avoid the whole family knowing or commenting on the fact that she's menstruating. Address this as a problem to be solved, and your daughter will be reassured that you understand her situation. Do set up some practical ways for her to manage pads and underwear. You may decide to put small bags and a lined bin next to the toilet so that she can dispose of her sanitary pads right away without bringing them out of the bathroom. Reassure her that it's normal for underwear to become stained sometimes.

Perhaps having her own personal laundry basket in her room will enable her to separate soiled clothes, then you can launder these discreetly without the whole family knowing the details.

Q When do I talk about contraception?

The sooner you talk about contraception, the better. This does not mean your child will immediately go out and experiment with sex: Being well informed has not been found to increase young people's sexual activity. Do refresh your own understanding

ESSENTIAL INFORMATION: PRETEENS

Baby fat and other issues
Achieving a healthy body image

Changes in body shape are an inevitable aspect of puberty. Your child may become very concerned about her appearance—including her size, skin, and pimples—and her rate of development, especially if she is earlier or later than her peers in showing signs of puberty. It is commonly said that children lose their "baby fat" at puberty, however this is not the case. If your child is overweight in the early years she is likely to continue to be large as she matures, unless changes in diet and activity level are made. An additional factor in weight change at puberty is that time spent playing sports and being physically active tends to drop as your child reaches middle school. This reduction in exercise can affect her weight while, at the same time, she is experiencing an increase in consciousness of her shape and size. Your role is to support your child's healthy lifestyle and sympathize with her worries without being patronizing or minimizing her concerns. This is no easy feat, and you may feel like you're walking on eggshells trying to be sensitive without implying there is a problem.

Help her gain a healthy view of her body

✳ Include healthy eating and regular exercise as part of your routine for the whole family. A balanced diet at puberty helps with general well-being and benefits adolescent skin conditions. When the whole family is involved, your child does not feel singled out or that you're implying she is overweight or unhealthy.

✳ Accept her no matter what. Compliment her on her achievements, appearance, and personal qualities to balance her own self-criticism.

✳ Watch what you say: Comparisons with others or joking comments about puberty or her appearance can be deeply hurtful to your child even though you don't mean any offense.

✳ Understand and be sensitive to her concerns about her appearance. Reassure her that you love her and how she looks, but acknowledge she may not feel this way herself. Offer practical help if she raises a specific problem. For example, assistance on a bad hair day or to conceal pimples is often appreciated, even if all you do is buy her the product she needs rather than fuss over the application.

I WANT TO BE LIKE YOU: If your child's concerns about her body cause her distress, for example becoming obsessed with skinny models in magazines *(left)*, get advice and support from a doctor or youth counselor.

HOW DO I LOOK?: Help your child develop a healthy body image *(right)*, by being sensitive and reassuring about her appearance.

of contraception before you speak with your child. Take a look at recent books and get advice from a health professional if you are unsure of the more up-to-date information. As well as giving information about contraception, bust some myths about how pregnancy happens. For example, many children believe that a girl can't become pregnant if sexual intercourse happens standing up, during menstruation, or if she jumps or moves around right after intercourse.

This is also an ideal opportunity to talk about pressure to kiss, touch, or have sex. Your child may believe "everyone is doing it" and feel he must keep up with his peers. Ease this burden by explaining that the majority of children of his age haven't done the things they claim and are as anxious about intimate contact as he is. Open up a discussion about what physical intimacy means in a relationship and that it is most enjoyable when there is love and only if both people want to take part. There is little joy if things happen only to prove something to others. Do encourage him to come to you if he's feeling pressured to do something he's not yet ready for.

Why is my child's behavior so unpredictable?

Like anyone under pressure and coping with a lot of change, your child might find her moods vary from hour to hour and from day to day. At times, the changes in her life may seem wonderful and full of opportunity while, at others, an increasing sense of responsibility can be overwhelming. It is unsettling for her to feel out of control of her moods, and almost as confusing for you, since you may not know what to expect or how to react.

Seemingly trivial disappointments may feel like major incidents to your child as she negotiates increasingly complex social relationships. For example, a friend not sitting next to her on the bus or not calling when expected can be interpreted as a major rejection. Similarly, she may feel unrealistically optimistic if something has gone her way, perhaps being asked on a date or complimented on her schoolwork gives her a moment of pure joy that

all is well with the world. All-or-nothing statements are common, such as, "Everyone is staring at me since I got these braces. They all think I'm a freak." Or "Nobody likes me, they're all laughing because I got in trouble in class." You may be tempted to argue against these interpretations, but doing so can prompt your child to defend her opinion. Often just listening, sympathizing, and making an offer to help are enough to put them in perspective.

What other emotional issues am I likely to encounter as my child becomes a teenager?

Your child has a lot of adjusting to do in the coming years: Striving toward independence, developing intimate relationships, and working out her own values and aspirations. It's no wonder, with all this going on, that her emotions and behavior may be erratic and unpredictable to you. Her developing body can have an impact on her confidence. She may feel out of proportion and embarrassed about her growth.

Other common worries for girls are about how to manage menstruation, weight, and shape. Boys can become concerned over height and penis size, and, as they mature, about erections being noticeable during physical education or in class.

One of the key tasks of the preteen and teen years is for your child to develop opinions and values separate from your own. To do this, she may actively challenge and reject your standards and attitudes, even taking on the extreme opposite views from your own in order to test them out and get your reaction. This is a helpful process for her, even though at times it may seem hurtful and worrying to you. More than ever, she wants you to trust her, to believe that she can make good decisions, keep herself safe, and live up to her own standards.

This drive toward independence can sit uneasily with your desire to protect her and to be cautious about giving too much freedom too soon. As a result, frequent small conflicts are common. Trust can only be built, however, if you permit her to test her independence through gradual increases in responsibility for herself.

Lazybones or workaholic?
your child's personality

My daughter just wants to spend time with her friends. Doesn't she need me any more?

As your daughter moves further into adolescence, her peer group will play an important role in helping her to become an independent, free-thinking young person in preparation for college and career. Learning to stand on her own two feet and developing an identity that is separate from her relationship with you is a necessary part of your daughter's development, so don't take this as a personal rejection.

Research shows that adolescents spend more than half their waking hours with their peers, and less than five percent of time with either parent. However, when children were asked to consider who they were closest to and who gave them the most support, parents still came out on top. Your daughter's friendships are becoming more important to her, but that doesn't mean that you are now less important. Your daughter still needs the loving care, safety, and security she is used to getting from home (friends can't replace that), but how she makes use of this will change.

I'm worried my son's friends are going to lead him astray. Should I stop him from seeing them?

If your son is trying to fit in with a new group of friends, he may get involved in a few high-spirited activities at first to show that he is "one of them." This behavior may be worrying, but remember that he is now choosing his friends based on qualities such as shared interests, attitudes, and values. When your son has gotten to know his friends better, he may feel that their behavior does not fit with his outlook on life, and will probably decide to look for a more compatible group on his own. However, if you challenge him on his choice of friends, he is likely to leap to their defence, and you risk pushing him even closer to this group. Discuss your concerns about his behavior and the possible consequences, but allow him the freedom to make his own choices—unless he is putting himself or others at serious risk.

Your son does not have to be a leader to stand up for what he believes in. With a little time and your support, he will make the choice that's right for him.

My daughter always spends her allowance as soon as she can. How can I get her to save up?

You may have thought that your daughter would grow out of the "I want it now" phase, but some preteens and adolescents take time to develop the ability to see the bigger picture. Delaying gratification in favor of a bigger but longer-term pay off is something that many adults still struggle with.

Some researchers have argued that adolescents find rewarding things more rewarding due to changes in how the brain processes rewards and pleasure. As a result, your daughter may be more driven to get a quick fix by buying something, and saving her money just isn't an option. Of course, your daughter's behavior is also shaped by her friends

Your child is beginning to make individual choices based on her own beliefs and principles about what she feels is right

ESSENTIAL INFORMATION: PRETEENS

Adolescent brain function
A second wave of development

It has been known for some time that young children experience a sensitive period of brain development, lasting from birth to around 18 months. During this time, a maze of connections is rapidly wired between brain cells (neurons). This process is known as synaptogenesis, and is followed by a period of synaptic pruning, in which frequently-used connections are strengthened, and little-used connections are removed. Young children should therefore be exposed to a wide range of learning experiences so they will retain as many new connections as possible. However, recent brain studies using magnetic resonance imaging (MRI) have shown that this is not the end of the story.

It is now known that different areas of the human brain develop at different rates. In the frontal cortex, which is responsible for functions such as planning, organizing, impulse control, reasoning, and decision making, there is a second wave of synaptogenesis that peaks at around 12 years for males and 11 years for females. Once long-term connections have been formed, they are made more efficient with a coating of myelin (insulation surrounding the synapses). MRI scans show that myelination begins at the back of the brain and moves forward, meaning that the frontal lobes may not be fully matured until young adulthood. Other brain areas, such as those involved in spatial, sensory, auditory, and language functions, appear largely mature in the teenage brain.

Research studies have also shown that teenagers are quicker than younger children at understanding the thoughts and feelings of others, but are not as efficient as adults. This suggests that the ability to see things from someone else's perspective and the quality of empathy continue to develop during adolescence and beyond.

What does this mean for my child?

✱ During this second wave of brain development, your child has considerably more control over his behavior than during the first, and can therefore do a great deal to help shape the connections that will be hard wired. Encourage your child to make the most of his talents and opportunities and support him if he shows a new interest, even if you feel it may be just a passing fascination. Expose him to new learning experiences, but avoid the temptation to force museum visits and enroll him in art classes unless he shows some degree of interest in these activities. Encouraging your child to make the most of his talents and opportunities will lay the foundations for important life-long skills.

✱ Some of the difficulties you may experience with your child's behavior are likely to be related to his developing frontal lobes. He is becoming more self-aware, reflective, and better able to understand

THERE FOR YOU: Your child's brain is continuing to develop, so she still needs your help and guidance.
ROCK STAR: Encourage your child to develop his new interests even if you think they may not last.

the thoughts, feelings, and behavior of others. However, these and other high-level cognitive skills, such as planning, thinking through the consequences of actions, and regulating his impulses and emotions, will take time to develop. This does not mean that you should let inappropriate behavior go unchecked: keep rules and boundaries firmly in place.

✻ Try to stay involved in your child's life—even though he may not seem as if he wants you to at times. Offer guidance and support when he needs it, listen to his point of view, and set consistent rules and guidance to help him stay on the right track.

A word of caution: This period of brain development is clearly important, but these biological processes are not the only factors that will shape your child's personality. Scientific understanding about the links between brain structures, their function, and their role in specific behaviors still has a long way to go. Your child's relationship with you, his home and school environments, and friends, not to mention the effect of all those hormones, will all play a role in the complex story of his ongoing development.

NOT JUST BIOLOGY: Your child's friends and family, as well as her relationships with school and others in her life, will all have a significant part to play in her ongoing development.

and the messages she gets from society, which tends to emphasize the commercial ideal that "You can have it all right now." This can be hard for a young person to resist when there are so many things they believe they simply must have.

Let your daughter make her own decisions about what she buys (within reason), but help her appreciate the value of money by talking through the costs and benefits of her choices. You can also teach her some smart shopping skills to help her money go further: Take her to look around second-hand shops, fleamarkets, and vintage clothing stores, which often contain hidden treasures at a fraction of the usual cost. If your daughter misses out on something she wants because she doesn't want to save, stay firm and try not to give in when she comes to you for a loan.

My son is spending more and more time alone in his room. Should I leave him alone?

Coping with the demands of adolescence requires a supportive and caring home environment, a stable school placement, good friends, freedom to grow, and privacy. As your son develops into a young teenager, he needs time and space to sit back, relax, and think about everything that is going on in his life, who he is, and who he wants to be. His developing sense of independence also means that he probably won't want to share everything with you in the way he once did, so time alone is very important to him. Unless you are concerned that your son is taking to his bedroom because he is distressed, anxious, or engaging in dangerous activities, allow him the time he needs to make sense of all the changes he is experiencing.

Try to keep your son involved in family life, let him know what your plans are, and invite him to join you if and when he wants to. Forcing him to come out of his room is unlikely to make for a very enjoyable evening for anyone. If you are concerned about your son's emotional health, find an opportunity to share your concerns with him and speak to your doctor if you feel he may need extra help and support.

Q My daughter seems overly focused on her schoolwork. I'm worried she's missing out.

Your daughter is at an age where she is beginning to imagine different futures for herself, and academic success may be an important part of her career plans. Alternatively, her study habits may reflect the peer group she belongs to at school, or they may simply show that she enjoys her work and derives a lot of satisfaction and self-esteem from academic success. If your daughter seems happy in herself, try not to worry that she is missing out on things. Her social life is important, but it is the quality of her friendships that matters rather than the amount of time she spends hanging around with friends. However, if you are concerned that your daughter

is withdrawing more from her friends, try to encourage a healthy work/life balance. Set an appropriate time limit for homework, and create opportunities for her to spend time with her friends. If you are concerned that your daughter may be spending extra time on her work because she is struggling to keep up, talk to her about this and speak to the school to see what support is available.

Q Lately my child argues with me about everything. Why is she being like this?

If you and you daughter have always gotten along well, her argumentative behavior probably reflects her developing verbal and reasoning skills rather than a problem in your relationship. Instead of simply accepting what she is told, she is now beginning to question things in her world much more—this is great for her academic development, but not so great when you are asking her to clean her room... again!

As a younger child, your daughter may have accepted what you were saying with nothing more than a comment under her breath if she disagreed. Now, however, you are getting the full force of her developing intellect. Try not to take this personally. State your case calmly and clearly and, where possible, avoid getting drawn into arguments. Let her have her say, but try to discuss problem issues when she is calm rather than in the heat of the moment. This will set the tone for how she uses her new-found skills in the future.

Q Our son refuses to help out at home. How can we get him to?

Children don't suddenly become lazy overnight—it takes years of practice! If your son has been able to get away with doing very little for a long time, there is no reason why he should suddenly start helping out. Many parents nag their children to do the dishes, clean their rooms, hang up their clothes, and so on— but end up doing it themselves for the sake of an easy life (and a tidy home). Similarly, many children who are capable of achieving far more find it is easy

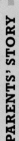

PARENTS' STORY

Like father like son?
letting go

To be honest, I was dreading my son entering adolescence—mostly because I remember the problems I caused my own parents. When he started puberty, I steadied myself for the onslaught of moods, arguments, and difficult behavior, so I wasn't surprised when it started. After a while, though, I began to realize that I was actually causing more problems than my son was. I was so scared about him getting into trouble that I tried to control everything he did and gave him very little freedom, which just made him argue with me all the more. It wasn't easy for me, but I started to give him more independence (with very clear limits) and tried to talk things over with him rather than just saying "No!" It helps us to work things out together.

We still have our disagreements, of course, but we also have plenty of laughs, and we now get along much better than I did with my father at his age.

to get away with doing the bare minimum at school. In this way, those who aren't bothered by a bit of nagging learn that laziness is rewarded in the end.

You can motivate your son by picking up on examples of behavior you want to see more of and praising him for these. You could also agree on some simple chores at home and link them to his allowance. Performance at school can be rewarded in the same way. Laziness is not a phase that your son will simply grow out of, but his behavior can and will change with the right motivation.

When my son is at home he just lazes around playing video games. Should I make him use his time more productively?

Everyone needs a period of downtime where we can relax and unwind from the pressures of the day, and this may be your son's way of doing that. Sharing tips and comparing progress on the latest video games may also be a hot topic of conversation among his friends, so your son needs time to keep up to date. Recent evidence on teenage brain development suggests that he is going through an important period of growth and development, during which high-level skills such as problem solving, planning, and organizing will be further refined. Those skills that are not used as frequently may not be hardwired in the same way, leading some researchers to call this the "use it or lose it principle."

If your son is spending all of his spare time on the sofa, you may need to encourage him to engage in other activities by setting a time limit on his gaming. Remember, though, that what you see at home is not the full picture of your son's life. He may be working hard at school and have other interests that test his developing skills.

I'm concerned because my daughter is very shy and only has a few friends.

From the earliest years of a child's life, individual differences in temperament affect how other people respond to her and how sociable she is. Clearly not

New beliefs
Environmental issues

Your child's developing cognitive skills now enable her to think about moral and ethical issues in a more complex and grown-up way. She may start to display new passions, for example, developing an intense interest in recycling and global warming. She may insist on shaping up your household recycling practices, or challenge some longstanding habits in your home. She's beginning to make individual choices based on her own beliefs and principles, and deciding on her own what she feels is the right thing to do. In addition to her attempts to improve the planet, you may also find her taking more of an interest in news and current affairs.

Use her enthusiasm to open up conversations with her about her activities, and try not to undermine her idealistic view that she can change the world single-handedly. We can all do our part for the environment; agreeing to a few changes at home will also show her that you support her beliefs, which helps to build her self-esteem.

everyone wants to be part of a crowd or is comfortable with being the center of attention— it's usually the same children who take the lead in the school play, while many are happy to stand at the back. As your daughter goes through adolescence, the changes she experiences may leave her feeling insecure and unsure of herself, increasing her shyness. However, being shy is not a problem in itself, as long as it does not prevent her from doing things she wants to do. If she has a few close friends, this may be enough for her needs, and you can't force her to take part in activities. In fact, trying to do so will probably make things worse.

Focus on building her confidence and self-esteem by praising the things she does well and offering her plenty of reassurance if she is critical about aspects of herself she does not like.

What's the fallout?
divorce and blended families

Q **My daughter sees her father every other weekend, but wants to keep photos of him all over the house. I would rather she did not.**

Your daughter has come up with a way to keep her father present in her everyday life. Maintaining a strong relationship with both of you is known to assist children adjust to family separation, so while this may be a difficult reminder of your ex for you, it's going to help keep this important relationship active for her. Find places she can keep photographs and

mementos of her other parent, especially in her room. There may be other ways she can be in touch during the week: phone calls, texts, and instant messaging between her and her father may also help her feel connected.

Q **I see my ex-partner when she picks up or drops off our son, and we sometimes argue on the doorstep. Is this bad?**

When your child is being picked up or brought home by his other parent, it may be the only time you see your ex-partner. However, raising sensitive or hurtful topics at this point can mean your child dreads these changeover times. Tension between parents can make your son anxious and unhappy. He may think that the only way to stop the arguments is to give up seeing his other parent, or that it's his job to step in and protect one of you. It is important that he's not forced into the role of the adult, trying to resolve or avoid your disputes. It is up to you and your ex to find other ways to communicate. Writing, emails, texts, and phone calls keep the heat of disagreements away from your child. If things are not resolvable this way, mediation or a solution through a legal process may be your best option.

Q **My son lives with me during the week. He's having some difficulty at school, but his mother seems to get left out of the loop.**

If your child is living primarily with one of you, it can take extra effort and organization for both of you to stay involved with his schooling. Ensure the school office and your child's teacher are aware that information and school reports need to be sent to both of you. At times of difficulty, increase communication between yourself and his mother.

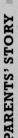

PARENTS' STORY

Changing places
avoiding frustrations

My husband and I separated when our son was only five, and we agreed he would stay with me for half the week, and his father, the other half. This worked well until he started middle school. Then, as his schoolwork and social life became more complex, frustrations kicked in. He'd leave homework or school gear at one home that he needed at the other, or he'd get frustrated if he started something on our computer then had to set up again on another. Frictions built up, and we finally made the tough decision to take a fresh look at the arrangements. We're now having a trial of him spending his whole school week with us but more of his weekends and holidays with his father to balance things out.

So far, he tells me it's easier to manage this way, and there are definitely fewer round trips to his other home to collect something essential that he's forgotten.

MYTHS AND MISCONCEPTIONS

Is it true that...

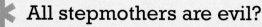

✳ All stepmothers are evil?

Happily, this is untrue, but stepmothers do have a major stereotype problem, created by children's fairy tales and movies. Help overturn the myth by showing your willingness to get to know and become known by your stepchild. Do avoid the trap of trying too hard to be a friend, since this can seem false and add to their suspicions about your "evil" motives.

✳ It's better to stay together for the sake of the children?

This is not necessarily true. If your adult relationship is characterized by conflict and resentment, your child will probably feel a sense of relief when you separate, since it reduces her exposure to tension or frequent arguments. Maintaining a positive relationship with both of you and your ability to cooperate concerning her upbringing predicts better adjustment to your separation for your child.

✳ Having a new baby in the stepfamily brings everyone together?

Many parents in a blended family decide to have another child. Having a new baby can certainly bring love into the family; unfortunately jealousy and resentment may also result. If you make this choice, it's essential to keep your child involved throughout the pregnancy. Reassure her that she's as special to you as ever, and act on these sentiments by setting aside one-on-one time with her every day.

ESSENTIAL INFORMATION: PRETEENS

When parents separate or divorce
Handling a difficult decision

Making the decision to separate is never done lightly, and trying to get it right for your child, while coping with change yourself, can be the biggest challenge. There is no doubt that even the most amicable separation will be stressful for you and your child.

Soften the impact

✳ Explain: Once you and your partner have made a definite decision to separate, tell your child. Give a clear explanation that focuses on yourselves and reassure her that she is loved by both of you. You might begin by saying "Your mom and I don't love each other anymore and we have decided to live apart. We both love you very much and always will."

✳ No fault: Your child will wonder if she did anything to cause the separation, particularly if she's been in the throes of mood swings or preteen temper tantrums or arguments with one or both of you. Don't wait until she raises the issue—reassure her that this is a decision based on your adult relationship, and be clear that she has done nothing to contribute.

✳ Keep in touch: Your child's most pressing questions will probably be self-centered: Will she still see her friends, be able to go to the dance, etc. Make arrangements right away so that she sees both of you no matter what stage of the breakup you are in. Your child's long-term living arrangements can be difficult to decide on—her needs and views, practical issues, and your own wishes have to be carefully weighed. Often the help of someone neutral, who's not involved with the breakup, is essential to make these decisions without putting pressure on your child to favor one or other of you. A mediator, parenting coordinator, or counselor could fit this role.

✳ Minimize change: You may be anxious for a fresh start, but hold back: Your child needs things to stay the same as much as possible. It will help her cope with changes in the family situation if the rest of her life is relatively undisturbed. If possible, remain in the same house or local area, since the familiarity of a place can be comforting. When she can stay at the same school, see her friends, and keep up with her hobbies and clubs she'll find other adjustments easier to handle.

✳ Argument-free zone: If the separation is not amicable, you may need to work hard to keep arguments away from your child. She can be very sensitive to, and distressed by, conflicts in your adult relationship, so take extra care to stay calm and avoid criticizing each other in front of her. When you talk on the phone it can be easy to overhear, so watch what you say even then.

✳ Keep it even: You and your partner may no longer care for each other, but your child still loves and admires each of you. She will want to be loyal

NOT IN FRONT OF THE KIDS: Try hard not to allow your child to overhear heated arguments between you and your partner; these conflicts will distress her.

to you both, so try to minimize times when she has to choose between you. For example, if she has an event at school, assume that you'll both attend rather than asking her to pick one of you. For birthdays and holidays, half a day with each parent or alternating years between the two of you may work. Make communication between yourself and your ex-partner direct to ensure your child doesn't become a go-between. Ideally, she will be able to maintain respect for both of you and not feel she must take sides.

✷ Get help: Even when separation is mutual, you can feel hurt, exhausted, and lonely. Just when you feel least able to give support to others, your child will need extra love and attention. Draw on the help of the wider family and friends to give you a little added care. The more support you have, the more available you can be to your child.

✷ Who to tell: It is essential that people involved with your child, such as her doctor and school, know all the new contact numbers and details for each of you for emergency purposes. You may also want to alert your child's school to the upheaval in her life so faculty can be supportive if it affects her behavior or studies. Let her know you are doing this, and ask that the information be treated sensitively.

NOT YOUR FAULT: If you decide to separate from your partner, explain this to your child and reassure him that it was not because of anything he did.

Regular updates on issues or school meetings to be attended may be tedious, but have to be scheduled. Face-to-face meetings work best to resolve issues, since they give an opportunity to talk around the problem, and suggest and refine solutions.

My child is spoiled by his father. How should I approach this?

It must seem very unfair when your ex lavishes treats and gifts on your child and even appears to be buying your child's affection. Before you approach your ex-partner about the issue, identify the key points that bother you. Perhaps you consider your child will become materialistic, pester you more for toys or sweets, or has an unhealthy diet. Is it that you worry your child is being lured away from you by all these goodies that you don't allow? Consider also whether these gifts are the way your ex-partner has learned to show his love, or if they are an expression of his insecurities about the relationship with his son.

Find a private moment to explain your concerns to your ex-partner. Stick to the issues for you, such as, "I find when he comes back from being with you, he expects me to buy him as many toys as you do. I can't afford to do this, and it puts me in a bad position." Rather than accusations like, "You make life difficult for me because I can't buy as much for him as you can." Accept that, while you can suggest moderation in what is bought for your son, you cannot force this to happen. Be reassured that, while treats are enjoyable at the time, it is your child's loving relationship with each of you that counts—not the material goods he can acquire.

I feel bad that I don't like my stepchild. Should I?

You won't automatically love your stepchild. You haven't had the help of a rush of bonding at birth or time with her in the early years to build an attachment, so it will take time for that affection to grow. Remember that your stepchild had little choice in your joining the family, whereas you have actively made this commitment—so it's up to you to make the effort to build this relationship. Start by treating her

What's in a name?
you're not my real father!

Before Luke and I moved in together, we talked about what the kids would call him. I thought it would incite a riot if we suggested my new partner be called "Daddy Luke," even though I wanted him to be seen as a father figure. My son, who isn't too pleased about the whole setup, wanted to call him nothing at all, and my daughter was comfortable going with just "Luke."

After a bit of family debate we've gone for Luke as the simplest option, and my ex-partner is pleased that he's still the only one called Dad. Luke's children, who stay on weekends, were asked what they want to call me and came up with Auntie Lisa, which I don't like much but I'm going along with to please them. In the end it's all about compromise and making sure no one is forced to use a name they want to keep for their real mom or dad.

of each other's background and values. However, there may be limitations that must be accepted as a result of these differences. Your partner's religious practice may mean that certain foods are forbidden, such as ham or shellfish, and can't be present in the home, and there will be different religious rituals and days of rest. Take such differences as an opportunity for the whole family to discuss the deeply held beliefs behind these practices. Be clear about what applies to everyone, and where there can be compromise. For example, it may be possible to agree that no one will eat or keep pork in the home, but when they're at a friend's house or at school, your children can still have these foods.

Make a family decision that each member of the household will respect the religious ceremonies of the others. This means learning about each others' observances and taking part if appropriate. For example, your family may decide to eat together to celebrate the start of Shabbat on Fridays, but that only your partner will have a day of rest on Saturday. Be clear, however, that it's not necessary to change anyone's beliefs to enjoy mutual respect and support.

My daughter is making life miserable for my new husband. How can I help them get along?

The key to solving this difficulty is discovering the fear, anger, or concern that underlies your daughter's behavior. There could be plenty of reasons she's acting out. She may be jealous about having to share your love and attention, or fear that she is being pushed out and is less important to you. She may worry that this marriage will end, and is creating barriers between herself and your partner so she won't be hurt by his departure. Alternatively, she may see refusing to bond with her stepfather as an act of loyalty to her father. You must also consider whether her angry or avoidant behavior toward your partner is a sign that he is harming her in some way. When you take a compassionate approach to this misbehavior and explore her feelings about your marriage and her place in your heart, you are likely to uncover what's bothering her. Simply dealing with

with respect, show an interest in what she's doing, and give yourself a chance to get to know her. See her point of view if she's not as warm to you at first as you would like. Perhaps she wonders if she's now second place to you and your children, or is waiting to see if the stories about evil stepmothers are really true. As you show yourself to be warm and caring, you may find, over time, she warms up to you too.

My new partner is Jewish and my children are not. How can I stop this from causing friction?

Bringing together people of different cultural or religious backgrounds can be one of the most enriching aspects of your new family life, but it requires reflection and compromise to be successful. Learning about and celebrating different traditions and festivals should create a greater understanding

this as a discipline problem can confirm her fears that you're "on his side" rather than hers. Once you've brought out what bothers her, make a plan to deal with the problem. Perhaps she does need more one-on-one time with you to show her you care. Discuss how she would like to be respected in the home, and how she can show respect herself. She may benefit from having her own private diary to express her anger or fears without having to act them out. If she does disclose that she is being hurt, act immediately to protect her and contact social services for support.

My new partner is furious that, as he sees it, I favor my own children over his. What can I do?

You may be having a protective reaction to your own children as you help them adjust to stepfamily life, and, without realizing it, you may tend to take their side. If possible, allow the children to resolve their own everyday disputes. They probably do have the negotiation skills to work out who will use the bathroom first, take a turn on the computer, or choose a TV show to watch.

If they continue to argue, take care to hear each side of the story before you act, rather than jumping to a conclusion about who's in the right. If this doesn't resolve the problem, take a more systematic approach: Agree some clear rules and consequences about acceptable behavior, sharing, and respect for each others' property, that will apply to everyone. When you apply these to all the children in the family, there is much less likelihood of favoritism.

We are having problems with privacy. Please help!

Privacy, or lack of it, can be an issue in any home, but especially so when new family members, with different expectations, move in together. Often the simplest solutions are the best. Do place locks on the bathroom doors and create places in your home where each member can be on their own to relax, study, or just think undisturbed. Introduce "do not disturb" signs on bedroom doors, and have a knock-

before-entering policy. Consider how you manage nudity in your home. If you have slept naked in the past or been comfortable walking around nude or semi-naked, this may need to be reviewed. It's often the case that your child, as she approaches puberty, will not find your nudity as acceptable as she did when she was younger, and will be more modest about her own body, so this is an ideal time to reflect on how much you cover up or not.

It can be difficult letting go of habits that have been natural to you for many years, but respecting the views of others on privacy and nudity will spare embarrassment and smooth family life.

How can I help my new family merge successfully?

Creating a blended family is a delicate business: Its basis needs to be the total commitment of the adults involved in establishing and making a success of things, no matter what comes. Your relationship with

---

Telling her friends
What to say

Separating from your partner is essentially a private matter but, in the end, other people will need to know. For your child, telling her friends can be a daunting task. She may not know what to say to them, worry they'll pity or taunt her, or think this makes her family look like a failure. Like many children, she may hope that you'll get back together and be reluctant to tell others because it makes the separation seem real and permanent. Coach her in what she could say, such as, "I want you to know my mom and dad are separating. I will still come to this school and be around like always. I feel pretty sad about it, so that's all I want to say right now." She may want to tell a few best friends first or go around during one lunch break to tell all her friends at once. This way they have nothing to gossip about; everyone is in the know.

your partner is the foundation for this family, and while the two of you may see this as the natural progression of your love, your children might be somewhat less certain about what this means for them. Be realistic about what you expect: It is unusual for stepfamilies to immediately bond, live in harmony, and never disagree. However, as relationships grow, stepfamilies do form a secure, rewarding base for raising children.

Being in a stepfamily brings change. You may want a new start in a new area, but to your stepchildren, moving to a new house, changing schools, and losing contact with friends are major concerns. Keep resentment to a minimum by keeping change to a minimum. Make decisions as a family whenever you can. Cooperation is easier to achieve if your children have had their say and influenced family decisions. Regular family meetings are an ideal place for opinions to be put forward.

What problems can I expect with my new family?

You may need to develop a thick skin. Children can say hurtful things to parents, but much of the time, the parents' memories of loving moments put these in perspective. You don't have this store of past experiences with your stepchildren and may find negative comments more difficult to shrug off. So next time you hear, "I hate you," or "You can't tell me what to do, you're not my mom," don't take it personally. See them for what they are: A burst of anger at all life's unfairness, directed at the easiest target.

When it seems like a battle between you and your stepchild for your partner's attention, it's time to reevaluate how love is expressed and time is shared. Children can fear that there won't be enough love to go around once they have to share their parent with you. Bring this issue into the open, and talk over what each person needs in order to be reassured of their importance. Otherwise, insecurities can fester if they're left unspoken. In your new family your relationship is very important. It's the reason this stepfamily has come together, and it offers stability as well as setting the tone for everyone. Keep your

relationship on track by finding time for each other every day, and talk to one another about more than practical issues or how the children are doing.

When times are difficult, remember this may simply be because you're in a family, and family members don't always get along. Not all the issues are about being a stepfamily.

How can my new partner and I parent together effectively?

Your child will be sensitive to any perceived favoritism or to discipline that varies from how things were in her original family. It can seem easier to continue parenting your own child in the old way and put the stepparent in a backup role. This rarely works, as it can cause the stepparent to feel sidelined and without authority in the home. Each of you will have your own parenting style, but it is essential that you parent with the same standards for all the children in the family. Rules and expectations need to be discussed with children and adults. And remember, parenting works best when it comes from both of you.

Ask yourselves these questions in preparation for parenting together:

* How will we show our children how special they are and reward them for their achievements?
* How will we make sure children get the same response from both of us when they have a request?
* What behaviors will be acceptable?
* How will we discipline our children if they misbehave?
* What sort of help around the house do we expect?
* Will there be any areas of parenting in which there is no room for negotiation, such as not using physical discipline?

If you can, have a similar discussion with your child's other natural parent. At the very least keep your ex informed about what approach you are taking. This will help cross over between homes and reduce confusion for children about what applies where. If you and your new partner can't agree on the details, attend a parenting course together. Whether you go to a standard course or one specifically designed for stepfamilies, you will find many issues are clarified.

Their time online
safe internet use

My child seems to want to be online all the time. Could she be addicted to the internet?

Using the internet can become a compelling and time-consuming pastime for your child. The excitement of making new friends, online gaming, and creating then refining a new persona for herself can keep her online. While experts disagree about the possibility of physical addiction to the internet, very high usage can dominate your child's free time to the exclusion of real-life socializing. There may also be signs of anxiety if she can't go online to keep up with her life there and maintain her contacts, games, or gossip. If your child's home life revolves around the computer, do take action. Gradually reduce her time online until you've reached a level that enables her to eat with you, socialize each evening with family or friends, and attend offline hobbies or clubs. Set specific time slots for computer use. She needs her sleep, so late at night or early hours of the morning are not the time for going online. Keep internet use in the family areas of the house only: This increases your ability to monitor, and makes it easier to spend time with her online yourself. You will probably meet some resistance at first, but increasing her satisfaction with her life offline should balance what she feels she's lost.

What can I do about my son's inappropriate searches?

There are few children, when egged on in a group or even out of individual curiosity, who won't put a rude word into the search box and dare to press "enter." It's the virtual equivalent of giggling over the underwear section of a clothing catalog, but the stakes are far greater. Forbidden behavior like this matches your child's stage of sexual development. For example, he might want to know what male and female bodies look like and explore the nature of sex while also having a sense that this is "naughty."

Whatever your child's motivation, such a search can lead to exposure to inappropriate images or explicit information, and needs to be addressed. It makes sense to treat computer rules like any others that are applied in your home: A system of rewards for sticking to the agreement for safe internet use, and consequences for flouting the rules may focus

---

PARENTS' STORY

Parental controls
different accounts

Our computer is shared between the whole family, and I use it pretty much every day. I was constantly playing around with the parental controls so that when the children were online the searches were restricted, but when I was on I could access all areas. Inevitably one night I slipped up and forgot to put the parental controls back on. Next day, the kids logged on and had free access to anything and everything. To their credit they didn't go too wild, and were so shocked by some of the pop-ups that they came and told me pretty quickly.

Shamefaced, I began sticking a note on the corner of the monitor to remind me to reset the controls. I've gotten even more techno-savvy recently, and used the administrator to set up different accounts for each of us with individual passwords and personal levels of control and filtering—so no more constantly adjusting the levels. Now all I have to do is keep my password secret, and remember it, of course.

ESSENTIAL INFORMATION: PRETEENS

Managing the internet
How to ensure safe, effective use

The internet invites your child into an arena of learning, friendships, and fun that can be rich and exciting. She can reach out to other children across the globe and interact in real time, peer into the world of others through YouTube, and share something of herself on social networking sites and in chat rooms. Helping your child make the most of her time online and minimize and manage the dangers requires the same skills and vigilance you would apply to any other aspect of your child's life.

✱ Freedom and limits: Agree with your child where she can go online and what's out of bounds. See this as co-management of her internet use, something discussed and agreed with your maturing child, rather than a rule brought down by you. Apply parental controls and filters to ensure that your child's searches come up with appropriate content and to avoid offensive pop-ups. If you're not sure how to set up controls effectively, seek help online. Check regularly that controls are still in place as your techno-rebellious child may try to take them off. Keep filters under review: As she matures your child may value access to sites, such as those giving advice about relationships or puberty, which need an adjustment of limits.

✱ Quality time: Using the computer doesn't need to be a solitary pursuit. You can search, play games, and watch movies or television with your child. Shared use means you can enjoy time together and get an idea of the sites your child enjoys.

✱ Train yourself: You'll be in the best position to help your child online if you are familiar and comfortable with the computer and internet yourself. Being e-literate, particularly when it comes to new and developing areas, allows you to understand and be able to talk with credibility about the sites your child visits. You can learn formally (often local adult learning centers run computer courses), work through a book, or seek the help of your knowledgeable child.

✱ Time: Do agree limits on your child's time on the internet to ensure she has space for activities in the "real" world. Internet sessions of around an hour or two a day, with a break to stretch every 20 minutes, will leave your child time to spend with you and her friends. Limit yourself, too: Internet use can be the thief of family time for adults as well as children.

✱ Supervision: As with anything your child does, she'll need some degree of supervision and guidance. This is easier if your computer is in a family area of the house with the screen facing the room. Having the computer in a well-used area means you can look in on your child as you go about family life. You may be under pressure to permit computers in your child's bedroom, away

TECHNO-SAVVY: The internet is becoming an essential part of everyday life. Supervision and a few rules will ensure that your child can use it safely.

from adult supervision. This is not recommended as it severely limits your ability to supervise content and monitor the amount of time spent online.

✱ **Trust:** You cannot look over your child's shoulder all the time, so it is essential to build up trust that she can use the internet safely. You will still need to supervise and check in with her but, by setting rules together and giving her some credit for regulating herself, you will build her sense of responsibility.

✱ **Personal safety:** There is no guaranteed way to stay completely safe online, but you and your child can work out how to minimize risks. Pin up a list of your agreed safety points next to the computer as a reminder. These could include:

✱ Stick to regulated, supervised sites.

✱ Anything being posted on a social networking site will be agreed between the two of you in advance.

✱ Keep personal details of herself, other family members, and friends to herself and don't share even with the closest online friends.

✱ Be respectful of others in what you write and post about them.

✱ Tell immediately if someone is pressing for intimate information or suggests meeting in the real world.

TOGETHERNESS: Computers can offer shared activity such as creating blogs together or watching streamed movies, so it need not be a solitary pursuit.

your son's mind. For example leaving his search history intact may earn an extra 10 minutes online, whereas deleting the history, so you can't see where he's been, could lead to 10 minutes off next time. Meet your child's need for more information about the human body and sexual development by giving him appropriate reading material or find factual sites online for him that he can then view with some privacy. If another child was involved in the risky searches, inform their parents of the problem so they can take action if they wish.

Q My son's homework looked much more formal than usual. It seems he copied from the internet. Is this cheating?

Your son is probably facing a tough job translating what he's found on the internet into his own words. Often online text is well written and may practically answer his homework question with little input from himself. However, taking information this way is plagiarism—passing off the work of others as his own without acknowledging the original author—and is a form of cheating. Help him understand the implications of copying by asking him to list the advantages and disadvantages of completing homework this way. He may have positives such as the homework looks better, has more facts in it, is quicker to complete, and may get higher marks. On the negative side, he could recognize that he hasn't really thought about or learned the information, he might be embarrassed if he's asked a question in class, he may be caught and disciplined. Taking material from the internet won't help him prepare for exams either: By not actively processing the information, he won't be learning it effectively. Talk over how you feel about cheating and help him recognize it isn't acceptable.

Get him to redo his existing homework, but ask him to tell you about the subject out loud and in his own words before he writes it out. This way he has to think about the topic without being distracted by the existing text. The temptation to cut and paste may be strongest when he's in a rush or doesn't understand

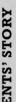

Family blog
an inspiration

I felt like I was getting nowhere talking with my son about internet safety. The rules and ideas weren't coming to life, and I wasn't confident he could translate them into action once he was online. Inspiration came when we were posting something on his school blog and it suddenly occurred to us to create our own family blog. It seemed an ideal way to work through safe internet use and develop something of value for ourselves. My son and I investigated how to set it up, designed it together, and now we each post almost every day. We do get into heated debates about the gray areas, such as what might be too personal or identifiable to post. We agree on posting about favorite bands and we're deciding if blogging about best holiday destinations would give away too much. I've learned lots about him in this process, and I think he's learned about me. I'm certain we both know more about safety online.

situations online when he overrides safety rules. Being able to use the technology does not necessarily mean he can keep himself safe.

Research has found that parents who are confident with the computer manage their children's internet use most effectively. Work to become a competent user of the internet yourself. When you ask your son to teach you these computer skills himself you can gain his respect without overriding his sense of pride that he knows more than you. Be open in telling him that you admire his skill but that you also have some worries. Check out the risks and rewards of time online by looking at child safety websites together. This way, your concerns are being backed up by information from the internet itself, and he should take them more seriously. Be realistic: If you over-dramatize the risks, he may disbelieve you or be tempted to test just how far he can go before he senses danger.

Do make it clear that attempts to outsmart you will not be acceptable. Use a family meeting to work together on reasonable freedoms and rules so everyone who uses the computer has their say. You could even have a written code of behavior for internet use that you all sign. Formalizing this agreement can mean it is taken more seriously.

the topic very well. Scheduling homework so he meets deadlines easily and giving your help on complex topics can go some way to addressing this problem. Occasionally, it is useful to transfer a picture, clip art, or short quotes into his homework. Educate him on how to use quotation marks and cite his source to show that he's taken material directly from websites or books.

My internet-savvy son ignores my rules about the computer. How can I regain some authority?

Your son is beginning to realize you don't know everything, and it may give him a kick to be able to fool you. However, it seems he's throwing his weight around and could be placing himself in risky

I found nasty statements about a friend on my child's social networking page. What can I do?

Spreading and repeating hurtful rumors or accusations toward someone else is bullying. Take immediate action by removing the messages from this and any other site your daughter has used. Listen to her reasons for her behavior, but make it clear that what she's done is unacceptable. Arrange for suitable consequences, which may include apologizing directly to the person she's targeted and posting a message on her networking page showing that she's truly sorry.

Using the internet to bully is an abuse of your trust in her, so you may wish to restrict her to using the computer for homework only for a time, perhaps a few days, followed by closer supervision of her

ESSENTIAL INFORMATION: PRETEENS

Cyber bullying
A growing form of abuse

Cyber bullying is when internet and mobile technology are used to spread malicious comments or embarrassing gossip, video, or photographs. It can be particularly distressing to your child, because there are few places she can gain respite from such messages. They follow her around through her mobile technology and invade the safety of home through her computer. Cyber bullying can also rapidly reach a very wide audience. This can increase the impact on your child as she becomes aware of the number of people seeing negative things about her.

If your child is cyber bullied:

✱ Agree that she will not reply to the messages or defend herself through IM's, blogs, or postings. Replying can give the bullies a buzz because it tells them she cares and is affected by their actions.
✱ Make it clear that she should not fight back by being abusive in return. Talk over how this reduces her to the same level as the bullies, and makes it more difficult to stop them if she joins in the same pattern of behavior.
✱ Ask her to save all negative items. She doesn't need to look at or read them, but they form the evidence needed to stop the bullies. Keeping a record of the time and date of each message is also helpful.
✱ Report the abuse to the authorities. It is illegal to threaten or abuse you or your child, and help is available. Contact your child's school to get them to apply their anti-bullying policy, which should include steps to stop cyber bullying. If necessary take your complaint to the police and alert websites that are hosting the forums where the malicious messages are posted.
✱ While action against the bully is taking place, change your child's email and mobile contact details and block email addresses so messages don't get through.
✱ Get her to take a break from her mobile technology. For a few hours a day, ask her to turn off her phone and use the internet only to research homework and not to IM, or access emails, chat rooms, or her blog. This way, she's not exposed to the negative messages and can relax for a while.
✱ Cyber bullies are often known to your child offline. They may target her in the real world, too, so ensure she is well supervised when not at home and knows who and how to tell if bullying occurs.

THREATENING TEXTS: Cell phones can be used by cyber bullies to send abusive text messages. Changing your child's phone number may help.
FRIEND OR FOE?: Although useful for many, the internet can become a means for bullies to distribute hurtful things about your child.

Accurate information
Sorting fact from fiction

The internet is a major source of information for your child, from facts and images needed for homework through to all she wants to know about puberty, relationships, fashion, and sports. However, it's largely unregulated, and the content varies from accurate to fanciful. Help your child develop a critical approach to internet information by teaching her how to spot the signs of a reputable website. Good quality information is usually on sites where:

* There are contact details for the author and host organization.
* Information is recent, as shown by the date of the latest review or postings.
* The information matches with at least two more sources, such as books and other websites.

* The site is neutral, not trying to convince you of something nor hosted by an organization or person with a particular point of view to push.
* The text is well written with few or no spelling or grammatical errors. Sloppy writing can mean sloppy fact-checking.

online networking until that trust is rebuilt. Help your child see the effect of bullying on others by asking her to imagine what is must be like to the subject of malicious gossip.

Take something unpleasant that she's actually posted and use it as a teaching aide by rewriting it together, replacing the victim's details with her own. Ask her to tell you all the thoughts and feelings she might have if this popped up on her computer and was seen by people she knows. Absolutely do not post it even for a moment, but do use it to get her to genuinely empathize with the person she maligned, and she'll be less likely to bully again.

Q My child argues that she can only make friends online if she shares personal information.

Your child is right—she does need to disclose some information about herself, including her likes, dislikes, experiences, and opinions, in order to make friends. These are the foundation of getting to know and being known by others. However, some of this

personal information makes her vulnerable. You can teach her the specific things to keep private and give guidance about what information puts her in most danger, and what is less risky.

Explain that personal information that allows her to be located and contacted in the real world is one of the problems. So, no sharing full name, home address, phone number, birthdate, or details such as school and specific clubs she attends. Giving out her deepest secrets or worries online is not advisable either; it amounts to pointing out her soft spots, and invites bullies to take advantage of her vulnerabilities. Remind her that sharing covers all aspects of her internet use, including when she posts a comment on a blog, uploads information or pictures to a social networking site, or responds to questions when instant messaging. Agree, as one of your internet rules, that she will write out the guidelines on what she can share online, and that if she wants to meet someone offline, then you will be fully involved, including being present at the meeting or able to veto it.

Wannabe?
clothes, makeup, older behavior

Q **I think that my daughter's friends are a bad influence. Can I forbid her from seeing them?**

Banning something usually makes it more attractive. Trying to ban friends is practically difficult and may well mean that the friendship becomes clandestine, making it deliciously exciting. The subterfuge will only distance your daughter from you further. It might be worthwhile to discuss with your daughter what she likes so much about these friends. They are satisfying a need in your child that may be satisfied in some other way. It could be that she feels safe and grown-up with these "unsuitable" young people, and you could address her insecurities together.

If they are influencing her to behave in risky, unacceptable, or antisocial ways, you would be right to try and discourage her from mixing with them. Explain your reasons for your concerns, and ask her to cooperate in trying to see less of them. Support her to make connections with more suitable friends.

Q **How can I teach my materialistic son the value of money?**

Preteens are a lucrative market, but at this age they are not yet cynical enough to realize that they are being targeted with subtle advertising. Brand names and the latest gizmos are signs of status that can mean a great deal within his peer group: The boy with the latest cell phone or MP3 player is top dog. They are probably at their most rapacious at this age, wanting possessions without any real understanding of their value or the hard work behind the money that pays for them. Encourage your son to earn some of the money toward purchasing these products. This might be doing some jobs for neighbors and extended family, and it certainly can apply to jobs he does at home. Pay him to clean the car or mow the lawn and encourage him to save his money for the things he wants. You can agree to match his savings to get the new game or pair of shoes. Also, consider with him how important possessions are in his judgments of his friends. Is it really all about the things they own, or is it more about their great sense of adventure or their hilarious jokes? Don't be afraid to say no to his constant demands, or to make him wait for a new possession: If he really wants it, he will value it all the more. If you give in every time, he will not learn the value of money.

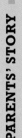

PARENTS' STORY

Making time to talk
transferring values

Since my children were small, I always insisted that we eat our evening meal together as a family. Whatever they are doing in the evening we sit down at the table together. Now that they are older and spending more time with their friends, I still try to ensure that we eat together on weeknights. This is our opportunity to talk, and it is so normal that they always do.

Now that we are heading for adolescence, our conversations move backward and forward from football and ballet to schoolwork, friends, music, smoking, Grandad's colorful youth, and the pros and cons of becoming a vegetarian. I can talk about difficult issues without having to announce a lecture and immediately lose their attention. It means that our parental and family values are filtering down to our children in an organic way, which just might ensure that they hear and remember them when having to make difficult choices.

Parenting tweens
The drive to be cool

School dances, girl and boy bands, pierced ears and fake tattoos, makeup, short skirts, high-heel shoes, boys, social networking… and she's only 11! The in-between years, when she's not quite an adolescent but not really a child, can be a wake-up call for the teen years to come. If you can get it right at this stage, you may have a head start for later.

Particularly in girls, puberty may start to bring about physical changes that make your daughter look older than her years and older than she feels. For this age group, developing maturity has an elasticity that can be confusing and stressful. Being "cool" and hanging out with others who are widely considered to be "cool" can be a masterful disguise for this internal tug of war.

* A new age: Looking like the pop stars and celebrities that she admires, mixing with peers who share the same interests, and doing things that older kids do, all serve to mark the end of childhood and the dawning of adolescence for your child. This means decisions about the suitability of the clothes she chooses and the way she wants to look. It also means choices of friends with whom she wants to mix. These can sometimes be unsuitable or older girls and boys, especially if she has had an early puberty. Finally, her behavior may start to change, with signs of challenges and difficulties such as lying about her whereabouts or being caught shoplifting. You may see these as the influence of the peer group, but they may be more a sign of your daughter's need to fit in. Try asking her what it is that she likes about her new friends—you may discover that they give her something, composure or quirkiness, that she feels she is lacking. Together, you may consider how she can develop these traits for herself without being totally led by others.

* Different identities: The rapid growth in her cognitive and emotional development has moved her from the spontaneous busy-ness of childhood to the beginnings of the more reflective self-absorption of adolescence. She will be trying out different identities, and experimenting with looks, companions, and behaviors. Her templates for all these different possible selves will be strongly influenced by what she sees in magazines, on television, and on the internet. She will want to look like her friends. The shops are filled with "tween fashion"—downsized fashion and glamour in colors and shapes meant for older, shapelier, girls. And into this swirl of glittering developmental confusion, there emerges for the first time a sneaking doubt in her mind: That you, her parent, may not know best and, worst of all, may not be cool at all.

* What's acceptable? While your son or daughter may be relishing the prospect of growing independence, new intimacies, lights, music, and action… you as her parent, may be feeling that it is all too much too soon. How do you steer a steady course through these first tensions of growing up while keeping in touch with your own judgment and values? The bottom line for the tween parent must be to remember that she is still a child underneath that first bra and lip gloss. The shift in your parenting doesn't need to be seismic, but it should subtly recognize changes from within and without. Behind the challenges to your authority and judgment are many doubts and insecurities that need careful handling, not a sudden imposition of military rule or a complete relaxation of family routine in the quest to become a cool parent.

* Being popular: Popularity and physical attractiveness are likely to be two issues most bothering your child. You can help her to think about what it means to be popular by putting it in perspective. Think with her about other young people and what makes them popular, consider whether these are admirable traits or not. For example, is it material possessions or having the latest gossip, or is it being funny or a trustworthy friend? Particularly in boys, there is a relationship between popularity and aggression, because aggressive boys are perceived by their peers as tough and cool. Allow your child to decide whether this is the sort of popularity that she is after. Popularity can be more valuable among a small group of good friends, rather than a large group of superficial acquaintances. Socially able children are more likely to come from families where there are clear rules about appropriate and inappropriate behavior. So don't stop teaching your child right from wrong now that she is starting to question you. Redouble your efforts, explain your reasons, and share a little of your own experience at a similar age. By imposing some limits on her appearance and behavior, you will help her to feel secure and more confident about her choices.

✱ **Fashion victim?** When it comes to choices about what to wear and how to look, take account of the enormous pressure on girls and boys to dress in a certain way from the media and from their peer group. Preteens are targeted just as much as their older sisters and brothers. However, your daughter will still look to you for advice and approval (and financing) of the clothes she wears. Look through magazines together and talk about what suits her, think about stylish (age-appropriate) role models, and help her to discover her own style. It might be a good idea to set a few rules about what you consider acceptable, such as: When she can have her ears pierced, how much makeup is OK, whether it's OK for her midriff to show, etc. Give some thought to what kind of a role model you are yourself. It is worth updating your knowledge and views about music, pop culture, and fashion. You could try exploring fashion and style together. By being better informed about the world your tween inhabits, you are more likely to earn her respect, to ensure that she listens to what you have to say and, ultimately, to keep her safe.

APPROPRIATE?: Think about what age you will allow your child to get her ears pierced or wear makeup and set rules to help her feel safe.

LOOKING COOL: The drive to be cool is very strong at this age, with his peers and the media influencing fashion and hair styles.

STAYING UP TO DATE: Try reading magazines together with your tween to understand her world. In this way you can show your interest.

For my daughter's 12th birthday she wants to have a sleepover. Is this a good idea?

There are lots of advantages to having a slumber party at this age: You know where the kids are, you are on hand if you are needed, and you can keep an eye on them while giving them time on their own. It is also a good opportunity for your daughter to learn about being a good host. Give her the responsibility of planning and organizing the party with your help and support. In order to preempt difficulties, set a limit to the number of guests she can have over. (Even numbers of guests are probably best.) Have some activities planned, such as a DVD, games, and make-your-own pizzas or ice-cream sundaes, and then leave them to their own devices. You may be called upon to deal with someone who is homesick or just plain sick—both are very likely. Talk about the ground rules with your daughter beforehand, and think about how you will communicate them to her guests. You might decide to show them around the house at the beginning, introducing them to the whole family and pointing out which rooms are out of bounds. You may want to restrict certain television shows and give them a time when things need to quiet down. They probably won't sleep much, but will definitely have lots of fun.

My daughter says she is fat and ugly, and it's my fault she's like that. What can I do?

This can be a time when youngsters seem to be beset with self-doubt, and you may observe this as a drop in self-esteem. This can be coupled with the development of a more curvy figure as puberty progresses, which may be quite a change from her previous childish shape and lead her to feel fat. However, she is still a child in many ways and is struggling to rationalize her emotional turmoil— hence the finger of blame being pointed at you. Try not to take this personally. Instead, take a deep breath and help her sort out what is real and what is distorted thinking. Help her to realize that she doesn't always feel fat and ugly, even from one day

(or hour) to the next. It's not that her body and face change dramatically, just the way she is thinking and feeling about it. Help her experiment with hairstyles, colors, and styles of clothes that make her feel better and, most importantly, get her busy doing things that help her to feel good in her skin. Physical activity may help; it produces endorphins, which have their own positive payoff for self-esteem and self-image.

My son and I are always arguing. Is there a way to defuse these shouting matches?

Arguments between you and your preteen may become more common as he challenges your authority on clothes, allowances, curfews, and the like. It is worth remembering to be patient, keep calm, and to hear his point of view. Get him to think through the advantages and disadvantages of his requests and come up with a balanced decision about whether to proceed with it. If it is safe, then sometimes learning through his own mistakes is the most effective lesson of all.

Try to stay positive, and avoid using guilt and emotional blackmail. It is more effective to say, "I felt put down by the way you talked to me in front of your friends," rather than, "You were rude to me in front of your friends." The former explains the impact of his behavior and may get him to think about it, while the latter is an accusation—he is more likely to become defensive. There will be times when he pushes the boundaries just to test you, so do not be afraid to say "No." He will be relieved to have you stand firm.

Being cool and hanging out with others who are widely considered to be cool can be a masterful disguise for mixed emotions

Arguments with your preteen

Your daughter has you cornered. She wants to dye her hair black for her last day at elementary school and you have said, "No! Absolutely not." She starts to plead with you, saying that everyone else is doing something: So and so is having braids and beads put in, another is having highlights. "Please," she says, "It's the last day I'll ever be at that school." You start to doubt your decision; you don't want your child to have dyed black hair all over the summer vacation, but you can't come up with a reason that she will accept. You stand firm, she cries with frustration, and storms from the room. You are left upset and bewildered, wondering if there was a better way to deal with her!

Part of the challenge of dealing with this age group is the unexpectedness of it all. It seems it was only a few weeks ago that you were struggling to get her to brush her hair at all. When faced with these dilemmas, try and give yourself some time to think your position through. Perhaps ask for some details about what she wants to do and what her friends are doing and say that you'll get back to her with your decision.

Perhaps a chat with another one of the parents might help you to understand what has been agreed. You can then make up your mind about whether this is a battle worth fighting or just a little harmless fun that will bring you together over the sink with some rubber gloves and a bottle of hair dye.

Q My son used to be very level headed, but now his behavior is so up and down. What's going on?

Development for any child is a slowly unfolding process. As your son's thinking and reasoning skills become more complex, you will see a steady increase in the mature, age-appropriate behavior you want to reinforce, mixed in with flashes of what you might expect from a younger child. You can help him with this process by not being critical of his fluctuating behavior, ignoring any silly or immature behavior as much as possible, and encouraging his developing skills by praising and reinforcing examples of the behavior you want to see more of. Try to role model behavior that you'd like to see, such as good manners. Your son is still young, though, so you should expect him to act without thinking at times—that's part of the fun of being a child.

Q My child shows absolutely no signs of growing up. Will he be left behind by his peer group?

Late-middle childhood is not a developmental stage, like adolescence, but a period of social and educational change. Many children, particularly boys, do not go through puberty until well into their teens, and remain looking and behaving like children while their peers develop and change around them. It can be difficult to be the only one who shows no sign of physical development but, if he is happy with his friends and in his activities, there is nothing to worry about. Boys often get very involved in particular activities during this preteen stage, such as sports or chess club or war games, and seem oblivious to the world of girls and pop culture. Let him enjoy his childhood; he will catch up in due course.

Teens
becoming an adult

* **Giving and getting respect**
  challenging behavior

* **Testing times?**
  the pressure of final exams

* **Highs and lows**
  moods and melodrama

* **She won't eat**
  all about eating disorders

* **When should I let go?**
  your young adult, relationships

* **Who am I?**
  exploring values and identity

* **Sex, drugs, rock and roll**
  when to worry

* **Moving on to responsibility**
  the world of work

Giving and getting respect
challenging behavior

Q My son has set up a diary on the computer and won't let me read it. Should I insist he let me?

Your son's diary is a dialog with himself that allows him to explore his experiences, hopes, and fears. Closing the screen is his way of snapping his diary shut to stop you from looking. No one has a right to access the private thoughts of another person, only to ask they be shared. As your son's diary is essentially his private world written out, demanding to read it could be seen as going beyond your rights.

Instead, share your worry that he may have things on his mind that you'd like to hear about and help with. If you are convinced there is something major troubling him, suggest that he tell you or someone else that he chooses. Sometimes teens find it easier to talk with a school counselor, a grandparent, or an older sibling rather than a parent. Reassure him that, no matter what is happening, you will stand by him, and that help is available.

Q My son wants to go and hang out at the park. What's the best way to supervise him?

While your teenager no longer "goes out to play" he probably wants to get involved in the more grown-up version: Hanging out with friends, often doing what appears to you to be absolutely nothing. It is up to you to decide how risky this is.

If the park is nearby, well lit and with no other problems in the area such as drinking or drug use, then this may be an ideal place for him to safely meet up with his buddies. However, if these risks are present, it is wise to talk them through with your child, explaining that you have faith in him, but don't want him to be caught up in other people's problems. Help work out an alternative place he and his friends can go. Perhaps you can play a part by offering to drop the group of them at a community center or basketball court, or make your home an open house once a week.

If this all seems too controlling to your son, then agree some basic rules for both of you to follow so he doesn't feel as though you are breathing down his neck. Start by setting a curfew and some acceptable and unacceptable places for him to hang out. Agree that you will monitor him at first by coming to pick him up but won't embarrass him, for example, by honking the car horn. If he sticks to the rules, you can gradually loosen them, if not, tighten them a little so you can rebuild trust. However, no matter how much freedom he has, a basic minimum for keeping him safe is to know where he is, who he is with, and when he'll be home. This should be non-negotiable.

Q I was horrified to receive a call saying that my child was caught stealing. What can I do?

Your first reaction may be embarrassment or disbelief, and your teenager could well feel the same. Often, stealing is done on impulse or as an act of rebellion, and she may not have considered the possible end result. Getting caught might be the best outcome for her, because it debunks the myth that shoplifting is easy and has no consequences. Your role may be a delicate balance of disapproval for the

Recognizing that your child can care for himself may be one of the hardest acts of parenthood

theft and support as your child faces the outcome of her action. If she is questioned or charged by the police, accompany her to all interviews and encourage her to be honest. This can be a distressing experience if she has not had contact with the police or legal system before. Ask plenty of questions yourself about what will happen, what your child's rights are, and how best to prepare her.

If she's not charged, you may arrange with the store that she return the goods, makes an apology, and do something to provide restitution. Examples might be making a small donation to a charity of the store's choosing, or doing some volunteer work. These positive acts can rebuild her sense of self-esteem and restore some of your faith in her.

My rebellious teenager does the opposite of everything I ask. I'm at my wits' end!

Resisting your rules can be very satisfying to your daughter; not only does she get a big reaction from you, but she also gets her own way. Reduce her opportunity for rebellion by considering whether you could say "yes" to a few more of her suggestions, or at least reach a compromise. For example, you might agree to a new hair color as long as the shade or style doesn't break school rules. This way the two of you don't go head to head so often.

When you must stand your ground, do so with good reason. For example, you may say no to a late night party because of safety, supervision, and difficulty getting home. Explain yourself fully and negotiate an alternative, such as having her friends over to your home or going to an organized event rather than a private party.

I was a wild child in my youth. How much do I disclose?

It is an individual decision how much of your past you tell your teenager. In general, however, it is wise to be honest and model the openness you want your child to display. This works best if you give general factual information without glorifying your wild ways or lecturing. Tell him what happened to you, a brief

PARENTS' STORY

Thick skin
rejecting my authority

This past year I've put up with a lot. My son started with a bit of defiance and built up to full-blown rants accusing me of not caring about him, ruining his life, and saying he hated me. I was even frightened he'd act out his feelings and hurt me. In the end I picked up a parenting book which said this was more common than many parents thought. Now I recognize it's my son's struggle to be independent, yet have to live within my rules and in my home, that starts him off. Pushing me away with words is just a way of rejecting my authority.

The rudeness is still not okay but I've grown a thick skin and tell myself that he loves me underneath it all. Because I react less strongly now, he seems less aggressive, too, and we've even had a conversation about talking to each other with respect.

explanation of why you got into harmful habits, and the reason you stopped. For example, you might say, "When I was 15 I started drinking. A group of us would meet up at the park and pass a bottle around. It began because I thought I'd look weak if I didn't join in and it wasn't fun being around my friends when they were drunk and I wasn't. I stopped because I got so fed up of hangovers and it ended up being boring rather than exciting."

Disclosure of your rule-breaking can bring you closer to your teenager if he recognizes that you have some understanding of the pressures on him to fit in and engage in the same behavior as his peer group. However, he may also question why he should obey you when you didn't listen to your own parents. An effective answer to this is to explain that you've learned from how you behaved, and that's why you've worked hard with him to agree rules and limits that keep him safe without overprotecting him.

ESSENTIAL INFORMATION: TEENS

Building trust
Teaching your adolescent

The trust that flows between you and your child begins at birth and changes as he grows and develops. In his babyhood and early years he must trust you completely to meet his emotional and physical needs. As he gets older, the balance shifts as you teach, guide, and accept that he can do more for himself until, when he moves through adolescence, it is your turn to trust in him to meet his own needs and make decisions for himself.

Your past experience of him, the fears or confidence you feel in yourself, and perhaps the successes and mistakes of your own adolescence will affect how much trust you place in your teenager. The faith he has in you comes from much the same basis as yours in him. If you have cared for and supported him consistently and done what you said you would do, he's likely to continue to trust you as he enters adolescence. Recognize, however,

that his physical, social, and emotional development is taking a leap forward and it's up to you to change along with him by offering him new opportunities to show you how trustworthy he is.

✱ **Be respectful:** The most powerful way to gain respect is to act respectfully to others. When you treat your teenager with courtesy and honesty, and have a high opinion of him, he is more likely to live up to your expectations. Model this in all your relationships, and your value for others will rub off.

✱ **Teach him:** Making choices that are right for him depends upon your teenager's ethics and morals, an internal barometer telling him what is right and wrong. Help him reflect on his values through casual conversations rather than lectures. Often, topics covered in the news or raised on TV can stimulate discussion about right and wrong. Talking about subjects as diverse as war, racial hatred, faith,

HIS OWN SPACE: Respect your teen's personal and private space, usually his bedroom, by knocking before entering to show your trust.

BUILDING VALUES: Talking about a range of subjects when they are brought up in the news or on TV will help your teen form his ethics.

START SMALL: Give your child responsibility for chores such as doing her own laundry to help her practice for the future.

human rights, and green issues can all help crystallize your teenager's perspective on how he should treat people, animals, and the environment.

✳ Take small steps: You will never know what your teenager can achieve unless you give him the chance. Start small: Give him opportunities to make his own choices and live with them. Whether he's picking the decor for his bedroom, taking responsibility for his chores, or choosing school subjects, each one is a practice session for good decision making. As he shows you that he is capable, gradually increase the level of responsibility you give him. Then it's your turn to practice respecting his decisions, even if you disagree.

✳ Expect mistakes: It is an extremely rare child who navigates adolescence without slip-ups, and it could be argued that mistakes educate your child more rapidly than successes. Your challenge is to minimize risks so that, when things go wrong, they're not catastrophic. Good communication and a clear idea of where your teenager is, who he's with, and when he's expected home means you know where to go and who to contact if there is a problem. Education about drugs, alcohol,

and contraception (see pp. 238–243) gives your teen the information he needs to weigh the risks himself.

✳ Stay calm: It can be terribly disappointing when your teenager does not live up to your trust in him. However, keep in mind the many times he has been trustworthy, and keep his transgressions in perspective. Focus on working out what went wrong and how to rebuild trust rather than overreacting with emotive statements such as, "I'll never trust you again."

✳ Get support: Share your successes and war stories with other parents who have teenagers. If parenting your teen is very stressful, access help and advice through books and websites, or contact your child's school for courses specifically for parents of teens.

✳ Finally: Your teenager will no doubt have many successes, make some poor choices, and learn from both. He may or may not make the same mistakes you did. You cannot fully protect him from these mistakes or take the consequences for him. His experiences as an adolescent shape the adult he will become, and in this phase of his development you are an important navigator—but no longer the driver in his life.

TAKE A CHANCE: The opportunity to make his own choices, for example, about his bedroom decor, will allow him to demonstrate his capability.

TALK ABOUT IT: Frequent and open communication with your child helps to guide her through the ups and downs of adolescence.

TOO SHORT?: Compromising on certain things, such as acceptable clothing, gives your child the chance to show that she can be trusted.

Rebellion: Exploring identity

You cannot stop your teenager from rebelling. Her rejection of family values and standards is part of her exploration of her own identity, a way of giving herself a clean slate so she can fully explore what is important to her as an individual. Fortunately, most teenagers do eventually return to some or all of the values you have taught them over the years.

Coping methods for this time:

✱ Stick to reasonable house rules. Your teenager still needs to feel the safety of clear boundaries at home, if only so she can kick against them.

✱ Keep a straight face no matter what your teenager presents you with. There is nothing so encouraging to her as your shocked or horrified expression.

✱ Avoid ultimatums: These act as a dare to your teenager to see what you'll do if she doesn't comply. Whether you want her to give up smoking, stick to her curfew, or get a job, you'll get a better result if she has a timeframe rather than a deadline.

✱ Find moments of closeness: Raising a teenager isn't 100 percent challenge and rebellion. Sit together in quiet companionship, respond to a request for advice, share a success, or be a shoulder to cry on.

✱ Recognize her strengths. Some of her most annoying characteristics are also the most helpful to her progress. Being opinionated and prepared to try new things can get her into conflict with you but help her to be assertive and grasp opportunities in her life.

✱ Ride it out: Understand that this period of rebellion will come to an end.

How can I stop my teen from putting herself at risk by breaking the rules? She sneaks out late at night to visit her boyfriend.

Once your daughter has developed a habit of disregarding reasonable rules, it can take plenty of negotiating to get things back on track. Open up an honest discussion immediately about your concerns; there is no need to interrogate her, simply state that you believe she's been breaking her curfew. Take the time to understand her reasons—perhaps she enjoys the excitement or feels the rules are meaningless or harsh. Try to reach a compromise so that her needs, for example, to spend time with her boyfriend, and yours, to ensure her safety, are both met. Perhaps you can allow her boyfriend to visit more often while she agrees to stick to her curfew. It won't always be that simple, and you may need to set up a contract and a reward system so that sticking to the rules becomes worthwhile for your daughter. Negotiate and write out the most important rules, and decide upon rewards for each time they are kept. Increase this contract's formality by both signing it. For example, agree that she will remain in her room after lights out and that you will check in on her each night. Find a reward that is meaningful to her, for example earning money to add minutes to her cell phone, credit for music downloads, or extra time with her boyfriend at the weekend. Keep monitoring the contract to see that it's working for both of you.

Let her know that you won't hesitate to take action, such as searching, phoning her friends and, ultimately, calling the police, if she does leave home late at night and you feel she is at risk.

ESSENTIAL INFORMATION: TEENS

Tough times
Helping with harmful situations

A small number of teenagers do go "off the rails" during adolescence and present you with exactly the situations you had always hoped to avoid. It is normal for your teenager to be impulsive, reckless, and consider himself indestructible, but not to deliberately put himself in danger, wilfully harm others, or repeatedly break the law. If this happens, you and your child need to take action and acknowledge there is a problem. Seeking help from outside the home, for example from health, drug, and youth services and (as a last resort) the police, will make things easier, and means you won't have to cope on your own.

If there is tension brewing:
* Ask your teenager to tell you the problem from his point of view.
* Listen without interrupting or offering unwanted advice.
* Under no circumstances fight back or use physical discipline with your teenager.

* Keep your body language open and the tone of your voice soft. Try to stay calm, even if he is deliberately trying to provoke you.
* Avoid arguing back or sarcasm.
* Keep your distance: getting too close and invading your teenager's personal space can escalate emotions.
* Find solutions together if at all possible. If tempers do not cool and you are at immediate risk of, or are being harmed, take the difficult step of calling the police for help. In the long term, call on your extended family or friends for support and contact youth services for assistance.

Aggression and violence It's rare but, occasionally, teenagers struggle against the limitations of home life by threatening or hurting their parents or siblings. Avoid getting to this point by being aware of pressure points that could lead to violence. Start a conversation with your child about his frustrations before tempers get too hot.

NOT JUST PLAYING: If your teen is hurting you or his siblings, you may need to seek advice from youth services or the police.

TALK IT OUT : Have a calm conversation with your child about her frustrations.

FIGHT: You will need to take action if your teen is deliberately harming others.

Testing times?
the pressure of final exams

Q **I don't want my son to make the same mistakes I did. How can I get him to understand?**

Exam time can be a very stressful period for parents. It's easy to put yourself in your teenager's shoes and imagine yourself sitting at a desk, nervously waiting for the examiner to tell you to turn over your papers and begin. However, it is important to remember that these are your son's exams. While it may seem helpful to try and motivate him by sharing your past experiences, this may add to his stress levels if he feels that he has to somehow make up for what you didn't achieve at school. Instead, try to motivate him by discussing his own aspirations, and the grades and qualifications he needs to pursue them.

Negotiating a reward for extra effort may help too. After all his hard work at school, you want your son to do the best he can, but he needs to set his own pace and make his own decisions. Learning with the benefit of hindsight can only happen once he has something to look back on. If he doesn't make the grades he needs first time, that is not the end of the road. He is likely to be able to retake his exams, or he could look at other options for further study or work.

Q **My daughter's approach to studying seems very laid back. What can I do?**

Just because your daughter is not spending every spare minute with her head buried in a text book does not mean that she is failing to study. Knowledge and understanding of how people learn has changed significantly over the last 20 years, so the study skills she is using may be somewhat unfamiliar. Some teenagers learn best in a quiet room with no distractions, while others may find silence deafening and want their music cranked up. The space your daughter uses for studying is also important. If her

bedroom resembles somewhere you wouldn't normally enter without suitable protective clothing, resist the temptation to sweep in (literally) and clear everything away as she may find this organized chaos helpful. Rather than challenging your daughter on her approach to studying, show an interest in the strategies she is using and ask if there is anything you can help with. Encourage her to organize her time effectively by drawing up a study schedule, and offer support as and when she needs it. Your daughter has spent years developing her skills: Try to trust her to do her best.

Q **How can I help my son? He is worried about what he will do if he fails, so is working long hours.**

Your son may feel that his hopes and dreams are on the line with every final exam. It's no wonder he is feeling anxious and putting in plenty of study time! Of course, the grades he gets are important, but they are not the only factor that will determine his future. As well as worrying that he may let himself, you, and others down, he may also be anxious about being left behind by his friends. Talk about his concerns and make sure his expectations are realistic, bearing in mind his achievements to date. Anxiety and tiredness

> Anxiety can be paralyzing, so help your son to focus on the practical things he can do to improve his chances

MYTHS AND MISCONCEPTIONS

Is it true that...

✳ **A certain amount of stress can help you perform better?**

Yes and no. A small degree of stress can motivate careful attention. However, excessive stress interferes with organization and concentration, and evidence suggests that it is associated with poorer exam performance on the whole. The exact effects of stress differ for different people.

✳ **Drinking coffee keeps you awake and alert?**

It may. Many people turn to coffee to help them stay up working late into the night. The active ingredient—caffeine (also found in many energy drinks)—is indeed a stimulant, but its effects are relatively short lived, so you need to drink more to sustain energy. Too much caffeine can result in headaches, loss of concentration, and feelings of irritability, which all make it hard to stay focused and work effectively.

✳ **Memorizing important facts and figures the night before makes it easier to remember them?**

No. Last-minute cramming for tests and exams means more stress and less sleep—both of which can lead to poorer performance on the day. It takes time for the brain to process and consolidate new information, so although some facts and figures are bound to stick, there is no substitute for a sensible study timetable.

ESSENTIAL INFORMATION: TEENS

Coping with exam stress
Top 10 tips

Signs that your teenager may be experiencing significant levels of stress include: Negative thoughts and self-statements ("If I fail this my life is over"); physical symptoms such as headaches, stomachaches, and trembling; and changes in study behavior such as avoiding or putting off work (more than usual).

All teenagers experience some degree of exam stress due to fear of the consequences of failing, judgments by parents, and repeated messages from others about the importance of final grades. Too much stress will hinder your teenager in study and exams. Discussing the following tips with him should help to keep his stress levels down.

✱ Plan a sensible study schedule in advance, allowing plenty of time to cover all subjects, and try to stick to it.

✱ Take regular breaks when studying: a 10-minute break every 40 minutes gives the brain a chance to process information and keeps attention and concentration levels up.

✱ Eat regular, healthy meals, get plenty of sleep (late night, last-minute cramming sessions are not usually helpful), and get some exercise—even if it is just a walk around the block.

✱ Get to the exam in plenty of time and pick a good spot: Sitting at the front means it may be easier to get the teacher's attention; sitting at the back means a good view of how others are doing and who is leaving early (not necessarily a good thing); and sitting by the exits may lead to disruption during the exam if others leave before you.

✱ Take a few relaxing deep breaths, read the instructions carefully, and jot down any key points. Read each question thoroughly and try to write down exactly what it is asking you.

✱ Answer easy questions first to settle into the exam, build confidence, and help with the recall of all the information that is bursting to get out.

LEFT: Excess stress will hinder study and exam performance, so try to help your teen plan sensible strategies. Ask if she wants your help and discuss what form this could take, for example quizzing her or just providing snacks.
MIDDLE: At the start of the exam, writing down key points for each question before answering it in full can help.
FAR RIGHT: Engaging in an analysis after the exam may be inevitable, but try not to get too worried about how others answered the questions.

* Resist the temptation to leave the examination room as soon as possible. Review work carefully, check that all questions have been answered, and proofread for spelling, grammar, punctuation (which may cost you points), and other simple mistakes.

* A postmortem analysis with friends is inevitable, and sharing the experience can be a good way to relieve the tension. Try not to engage in too many question-by-question comparisons, though, as it's a surefire way to raise stress levels and undermine confidence. There are bound to be differences in how questions are answered, but try to leave the grading to the professionals.

Tips for parents:

* Try not to crack the whip too hard along the way. Promote a healthy work/leisure balance and reward efforts rather than performance to keep motivation levels high.

* Keep things in perspective—exams can feel like the most important thing in the world at the time, but soon enough they will be a distant memory. If one has gone especially badly, remember your child may be able to retake it or submit extra work as a substitute.

can be paralyzing, so help your son focus on the practical things he can do to improve his chances and manage his stress rather than worrying about the "What if... ?" factor. If he does not achieve the grades he needs, be sensitive to how he will be feeling and try not to look too disappointed. There may be opportunities for him to retake his exams so that he can keep up with his friends and stay on track with his plans. However, this could also be an opportunity to rethink where he is going and to look at options he may not have considered otherwise.

I'm eager to help my child prepare for her exams in any way I can. Do you have any tips?

During this potentially stressful time, there are many things that you can do to help your teenager stay calm, study hard, and do her best on exam days. However, there are many equally unhelpful but well-meaning acts that will serve to aggravate your daughter, cause arguments, and give her plenty of ammunition to retaliate with.

Discuss and agree the rules around study and leisure time in advance, particularly with regard to the time allowed on major distractions such as TV and video games. Focus on achieving a healthy balance; placing too many restrictions on your teenager's social life may lead to feelings of resentment, and is unlikely to make her study harder. Discuss with your child what kind of support and help she would like from you (if any) with her work. Trust her judgement on this—not everyone finds it helpful to be quizzed by their parents the night before an exam.

Research shows that exam stress can lead to loss of appetite, so try to feed her meals that she likes to eat (and which are healthy, if possible). Increasing her quota of favorite foods will show that you are thinking about her and make it more likely that she will eat. When she is stuck in study mode, keep the snacks and drinks coming regularly too. Relax the rules on household chores or maybe relieve her of these responsibilities completely until exam time is over. This will free up more time for studying, and shows that you are doing what you can to take some of the pressure off. Pick your battles and try to avoid arguments—things are far more likely to escalate during this time. Finally, offer plenty of heartfelt, genuine praise for all of your teenager's efforts.

Q My daughter is behind with her research projects, but it doesn't bother her. What can I do?

There is a commonly held view that having coursework to complete is somehow less stressful than sitting for a final exam. Some might even see this as a "soft option." The reality is that coursework is often equally, if not more, stressful than sitting tests and exams. Your daughter may be working as part of a group (which can be difficult in itself) and is probably involved in a range of tasks such as reviewing the literature on a particular topic, collecting data, and presenting her findings— while juggling several deadlines, her other schoolwork, and exam prep!

If you challenge her on why she has not submitted her work you will probably get an angry and defensive reaction, that will leave you none the wiser as to what is going on. Instead, try asking her what needs to happen in order for her to finish her projects. If there are extenuating circumstances, your daughter may be able to apply for an extension to her deadline. However, it may be that she is dragging her heels because she has little or no intention of completing her work—despite your best attempts to motivate and reward her efforts. If this is the case and she understands the consequences, there is little you can do. Being independent means taking responsibility for her actions—whether you agree with them or not.

Q My son is not doing well in his review sessions. Now he says it's not worth trying in his exams.

Your son is bound to be feeling down after having his confidence knocked, and he needs time to reflect on what happened. However, don't let him wallow in self-pity for too long. Your son's reaction shows that he genuinely cares about his performance at school, so be sensitive to how he is feeling but try to problem solve what happened, put it into perspective, and gently help him move on. Discuss his study habits, preparation, and approach to the review sessions themselves. Ask what he thought he did well in, were there any areas where he did better than expected, what could he do differently this time, and what support and help does he want from you.

Achieving less than glowing practice-exam results often serves as a timely wake-up call for teenagers who might not have been giving schoolwork their full attention. Having tasted failure once, your son may now be spurred on to achieve the results he is capable of.

Q I'm worried that my child's choices of easy subjects will affect what she can study at college.

Certain subjects may be perceived as easy choices because they don't lend themselves to a traditional assessment by written exam. However, your daughter's knowledge and skills will be thoroughly assessed in whichever subjects she chooses. In fact, she may find that some forms of assessment require as much preparation as written exams, and can be more anxiety provoking, for example, preparing a portfolio, oral exams, and group presentations. With regard to the possible impact of your daughter's choices on her future studies, discuss which subjects she would like to pursue and check with the college of her choice that her curriculum will adequately prepare her. As long as she is covering the minimum prerequisites for her preferred course of study, you should be able to reach a compromise and allow her some freedom and flexibility in her other choices. Your daughter may be genuinely interested in exploring other subjects, and she may even discover a hidden talent. However, if she is motivated more by the idea of easy assessment, rather than interest in the subject itself, she may find some of her options far more challenging than she expects. There is no such thing as an easy qualification, but this is something she needs to find out for herself.

Highs and lows
moods and melodrama

Q My child and I always clash over her sleep patterns—she says I don't understand. Who is right?

You both probably are! It is true that it is typical for teenagers to shift to a sleeping pattern of later bedtimes and later rising over the weekends. However, overall she may be getting less sleep than if she had a consistently earlier bedtime. But staying up late is about watching late-night TV, going to parties and clubs, being awake when all the adults are asleep—it's exciting and it's what teenagers do. There is also some evidence that young people's brains function better later in the day.

If you think that she is sleep-deprived and that this is affecting her mood and her schoolwork, you may need to find a compromise. Try working out how many hours sleep a week you both think she needs, and see if you can agree on a figure somewhere in between hers and yours. Then agree an earlier bedtime on school nights and later rising times over the weekend. Give it a trial for a week or two and see if you notice improvements.

Q My daughter's first serious boyfriend has just broken up with her and she is inconsolable. How do I help her get over him?

The pain and heartbreak of your daughter's first rejection by a boyfriend is something you can't prepare her for. Since she has nothing to compare this experience with, your daughter may feel overwhelmed with emotion, so take this loss seriously. At first she may feel as if her whole world has collapsed and there is little you can say to make her feel better. Pearls of wisdom such as, "There are plenty more fish in the sea," will not help! Also resist the temptation to sound off about the cruel and heartless teenager who has upset your daughter,

since she will still have very strong feelings for him, and this could put you in an awkward position if they get back together. Once her first tears have passed she may want to discuss what happened or she may turn to friends for support. Keep an eye out for any behaviors which suggest your daughter is struggling to deal with the loss of this relationship. It is reasonable to expect her to take to her room and play favorite songs on repeat, but self-punishing,

PARENTS' STORY

Loner?
an unhappy child

It wasn't that he just wanted to be alone for a while, it was hours and hours in his room. I'd knock and open the door, and there he was, lying on his bed, staring at the ceiling. He stopped going out with friends, saying he was tired, and he did sleep an awful lot. But then I'd hear him moving around in the early hours of the morning. His appetite dropped off. He would also get really angry and shout and yell. He once punched the wall so hard he made his knuckles bleed. People said it was his age, teenagers are like that, let him be, give him some space. But I knew something was really wrong. I thought maybe he was taking drugs, but he just seemed awfully, constantly sad.

Finally I spoke to my doctor who said that parents usually know when there's a problem, and she referred us to a local therapist specializing in adolescents. He is now having individual therapy and we are having some family meetings. He seems a little brighter and more hopeful.

PARENTS' STORY

Tearing out my hair
remind you of anyone?

Parenting my teenager was really getting me down, from getting her to clean her room to her negative attitude. It seemed like a fight every step of the way. I was tearing my hair out. One time, when I'd had an especially bad day, my mom took me aside and asked me if my daughter reminded me of anyone? Funnily enough, my automatic reaction was to smile and say "Yeah, me." Mom and I sat there all evening, reminiscing about the things I did, laughing at my antics. It made me realize that sometimes, when I fight with my daughter, I could choose to help her instead. Even tough jobs like cleaning her room would be quicker if we did them together.

I feel more of a connection with my daughter knowing we both went through this phase and, if I hang in there with her, she'll come through it, just like I did.

emotional expression. The obvious is the cool nonchalance of the "no problem" teen attitude, masking the inner teenage turmoil of anxiety, self-doubt, and distress. She will get better at showing acceptable levels of emotion in her peer group, because she will want to learn the rules in order to be part of that group. In fact, it can be a useful way of learning how to manage inner feelings.

"Fake it till you make it" really works: Acting as if you are calm and cool has the effect of reducing anxiety. She will also find that others will react positively to her for putting on a strong front and thus "reinforce" this behavior, making her want to develop the skill more.

Q My daughter is so impatient to be grown up she makes herself miserable. How can I help her to slow down?

Wanting immediate gratification can be very frustrating when it's a future that she is after! Try exploring her dreams with her and finding the steps she needs to take now in order for her achieve her future goals. If she can see the route she is following and know the importance of each step, she may feel more satisfied with her life now. For example, if she wants to study medicine, taking a first-aid course now would be really interesting and possibly helpful. Or if she wants to look into culinary school, she could try cooking the family meal once a week.

Perhaps you can encourage a little "mindfulness" in your daughter. This is the ability to live in the moment, mindfully. Encourage her to pay attention to the things around her right now. Get her to describe them as she experiences them, but without making judgments. If she gets distracted and asks what is for dinner, or says she is bored, that's fine, redirect her attention back to now. See what she discovers. Get her to study something ordinary in her everyday life in this way—a pencil, the front door, her watch, anything. Get her to tell you what she notices. If she is prepared to try this with you, she'll be amazed by what she discovers. She will notice colors, textures, sensations, smells, tastes, and sounds that she never

risky or revengeful behavior will not help. Make sure you keep the tissues handy, be free with your hugs, offer a shoulder to cry on (literally), and indulge her with a few extra treats. A shopping trip for new clothes or a joint haircut or beauty treatment will give you an opportunity to chat away from the situation and help her feel good about herself.

Q My daughter wears her heart on her sleeve. I am worried this may make her vulnerable?

The ability to feel an emotion but not express it is quite a sophisticated skill and actually, teenagers are not very good at it. It is a developing skill, and she may learn to tone down the intensity of her expressed emotion, or learned not to blurt out emotionally laden words, but has not yet learned to hide it completely or substitute a more acceptable

noticed before. You may have to reassure her that you have not taken leave of your senses! Mindfulness is a combination of Eastern philosophy and Western psychology that is used for people with various kinds of physical and mental-health problems. But it is also helpful for ordinary people to give new meaning to everyday life. It may help her feel more open to discussing all the wonderful and important things she is doing now in preparation for her exciting future.

What can I do about teen blues?

"Everything is wrong, I'll never do anything special, and there's nothing anyone can do about it." Teenage blues can be catching. You make some bright suggestions, he looks at you wearily and responds

that he will never be what he wants to be, and you start to feel depressed yourself. His thinking is general, global, and negative. What you can do to help is to turn his thoughts into something specific, individual, and positive. Get him to think back to yesterday or last weekend, the last time he was more cheerful, and go through hour by hour what he was doing. Get him to score each activity (including lying on the bed looking at the ceiling) according to how much he enjoyed it and how much it gave him a sense of achievement. Now get him to choose one of the activities that scored highest on both counts, maybe playing his guitar, going for a run, or having a friend over to tinker with the car. This can help reposition his thoughts and help him to plan his whole day around pleasurable, productive activities.

Dealing with emotions

Adolescence can be a time of intense and sudden bursts of emotion. Even the most everyday situations can be experienced with more extreme feelings than they were as a younger child. This can be very difficult for parents to deal with. Unlike toddlers, who can be easily cuddled, teens require a more complex response that does not always come naturally.

Listen, check, label: If your teenage daughter is winding herself up into a state of high anxiety and distress, stop what you are doing and pay attention to her. Listen to what she is saying. Try not to interrupt or contradict or instantly make her feel better. When she is finished, check that you have the story right, for example, who called who first, what exactly was said, and so on. Now try and put a name to her emotion and check whether you have got it right. You might try something like: "It sounds as though she has made you really angry." This gives your daughter a chance to stop and think. She may adjust the label to match exactly how she feels: "I'm not angry, I'm furious."

This careful listening, checking the story, and labeling the emotion can be very helpful. Now you

can ask your daughter what she wants to do. If she is still angry, you might suggest some calming-down time and agree a time to talk later. She may want to talk now and get your help in coping with her feelings, or she may want to try and solve her dilemma herself. Together you can look at the problem and her possible options for a solution with their likely consequences, and she can decide, with your help and support, how she is going to proceed.

ESSENTIAL INFORMATION: TEENS

Teaching emotional intelligence
Helping with adolescent worries

Over the last 30 years we have seen increases in emotional and behavioral problems in young people. Support agencies report dramatic rises in self-harming behavior. In the 11-to-16-year-old age range, 13 percent of boys and 10 percent of girls have a mental disorder.

✱ Emotional intelligence: This fairly new concept is made up of three key areas: self-esteem, coping skills, and social support. Growing up in a stable and positive home and family might be enough to learn these skills. However, where poverty, illness, family dysfunction, or disability undermine emotional resilience, intervening through home or community programs to prevent emotional and behavioral problems is possible.

✱ Self-esteem: Reflecting an accurate and positive picture of your teen by using praise and positive feedback will help build her self-esteem. You might comment on a small act of kindness to an older person and how much it was appreciated or point out how funny she was at a family gathering. Use criticism rarely and constructively. Always focus on the behavior not the person. For example: "I was worried that you ignored Emily last night, she may have felt hurt by that." This invites self-reflection and discussion rather than defensiveness.

✱ Coping skills: Encourage her interests, activities, and social connections. You may not have chosen hip-hop music and street dancing, but give it a chance and seek out the talent and creativity that it brings out in her. Model an optimistic view of the world and her place within it. Each time you encounter a problem, you can show her that there is a way of overcoming it. A failed test is a learning experience and a wake-up call. A family illness or death brings people together and shows what can be endured when you support each other.

✱ Communication: Encourage independence and autonomy through small steps of increasing

LEFT: Encouraging your teen's interests and praising him for effort and achievements will help build his self-esteem, making him feel happier about who he is.
MIDDLE: Offering physical affection is a good way to help your teen to label and reflect on her emotions in a safe space while she is upset. This may help to increase her emotional intelligence.
FAR RIGHT: Your teenager's social support network, formed of friends, and family, reflects an important aspect of emotional intelligence: Empathy.

responsibility. Get her to make her own hair, dental, and doctor's appointments.

If you are angry or upset with her, tell her how you feel about her behavior: "I am angry with you for not letting me know where you were last night" is likely to produce an apology and a discussion about what she will do next time whereas, "You are so selfish, how could you do that to me?" will elicit a denial and a personal insult in return. Listen to what your teen has to say, be prepared to be wrong, and be aware that she is rapidly becoming your intellectual equal.

✱ **Social support:** Finally, to feel safe and secure in the world, she must be able to make relationships with other people outside the family. She needs to learn the important skill of empathy, of putting herself in other's shoes. She must learn to give and take in social and romantic relationships. Acting out situations where she takes the role of someone else and you pretend to be her can help to clarify things for her. For example, if she is struggling with a possessive friend, role playing can help your daughter work out some strategies for letting her down gently and give her insight into how the friend feels. Ultimately she must achieve autonomy and independence, and be able to rely upon herself.

Afterward he may be able to see that by changing the way he is thinking, he can pull himself out of the doldrums and feel much more positive about himself, his future, and his ability to achieve his goals.

How can a few pimples be the end of the world?

Teenagers can be very self-conscious and catastrophic in their thinking. A small pimple might lead your teenager to think that she is hideous, that nobody will want to associate with her, and that everyone is looking at her with a magnifying glass. Adolescents are characteristically self-absorbed and self-conscious, and tend to think in sweeping, negative, and extreme terms. So how can you help?

Perhaps you can get her to consider some of the individuals she knows and likes, who may also have the odd zit or two. Then get her to describe how many pimples they have. Firstly, she will probably not be able to say in any detail, demonstrating that she does not apply the magnifying-glass test to her friends and suggesting that she may be overestimating the scrutiny they give her. Secondly, if she can describe their pimples, she will have to recognize that, despite the state of their skin, they are still likeable, attractive, and her friends.

Be patient, use humor sensitively, help with acne treatment and concealer, and show her that the world will not end.

Is it OK to allow my child to spend ages alone in her bedroom?

It is normal for teenagers to want to be alone and to guard their privacy. They are often moody and unresponsive. Retreating to her bedroom following an upset at school or at home is a good way of having space and time to sort things out and cope with her emotions. Spending hours alone in her room, listening to music, staring out the window dreamily, sleeping, planning her brilliant career, imagining… then emerging as if nothing has happened, refreshed and ravenous, is perfectly normal. Her time alone is important, and you are right to respect it.

She won't eat
all about eating disorders

Q I'm worried my child might be developing eating difficulties. Is there anything I can do?

Parents may feel alarmed by the dangers of eating difficulties and disorders, and feel powerless to prevent them from happening, as parental influence and control diminishes in the teenage years. However, there are many simple and sensible steps you can take to support your teenager's healthy eating and perception of her weight and size.

Establishing regular mealtimes and a requirement that your daughter eat at least one meal a day with the family promotes both healthy eating and the opportunity to communicate as a family. Try to make mealtimes enjoyable occasions where you talk about interesting, amusing things in a relaxed atmosphere. If you have to admonish her for some misdemeanor, don't do it at the dinner table; find another time to speak to her alone. If she appears uncomfortable or anxious at meal times, ask her about it later, not in front of the rest of the family. She may say she is concerned about homework or a friend, but it may be related to eating.

Encourage your daughter's involvement in choosing and preparing meals for herself and the rest of the family, if possible. Give her some freedom to choose what she eats, help her with a healthy diet, and share your knowledge about nutrition. She may choose to be a vegetarian, or to eat different food from the rest of the family. This need not be a problem, as long as she helps a little in the preparation and is having a balanced intake.

Q What are the warning signs I should look out for?

Warning signs can be loss (or excessive gain) of weight, or certain behaviors such as cutting her food up into tiny pieces, avoiding mealtimes, or rushing through her food and leaving the table to go to the bathroom, possibly to vomit. If she is unhappy or anxious about food, has stopped mixing with her friends, has not had a period recently, or has dry skin, hair loss, or itchiness and rashes, seek professional help. It is better to get help early than try and cope on your own. The earlier you start therapy, the more likely it is to be successful. Your health-care provider can direct you to the most appropriate service in your area. If your daughter would prefer not to involve her doctor, then look for an accredited counselor with a specialty in eating disorders.

It is not just around eating that you can intervene. Support your daughter's transition to autonomy by giving her choices, encouraging independence, and promoting her sense of herself as strong, capable, and confident. Do not undermine her with personal slights even if you are provoked. Be careful not to transmit your own distorted thinking about weight and size. Family functioning affects girls' development of satisfaction with themselves more than boys'. So as the parent of a teenage daughter, be particularly sensitive to the impact of marital disharmony on her. Have your arguments in private, or show her how you both can resolve them satisfactorily without damage to anyone.

Q Can boys suffer from eating disorders?

Anorexia nervosa and bulimia nervosa are predominantly female problems, but males do suffer from them as well. Once established, the disorders affect male and female sufferers similarly.

However, the ratio of males to female who have an eating disorder is 1:10–15. Among prepubescent children, the ratio is much more equal. There is some evidence that the incidence of so-called "manorexia" is increasing. Presentation in boys seems to differ

Obesity

Obesity is on the rise. Dieting increases binge eating, which leads to unstable eating and obesity.
There may be complex causes of obesity, but in general they are fairly straightforward. For the most part, it is not that we eat more, but that we exercise less.

There are genetic factors in the origins of obesity. However, theories about lower metabolic rate leading to being overweight have not been borne out. In fact, evidence shows that overweight people have a higher metabolic rate. Also, the theory that there is a genetic predisposition for overweight people having more fat cells is unsupported. It seems that the more we eat, the larger are our fat cells, and the more we have of them. The bottom line is that obese people, in general, have a higher energy input than energy expenditure. Young people are experiencing unprecedented car use and sedentary digital entertainment. Psychological factors underpin overeating just as much as they do for undereating. There is some support for the hypothesis that overweight young people are less responsive to internal cues of hunger and satiety than average-weight youngsters. There is also evidence that they eat as a response to emotional triggers such as boredom, depression, and emotional emptiness. Parents can help with overeating by involving their teenagers in a frank discussion about their eating habits. Taking responsibility for their eating behavior and understanding the consequences of overeating can simply be a matter of education. However, if there is an emotional trigger for overeating or bingeing, together you may be able to pinpoint danger times such as getting in from school before everyone else has arrived home. A simple plan for a healthy snack may easily resolve this situation.

If the psychological factors are more complex and involve dieting, bingeing, and purging, professional help is more likely to be needed. Nonetheless, as parents of an obese teenager, regular mealtimes, healthy menus and good role models are all crucial building blocks to a healthy weight and size.

from girls in that boys are more concerned with shape than weight, and fear being flabby and unfit rather than fat. Boys may suffer from a delay in referral, diagnosis, and treatment because of a lack of awareness that this condition occurs in males.

It's hard to argue with someone with an eating disorder. Don't we all think a bit like that?

It is true that most western females of all ages have some dissatisfaction with their weight and shape. It is not uncommon to hear women exclaim in highly emotive terms how bloated they feel after eating something fattening. Teenagers are particularly self-conscious, and commonly judge their self-image harshly, as do eating-disordered young people. However, the distortions of thinking in someone with anorexia are extreme. She may be emaciated to the point of starvation, but will see a fat person in the mirror. The more her mood is affected by her low self-esteem and distorted, unsatisfactory body image, the more likely she is to hear and believe negative information about herself. She will also discount and deny any positive information. Thus a negative cycle is established and maintained. Along with feelings of depression, she may start to experience panic when she eats and gains weight. She may start to think that she can put on weight by touching food or thinking about food.

A further feature of this disordered thinking is how difficult it is to change. It is hard to get someone with an eating disorder to think reasonably, whereas the general population may be more willing to hear a balanced argument. It is important to take account of the impact of starvation on the ability to think flexibly. This is why treatment for eating disorders focuses primarily on getting a sufferer back to a healthy weight before starting to challenge her thinking.

Why do eating disorders develop?
A combination of many factors

Our teenagers are exposed to the Western societal anxiety about healthy eating, body weight, and exercise. Our daughters read magazines and watch television shows and movies that promote thinness as desirable and attractive. They therefore grow up with an ideal of female beauty that is unrealistic and unachievable. An average teenage girl would need to be two and a half inches (5 cm) taller, increase her bust size by five inches (12.5 cm), and decrease her waist by six inches (15 cm) in order to resemble Barbie! Boys are also coming under increasing pressure to conform to movie-star ideals.

Different pressures: There are a considerable number of factors involved in the development of an eating disorder. These are characteristics of the individual young person, features of her family, and socio-cultural pressures. They combine in complex ways, initially to make a young person more vulnerable to developing an eating disorder, then to tip her from just having difficulties around eating into what would be recognized as a clinical and, sometimes, life threatening, condition and finally, to establish and maintain the disorder as part of her life. This makes it hard to definitely say what causes the disorder and what is a consequence of the disorder.

Each of these factors on its own is not enough to be dangerous, and in many cases, can be seen as normal adolescent issues. It is the complex interactions that lead to the worrying results.

✻ Genetic causes: A girl may have inherited a vulnerability that predisposes her to eating problems. If a close relative has had eating difficulties, she has a higher risk of developing a disorder, but it doesn't mean that she definitely will.

✻ Body image: Eating disorders often develop around puberty, when a girl will typically experience an increase in body fat. This can lead her to perceive that she is fat. She may start to diet and exercise and experience a dip in her self-esteem. Having a distorted body image, particularly thinking she is fatter than she is (and feeling unhappy about how she looks), is a key factor in the development of a disorder, but on its own is not sufficient. Underpinning this state of affairs is her belief that appearance is vital to her self-image and the approval and acceptance of others.

✻ Dieting and exercise: She may try to diet to change her body weight and shape. Typically this is not successful, and may lead to her feeling depressed about her inability to change herself and feel good about herself. Dieting is pretty normal in adolescent girls, but it is particularly common among girls with a distorted body image.

MEDIA INFLUENCES: Reading magazines that promote thinness and focus on body image may be one of the factors involved in eating disorders.

Dieting also leads to binge eating which can be the beginning of a vicious cycle of bingeing and dieting or purging. She may try using strenuous exercise to alter her body weight and shape, and in a vulnerable girl this may become obsessive in time.

✳ **Family interactions:** All of these individual characteristics combine with particular family interaction patterns and parental influences to further increase the risk of an eating disorder developing. Her mother may have had an eating disorder herself or at least have had some of the characteristics. She may learn about dieting and extreme weight-loss measures from emulating her mother. She may have experienced critical comments from her parents about her weight or appearance. She is more likely to have a family that does not feel secure. They may not communicate very effectively with their adolescent daughter and may have a variety of other family difficulties, such as having lots of negative emotion being expressed without reaching comfortable resolutions. This young woman will be driven to please others more than achieve a set of her own goals. She is struggling to develop her own identity. She will not feel she has or is able to achieve autonomy from her parents, who show ambivalence about relinquishing control to their developing daughter. She will respond to their mixed messages of overprotection, over-control, and under-concern with her own version of self-control: Extreme control over her eating.

✳ **Cultural influences:** Western society has produced the myth of the superwoman: Someone who is physically attractive and successful in her career, as well as being a good partner and mother. These enormous and conflicting demands place extra stress on an adolescent who wants to achieve perfection, who is struggling with her identity, who overvalues the views of others, and who has not had an easy nurturing experience. Her response to this stress is to apply more pressure to be perfect and to apply more control to the thing she can control, her body.

How all these factors combine is not yet known. Some think that the normal stress of adolescent transitions—puberty, identity formation, sexual development, academic demands—and overvaluation of thinness in a young person who lacks a solid family base and strong sense of self, all combine to produce disordered eating of enough severity to constitute a clinical illness.

THINNER: Although dieting is common in teenage girls, it can become obsessive.

"MANOREXIA": Boys are also vulnerable to eating disorders, for much the same reasons as girls.

IRRITABLE: Lack of food, or dieting and bingeing, can affect emotions, leading to mood swings and irritability.

Anorexia and bulimia

Anorexia nervosa and bulimia nervosa are the two main categories of eating disorder. There are many similarities between the two groups: As many as 40 percent of sufferers of anorexia engage in binge eating. However most binge eaters do not go on to develop anorexia. The neat differentiation between different types of eating disorder is more imposed than real, and current advances in psychotherapeutic treatment tend to cross the diagnostic categories.

The key characteristics of anorexia are a morbid fear of being fat, significant weight loss (BMI of under 18), perceived distortions of body weight and shape, and cessation of periods. Bulimia is characterized by normal or above average weight, binge eating, regular vomiting or laxative abuse, loss of control over eating, and worries about body shape and weight.

A UK study of 13 to 19-year-old females found that there was an incidence of 50 cases of anorexia per 100,000. Bulimia is thought to affect 0.5 percent to 1.0 percent of young women.

Q My daughter is a little bit chubby. Is there any danger in letting her go on a diet?

Dieting is pretty normal in adolescent girls, but it is particularly common and concerning among girls with a distorted body image. Anorexia sufferers often say they started dieting after a comment about their shape or size from a family member. So you will have to be very careful how you talk about her weight and shape, because your attempts to help may be misinterpreted. In vulnerable young people what starts as a regular diet of calorie counting and cutting out sweet and fatty foods can turn into a campaign of food reduction and obsession about diet and eating. She may move on to smaller and smaller portions, skipping meals, eating very slowly, cutting food up into tiny pieces, smearing it around her plate, in her hair, or hiding it up her sleeves and in her pockets. When these efforts do not produce the expected changes in her view of herself as fat and ugly, she may try excessive exercise, vomiting, and laxative abuse. Although she may deny being hungry, she is may be preoccupied with food and its preparation. She may not be vulnerable, but dieting often leads to binge eating and a vicious cycle of bingeing and purging is quite easy to establish. Rather than start down this road, you would be safest to encourage your child in healthy eating habits, regular exercise, and a realistic positive attitude to her body.

Q My daughter has an eating disorder. I feel as though it's my fault.

Ironically the pressure on you as a mother to be all things to all people and then blamed when things go wrong, may contribute to your daughter's eating disorder. The desire to be a perfect mother, wife, beauty queen, career woman, and so on, often drives young women to over-control their eating in a misguided attempt to totally manage their lives.

Families and their patterns of interaction are implicated in the development or maintenance of eating disorders, but this does not mean that parents or families cause the disorder. On their own, the patterns of interaction or the characteristics of parent–child relations are not sufficient to produce the disorder. All families have their dysfunctionality, and many parents struggle with their children's quest for autonomy and independence. Many parents can't find a way of communicating with a silently hostile, intense, and secretive teenage daughter. And many couples with children negotiating puberty and adolescence are struggling with their own developmental processes as they reach middle age.

Blame and guilt won't help—little is solved through them. The development of an eating disorder is a complex interplay of many factors. The response required is equally complex and needs to include more open, positive family interaction, supportive, non-judgmental relationships, sensible patterns of eating and exercise and, often, a qualified therapist.

When should I let go?
Your young adult, relationships

My son keeps threatening to leave home whenever we argue. How can I deal with this issue?

Much like the young child who learns that throwing his toys around will get him out of a situation he doesn't want to be in, your son may have figured out that threatening to leave home is a very effective way to end, and win, an argument. Playing on your anxieties about him not being able to cope and the strength of your feelings on the subject is the unbeatable ace up his sleeve. Rather than arguing that he is not ready to leave home or begging him to stay, try taking a different stand. Tell him that you don't want him to go, but it's his life and his decision.

Of course, you want to know that he will be safe and secure, so ask him to put together a budget and show you on paper how he will survive without your financial support. In the heat of the moment your son may genuinely feel that moving out is an easy option, but confronting the reality of how much it will cost should reduce his enthusiasm for leaving home. In this cooling-off period, avoid the temptation to turn the tables and make him feel like your financial power gives you control, since this will only serve to push him away all the sooner. Put the argument behind you and let him know you are glad that he has decided to stay.

My son wants to stay at home with his friends when we go away for the weekend. Good idea?

Sooner or later all teenagers vote with their feet and most will opt to be somewhere else rather than spend time with their parents if given the choice. However, staying home alone overnight is a big step, and you need to know that your son is ready for this responsibility (and, more importantly, that he won't have a wild house party in your absence!). Agree some clear house rules with him and give him at least one opportunity to prove he can follow these by staying out somewhere local, so you can return home quickly if you need to. If you decide your son is independent and mature enough to handle this, make sure he has plenty of easy-to-prepare food available to avoid any cooking accidents, and a list of emergency contacts just in case. Call and check in with him at agreed times, and try not to use up your text allowance in between phone calls or he won't feel independent at all.

If you don't feel the time is right, you can either drag him along on your break—which may not make for a pleasant time for anyone—or perhaps arrange for him to stay with a friend to soften the blow, and agree to review the issue soon.

My daughter just uttered the three words every mother dreads to hear: "Mom, I'm pregnant!"

This is probably not the news you wanted to hear for several years yet, with thoughts of being a grandparent reserved for the time when your daughter is in a happy, stable, long-term relationship. You may be feeling angry, disappointed, frustrated that all your warnings and good advice went unheeded, and sad for the loss of the hopes and dreams you had for your daughter. However, your daughter probably didn't plan this, and she needs your support now more than ever. Remember how scary it was when you found out you were pregnant?

Try to stay calm so your daughter will feel she can talk to you. Your first thoughts may well turn to, "Who's the father?" but be prepared for the fact that she may not want to say. Respect her wishes and concentrate your energies on supporting her through the current situation. Make sure your daughter has a checkup at the doctor, and try to open up a discussion about her options: keeping the baby, adoption, or termination. Offer to accompany her for moral support, but don't insist: She may want this to be a private time for her to think about her choices. This may be one of the most difficult conversations you will ever have with her, and you may not agree with her choice. Whatever your daughter decides, she will need you with her every step of the way.

Q My son shares a bed with his girlfriend at her house and now he wants her to sleep over. I just don't think it's right.

Being confronted by your teenager's sexual maturity is difficult for any parent to deal with, and it may be easier to deny your son is in a physical relationship by adopting a policy of "Not under my roof."

However, if you do take this stand then your son will simply spend more time staying at his girlfriend's, or may even have sex in risky and less comfortable places, such as in a car or in the park. Before making a decision, it may be worth talking to other parents to see what their thoughts on the issue are. As difficult as it may be for you to say "yes" to his request, there are certain advantages. For example, you will know where he is and who he is with, and it will give you some leverage in discussing issues such as safe sex and also potentially risky behaviors.

The fact that your son is asking for his girlfriend to stay over also suggests that he may want you to build some sort of relationship with her, which is no small step for anyone. You could suggest a compromise: Allowing them to sleep over but in separate bedrooms. Either way, this does not mean that you have to turn over your house to the happy couple. Set some clear limits and rules on things such as curfews and minimum required clothing to avoid anyone feeling uncomfortable or embarrassed. If you feel you just can't agree to your son's request, take the time to explain your reasons rather than simply refusing. The landscape of sexual behavior

Communicating with your teenager

Good communication is the cornerstone of any strong relationship. As your teenager gets older and enjoys greater freedom and independence, you will come to rely on your communication skills all the more to help you stay in touch with her life. You have spent years talking to your child, but the head down, no eye contact, one-word answers, shoulder shrugging approach to communication practiced by some teenagers can make it difficult. Consider the following ideas to help you keep conversation flowing.

✻ Listen attentively to your teenager when she speaks—don't just talk at her.
✻ Ask questions, but remember her privacy is important: She won't share everything with you.
✻ If you are having to say "No," always explain your reasons why.
✻ Work on solutions to problems together—ask for her ideas and opinions.

✻ Talk when she is ready and try to use open questions (who/what/when/where/why/how?) as it is harder to give yes/no or short answers to these.
✻ Be positive and try to avoid being critical.
✻ Don't forget to praise whenever you can.

has changed significantly over the last few decades. You do not have to agree with your son's behavior but try to respect his choice as he must respect yours.

My 15-year-old daughter's new boyfriend is more than twice her age. What can I do?

Your daughter probably feels very flattered by the attentions of an older man who treats her like an adult and buys her things that boyfriends of her age simply can't compete with. However, the thrill of this relationship may be blinding your daughter to his true intentions, and she needs you to keep her safe and protect her from being exploited. Speak to them both individually and try to remain calm, since you risk pushing her closer to this man if you lose your cool. Ask him whether he realizes your daughter is underage as she may have tried to appear more mature and lied about being 15 or at least kept it quiet. If he is aware of this or doesn't seem bothered, you may want to check whether he is known to the police, and tell him that you will do so.

The bottom line is that you need to ask this man to stay away from your daughter. She may not want to hear what you have to say and may well accuse you of interfering and deliberately ruining her life (again). However, you need to explain your concerns and help her to see how inappropriate and potentially risky the relationship is. What would she think if you began dating one of her friends? Your daughter is unlikely to be thankful for your intervention right now, but one day she will look back and breathe a big sigh of relief that you were looking out for her.

My daughter wants to go on vacation with her friends. Should I let her go?

The prospect of going on a trip without their parents is a real watershed moment for any teenager, and is likely to push your anxiety and your daughter's excitement levels through the roof. Before your protective instincts kick in and you give a firm and flat "No!" to her request, find out exactly what is

Not my baby anymore
overprotective?

I thought when my daughter became a teenager I'd be less protective. I willed myself to let go, but whenever I looked at her I saw my little girl, not the "almost woman" I knew she was. The tide turned one day when I was out shopping and noticed her with some friends across the street. She stood there, happily chatting, tall and confident, and I saw one of the group giving her a very admiring look. In an instant it was as if I saw her through the eyes of a stranger, and I got such a clear perspective. There was a girl who appeared the image of self-assurance; friendly, yet in control of the situation.

Since then, I remember that vision of her whenever I'm tempted to treat her like a child. It's helped me to see how far she's come and what a credit she is to me.

being planned. Ask who is going; where they are heading; what the accommodation is like; how they will get there, and so on. If you don't know all of your daughter's friends, ask her to invite them over so you can meet them and see how they get on as a group.

Speak to the other parents to check out their thoughts too. You are bound to have a long list of concerns about vacation temptations and possible risks to your daughter's welfare. Work through these together and agree how she will manage each of them. Set clear boundaries on smoking, drinking, and sex and get a verbal commitment from your daughter that she will stick to them. There is no guarantee that she will stick to this agreement, but making a promise out loud and face to face will certainly make it more likely. Ultimately, you need to decide if your daughter is mature and responsible enough to look after herself, which may mean giving her an opportunity to prove it to you.

Who am I?
exploring values and identity

Q My son is an "emo." Should I be worried?

Subcultures of youth culture develop around musical styles, political positions, fashion trends, ethnic groups, and sex and gender roles. "Emo" stems from the word "emotional," and is a broad title that covers many different styles of emotionally-charged punk rock and the more light-hearted pop-influenced music that emerged from this, along with its associated fashion. Emo fashion tends to feature heavy black eye makeup for both boys and girls, skinny jeans, and dyed black hair in a particular style: long bangs brushed over to one side, sometimes completely covering one eye. As part of developing his identity your son has chosen to associate himself with the overt expression of emotion through this style of music and fashion. He might have chosen to grow his hair long and listen to heavy metal, or cut his hair short, play sports, and drink a lot of beer. This is one possible identity among many, but if your son is otherwise getting on with his life, education, friends and his family, there is no reason to be worried.

There is a reported darker side to the emo genre that associates some young people with self-harm. It is possible that these interests can be powerful and dangerous to vulnerable people who are seeking to address deeper psychological problems through this subculture. Communication is the key. By talking to your son about his music, and about being part of this particular group, you will be able to gauge whether there is any need for concern. Remember that he is expressing his individuality through this identity, so don't treat him as a stereotype.

Q My daughter has a chronic illness. How can I help her develop normally, like other teens?

The key is to focus on all the other aspects of your daughter as well as her illness, which will inevitably be a defining influence on her. It's a tricky balancing act, and you can't deny the fact of her ill health—others may need to know about it and it will have had an enormous impact on your relationship and your communication. However, she is so much more than her illness. An illness is not an identity, but her response to being chronically ill is a manifestation of her personality. Her courage, her rage, and her humor are all part of her identity. If you look beyond the illness, you will see the normal adolescent-development process and her search for an identity.

Encourage her to be as adventurous as she wants to be, to entertain the same hopes and dreams as everyone else. But do impose boundaries when lines are crossed. She needs and deserves the same guidance as any other adolescent. If she takes on extreme causes or a radical fashion style, she may be challenging you and the world, to see if you treat her differently from her healthy siblings and peers. She may be insulted and incensed by this double standard. Or she may take advantage of your soft-heartedness. If, for example, you don't want your daughter to have multiple piercings, don't give in because you feel sorry for her or guilty that she suffers from a chronic health condition. Tell her that

> Our identity is formed by our sense of personal uniqueness and the recognition we get from people who matter

ESSENTIAL INFORMATION: TEENS

Forming an identity
Development in the teen years

The physical, psychological, moral, and social developmental advances in teenagers allow and shape the mixture of personality characteristics, beliefs, and values that makes up identity.

✳ **Crisis or development?** The belief that this process is a "crisis" is not really accurate, but there is no doubt that adolescents go through stages of identity development. Teenagers may experiment with different possible identities: the practical joker at home, the quiet studious pupil at school, the day-dreaming delivery boy. He gradually settles for a good fit between his future career, his ideological values (whether they be political, religious, or philosophical), and his sexual role. This process can go on well into adulthood, and although some adolescents seem to simply take on the roles and values of their parents, others are still changing and developing in their twenties.

✳ **Peer influence:** The influence of friends is a crucial part of this process. Learning to make close friendships and romantic/sexual relationships helps to define and reflect who they are. Teens typically go for good looks and nice clothes, but

they also admire a good person. All those hours on the telephone or online with friends they have only just left at school are for exploring what others are like and, therefore, what they themselves are like. So give them time and space to experiment with who they are.

✳ **The role of parents:** Despite the influence of friends, the parents' role in this process is actually very important. It is the bedrock upon which a healthy self-image and identity is formed. Parents should expect age-appropriate behavior and place reasonable limits on their teenagers, but be open to reasonable change. This will encourage healthy identity and self-esteem.

For example, enforce a curfew… within reason: Parents who allow the occasional, negotiated late night over the weekend are likely to produce a responsible young adult. On the other hand, families with lax rules and an indulgent style tend to produce children with irresponsible and immature attitudes. Authoritarian families produce dependency in their offspring that can be the precursor of psychological difficulties and disorders underpinned by poor self-esteem.

FAR LEFT: The influence of peers is important for identity, so give your child time and space to develop friendships. **MIDDLE:** Discovering attractive and unattractive traits in others helps your teen to discover something about herself. **RIGHT:** Set boundaries but be prepared to compromise if your child shows you can trust her.

Idealism and realism
Gaining values and beliefs

Before he had the capacity to think maturely about responsibilities and obligations, your teenager probably thought of right and wrong as the difference between avoiding punishments and getting rewards. As he gets older he starts to question society's values, and may decide that in his view they are morally questionable. He also begins to consider the impact of his own behavior on others. He may feel very strongly about globalization, stem-cell research, or intensive farming, and consider his own values morally superior. He will often feel very strongly about issues of justice and injustice and be critical of his parents' apparent "hypocrisy."

* **Still a child?** On the other hand, he may not help with the recycling or treat his younger sister with much humanity, and you may think that, far from being a principled young man, he is in fact just a self-centered and confused child. Actually,

he may be both. In this time of growth and change in his knowledge about himself and the world, he may express clear moral judgements about some things and yet be very focused on his own personal goals in other situations.

There is no harm in gently pointing out that charity begins at home while engaging in an ideological debate about the third world. But there is no need to crush his new-found values in the process of insisting on family rules and beliefs.

* **Avoiding hypocrisy:** As ever, parents who set a good example by treating each other and family members justly and who approach their role in their communities responsibly, will stand a better chance of seeing this behavior in their children. Unfortunately, moral development in adolescence has a particularly sensitive nose for hypocrisy. Parents need to be able to justify their decisions rationally and be able to be challenged on their own values and identity.

EMERGING MORALS: As they grow, teenagers are likely to start to question society's values and develop strong opinions on the various controversial issues they read about in the news.

DO I HAVE TO CLEAN UP?: While your child may be very vocal about global issues, he might not care much about family values or helping with chores. Do encourage him to develop values that reflect both of these areas.

Lesbian and gay adolescents

The process of forming a sexual identity is begun at conception, but gay and lesbian adolescents generally do not identify themselves privately until they are about 15, and publicly until 16 years old. At first they just feel different from their same-sex peers. Then, when puberty is established, they find that they are attracted to same-sex peers, with all the confusion and upset that comes with such a realization. At some point after this, they will reveal their feelings to chosen family and friends.

Parents may react with initial shock and denial, and a sense of loss of an expected future of traditional marriage and family. To move beyond this requires courage, honesty, love, and a desire to maintain close family bonds. Remember that gay relationships can be just as rewarding as heterosexual ones. Although your child may never get married in the traditional sense to a partner of the opposite sex, same-sex couples can still be a family and have children, either via adoption or donation (for lesbians). As a parent, it is likely that you had an idea that your son was different in some way. Think about the anguish he may have been through and the courage it has taken for him to come out. Keep your communication going whatever your sense of personal hurt. Adolescence is hard enough: Being gay will inevitably present extra challenges for him. What he needs is your support and acceptance, in whatever identity he chooses.

you don't want her to spoil her beautiful skin and regret it when she is older. Your concern will make her feel valued, even if her first reaction is anger.

Q My 16-year-old son isn't very manly. Does this mean he's going to be gay?

Society seems to be much more tolerant of girls who enjoy doing things typically thought of as male interests and activities, than it is of boys getting involved in traditionally female activities. Girls doing motorcycle maintenance is considered refreshing and cool, while boys doing needlework is not.

The first consideration is what you and your family think of as manly. If it is that he is interested in more traditionally female activities, this preference would seem to have little to do with sexual orientation, but rather shows a sensitive, gentle character who likes making things rather than throwing balls or play fighting. If he likes style and fashion, designs his own clothes, spends hours doing his hair, and wears a little makeup, he may be creative and artistic, but this still does not tell us anything about his sexuality. Rather than measure him against your particular standard of manliness, try to pay attention to his interests and give him recognition for his talents. It's possible that your concerns about his identity are getting in the way of your relationship with him.

Q My child's sense of style is very odd. Is this okay?

Experimenting with clothes, makeup, and hair is one of the enjoyable aspects of feeling, and wanting to look, more grown-up. Your daughter's new shape gives her the excuse she needs to change her image but, like any experimentation, she may occasionally misjudge her look. However, if you think your child regularly dresses inappropriately, talk it over with her. Try not to suggest she gives a cheap or trashy impression as this will only confirm that you don't understand her or her look.

Instead, take a moment to think about what she's trying to achieve with her appearance and support her in expressing her individuality. Remind her to match her clothes to where she is going and what she's doing. For example, if she's going to school she needs to abide by the school dress code, but at parties or on vacation she can have more opportunities to dress up or look different.

Sex, drugs, rock and roll
when to worry

Q **I heard my son being teased by his friends for being a virgin, and I had very mixed feelings about this.**
This would no doubt make him desperate to lose his virginity, and you can probably empathize with that. On the other hand I am sure you do not want him to rush into having sexual intercourse, just to be one of the gang. Peer pressure is massive when it comes to sex, drinking, and drugs. On the whole, boys are glad to have lost their virginity while girls are more likely to have mixed feelings, and a small percentage really regret it. It probably would not be a good idea to directly discuss this overheard incident with your son.

However, you may be able to engineer a conversation later that generally covers the topic of sexual experience and peer pressure. It is doubtful that all those doing the teasing were as experienced as they may have seemed to him at the time. You may be able to get him to think of all the boys he knows who are still virgins and why so much pressure is put on them to have sex just for the sake of it.

Q **I worry about my daughter's safety. You hear so much about date rape. What advice can I give?**
Victims of date rape are almost always female, so sexual safety is an important topic of conversation with your daughter. Your general message should be that her body is her own and that she should be alert to other people's assumptions that they can do what they want with it. The advice you gave her as a young girl, that no one has the right to touch her, applies just as much now that she is a teen. However, now she needs to be particularly aware of how her behavior may be misconstrued, especially on a date. She must be clear with her date about what she wants to do and what she does not want to do. Young girls often believe that once you start a sexual activity, you have

to go through with it. Impress upon her that she can say stop at any time and she can say "No" to sex even if she has had sex with that person before.

Alcohol safety is another aspect of staying safe when out. Even if she doesn't drink, your child can be victimized by a spiked soda. Advise your daughter and her friends not to leave drinks unattended, and to stop drinking immediately if a drink tastes odd and they think it has been spiked. If any one of them begins feeling odd, they should make sure to stay together and look after her. Encourage your daughter not to drink or take drugs, as this will interfere with her ability to make sound decisions and keep control of the situation. Finally, discuss emergency escape measures, should the situation become more coercive or violent. Screaming, fighting, and running away may be options. Self-defence training is a sensible course of action for any young female; it will train her in strategies to disable an attacker. However, sometimes fighting is not a viable course of action and can make the situation much worse—if, for example, the attacker is armed. In this situation, survival is all that is important. Tell her it is not her fault and help her to report the rape to the police.

If you are also the parent of a son, educate him to respect girls and their decisions about their bodies. Boys must learn sexual self-control and understand the consequences of their actions, including the legal ramifications of rape.

Q **My daughter is sleeping around. What should I do?**
Is it possible that your daughter is using sexual promiscuity as a form of rebellion against you? It could be a way of challenging your control and establishing her independence from you. You are right to be concerned, as it is a high-risk form of

rebellion. However, confrontation is probably not going to help. The best course of action would be to find a way to talk with your daughter in a calm and caring manner. It may be the case that you have had difficulties in your relationship prior to her current sexual activity. This could be part of the reason that she needs to rebel in such an extreme way. This may be the time to seek professional help for you both to look at your relationship and for her to think about the meaning of her behavior.

What if my child uses drugs?

Two out of three young people have tried marijuana before the age of 18. You cannot prevent your teenager from having access to illegal substances, but you can make sure that you have information about different drugs and their effects, and the confidence to help her make good decisions when she encounters them. Talk to her about drug use in a calm and open way. Don't exaggerate or lecture, or you'll risk putting her off having these conversations with you—and they do need to be ongoing. Explain the harm drugs can do, both physically and psychologically. She might be surprised to hear how even such a widely-used drug as marijuana can cause damage to mental health. Talk about the harm it does to others, parents and siblings particularly, but also to friends. You could also mention links between the drugs trade and organized crime. It is worth being clear, informed and factual about the legal implications of being caught with different types of drugs. There are excellent websites with this information available. Discuss peer pressure as this has an influence on your daughter's decision making. You might work through a typical scenario with her: You're in the park with your friends, somebody offers you a joint, everyone else is doing it, what do you say? See what she suggests. Maybe she'd just take it and pass it to the next person. If her friends pressure her, she can say something like, "no thanks, I don't smoke." Help her to be prepared with a rehearsed defence if she feels she may be put under pressure.

Drug use: signs to look out for

Many of the signs of drug use on their own may be perfectly innocent, typical adolescent characteristics, so go carefully and do not jump to conclusions. However, unless you actually witness your teenager in the act of drug taking, it can be hard to be sure. The following may help. Physical signs such as red or altered eyes (dilated or constricted pupils), rashes or spots, general ill health, colds and coughs, bruising, weight loss or gain, not caring about appearance and hygiene, and poor sleep. In extreme cases, you may see track marks from injecting (although, if your child has these she is likely to conceal them under clothing).

Behavioral signs might be: Lying about activities and whereabouts, secretive phone calls and activities, loss of interest in usual activities, going out every night, new friends, deteriorating performance in school, missing alcohol or prescription drugs from home, frequent requests for or missing money and valuables, mood swings, hyperactivity and aggression, withdrawn behavior, locked doors, unusual smells on clothing or breath, or unusual wrappers or containers, such as plastic "baggies" (ziplock bags, occasionally with logos) in pockets.

ESSENTIAL INFORMATION: TEENS

Potentially risky behavior
Smoking, drinking, and sex

Most teenagers experiment with smoking, drinking alcohol, and sexual activity. Initially this is out of curiosity, because everyone else is doing it, and because it is pleasurable. How do parents know when experimentation becomes a problem?

Smoking: Preventing your youngster from starting to smoke cigarettes may be considerably easier than preventing him from drinking alcohol because of the clear anti-smoking messages in most societies now. His reasons for trying tobacco will likely be that it looks cool, his friends are doing it and, once he has got over the initial unpleasantness of the taste of nicotine, the nausea and dizziness, he will find it hard to stop. Smoking is also a bonding activity that has been enhanced by anti-smoking laws which require smokers to gather outside in huddles. Start early with your anti-smoking message to impress upon him that avoiding smoking is an important and desirable thing. It is wise to concentrate on short-term consequences, since teenagers are not good at taking long-term health risks into account when making decisions about current behavior. Highlighting the cost of a pack of cigarettes and what else he could buy with the money may be much more persuasive than a warning about lung cancer 10 years down the line. Or how bad it makes her breath smell, and that it stains her teeth and fingers (however, to some teens, stained fingers are cool). In order to educate your teenager about the longer-term consequences, you may need to be more creative. The ravages of smoking are much clearer on older people who have been smoking all their lives, so seeing Grandad struggling with respiratory problems or comparing the wrinkles of smoking and non-smoking family members, may serve as a warning.

Being a good role model is crucial. If you are a smoker, you may have been a powerful deterrent to him when he was young. But now that he is a teenager you are more likely to be an excuse for him to smoke as well. Now is the time to kick your habit. Your experience may serve as a powerful lesson for him to learn about the addiction to, and withdrawal from, nicotine.

Drinking: Experimentation with alcohol is complicated by the mixed messages that exist in society. It is very challenging for parents to give clear guidance to their teenage children about drinking when they are not abiding by it themselves. Whatever the reason was for starting drinking, teens end up doing it for the same reasons as their parents: To party, to be more socially attractive, to forget their troubles, to lift their mood, and to cope with shyness, anxiety, and stress.

As parents we should probably be tougher and clearer on alcohol use and abuse than any other drug. It is the most pervasive and destructive. As with other conversations about substance misuse, the advice is to keep talking, keep calm, be informed, and be a good role model. Make clear what you consider to be acceptable: A couple of beers at a family party or total abstinence before the legal drinking age. Explain your limits and your consequences. For example, being brought home dishevelled and disoriented after being on the winning team at school may elicit only a warning the first time. When it happens a second time, you may want to impose a consequence such as being grounded for the next Saturday night. Parents will have to take account of their own behavior and values, but need to take care not to confuse their children with their own displays of drunken behavior and jokes about it in others. Worrying signs in a teenager might be denying that they are drinking too much, being too interested in opportunities for a drink, and making excuses for needing one. If you find your child drinking and not being able to remember what he did the night before, it's time to act. There are excellent services for young people struggling with alcohol and drug problems and they are usually easily accessible by young people themselves. If you are struggling, ask your doctor to direct you to them.

Sex: For parents, sexual experimentation brings with it fears of pregnancy, sexually transmitted diseases (STDs), and a fundamental challenge to your parenthood: Your child is becoming a sexual being. Teens now have sex younger and with more sexual partners, which serves to increase the risks and your fears. Sexual experimentation starts early with masturbation. Girls and boys masturbate, often using erotic fantasies about film stars and celebrities from music and sports. Masturbation and sexual fantasy is normal and acceptable in the right place at the right time. You could see this as practice for the real thing later, with real people. Your attitude to masturbation as parents will set the scene for how your child approaches sexual activity later. If she feels guilt and shame, she may approach sexual encounters with a less-healthy attitude. Talking about sex can be embarrassing and awkward for parents and teens. Try to be proactive and factual when talking about sex. Don't wait until she approaches you; it may never happen. Talk about her right to say no and the age-old ploys that will be used to put pressure on her to have sex: "If you love me you'll sleep with me." Boys and girls have different approaches to sexual relationships: Boys will have sex if the opportunity arises; girls are more concerned with sex as part of a meaningful relationship. Give her information, advice, and practical help about contraception and prevention of STDs. Talk about the emotions involved in an intimate relationship. Emphasize that intimacy is not all about intercourse; there are many other ways of being intimate. However, do not be too intrusive, choose your timing for these conversations and respect her privacy. Finally, if she approaches you with a question that alarms you, about HIV, for example, try not to freak out before you calmly find out the context of the question. As long as your teen is well informed, prepared, and protected, deciding to have sex is a choice she alone can make.

SMOKING: Many try cigarettes but will not continue past adolescence.

ALCOHOL: Teens drink for the same reasons as their parents.

ROLE MODEL: A healthy attitude to sex will help your teen to be prepared.

ESSENTIAL INFORMATION: TEENS

Commonly used substances
Slang names, effects, and risks

The best way to communicate with your teen about drugs is to be well informed and to keep it casual.

Alcohol
Effects: Relaxation, exaggerates your mood so can make you maudlin, aggressive, euphoric. Hangover the next day.
Risks: Slurring words, falling over, vomiting. Increased vulnerability to rape, robbery, aggression. Physically and psychologically addictive. Heavy and long-term use leads to liver damage, cancer, heart disease.

Tobacco
Effects: Relaxation, reduces hunger, increased heart rate and blood pressure, satisfies craving for nicotine.
Risks: Nicotine is extremely addictive and very difficult to give up. Increased vulnerability to coughs, chest infections, cancer, emphysema, heart disease. Risk to others from passive smoking.

Marijuana
Street slang name: Weed, dope, grass, herb, ganja, marijuana, joint, skunk, buds, (and many others).
Effects: Relaxed, happy, talkative, mildly hallucinogenic, increase in hunger.
Risks: Anxiety and paranoia; can become dependent; increased risk of mental illness in those with a previous or family history; affects learning and concentration.

Solvents
Gas (for example, butane from cigarette lighters or butane gas lighter refill cans), glue, aerosols, nitrous oxide (N_2O) from whipped cream canisters.
Street slang name: Thinners, gas.
Effects: Drunk, dizzy, giggly; can hallucinate, enhanced sounds. Hangover and headaches, sometimes red rash around the mouth.

Risks: Suffocation if using plastic bag to inhale; vomiting and blackouts; heart, brain, liver, and kidney damage from prolonged use; coma from overdose and death due to reckless behavior.

Ecstasy (active ingredient: MDMA)
Street slang name: E, XTC, pills, X, sweeties, M&Ms, eckies, brownies, doves.
Effects: Enhances sounds and colors; makes people chatty; full of love and empathy for others. Full of energy or desire to sit cuddling. Increase in heart rate and body temperature. Can experience a marked come-down following taking E.
Risks: Anxiety, panic, confusion, paranoia. Sleep deprivation. Danger of overheating and dehydration or overhydration. Often cut with other substances. Mental health problems. Liver, kidney, and heart problems due to excessive use or if mixed with other substances.

Cocaine and Crack
Street slang name: Cocaine: coke, Charlie, snow, dust. Crack cocaine: crack, rocks, stones, base, white, freebase (although freebasing has a different method of manufacture).
Effects: Short, intense high. Hyperconfident and wide awake. Increases heart rate, body temperature, reduces appetite. May increase libido. Followed by hangover, low mood (which may include paranoia), and intense cravings.
Risks: Extremely addictive—temptation to achieve the high and avoid the come-down. Risk of overdosing, can cause fits or heart attacks. Encourages risk-taking behavior. Panic attacks, anxiety, and paranoia. Smoking (usually crack) and injecting (which is rare) have risks of infection and respiratory problems. Combinations of cocaine and other drugs increases risk, especially with tranquilizers.

Amphetamines

Street slang name: Speed, phet, uppers, billies, dexies, paste, base. Base tends to refer to "uncut" speed, which hasn't been watered down with another substance, typically glucose, yet.

Effects: Creates a wide-awake, energized feeling. Users appear buzzy, restless, talkative. Reduces appetite.

Risks: Addictive. Hard to come down, irritability, anxiety, depression. Combinations of amphetamines with alcohol or antidepressants or relaxants such as benzodiazepines or heroin can be fatal.

Crystal Meth/methamphetamine

(type of amphetamine)

Street slang name: Ice, glass, Christine, yaba, meth, crystal, crank.

Effects: Euphoric stimulant. As above, but more intense. Usually smoked or injected. Rapid heart rate and increased blood pressure.

Risks: Particularly addictive if injected. More dangerous than speed. Confusion, agitation, paranoia; violent behavior. Long-term use may lead to psychosis. Overdose can cause stroke, kidney, lung, or gastrointestinal damage, coma, death. Increases sexual activity with risk of infection. Dangers of infection from injecting with dirty needles. Dangerous if taken with MAO inhibiter antidepressants.

Heroin

Street slang name: H, horse, brown, gear, smack, skag.

Effects: Intense euphoria, warmth, and well-being. Dulls psychological and physical pain; induces relaxation, sleepiness. Slows down bodily functions.

Risks: Very addictive, as a tolerance quickly develops. Dizziness and vomiting. Choking on vomit, as suppresses gag reflex. Overdosing causes respiratory depression, leading to death. Dangers from injecting with shared or dirty needles: Gangrene and HIV/AIDS, hepatitis.

LSD

Street slang name: Acid, dots, Lucy, drop, tabs, rainbows, paper mushrooms.

Effects: Distortions of color, sound, time, vision. Heightens mood. Can have good and bad "trips."

Risks: A bad trip can be traumatic and last for up to 12 hours. Users may experience flashbacks weeks or months later. Can trigger preexisting mental-health problems.

Tranquilizers

Street slang name: Benzos, vallies, downers, mazzies, jellies, eggs.

Effects: Calm, relaxed, sedated. Higher doses may cause a deep sleep. Slows down the body's functions.

Risks: Highly addictive, particularly benzodiazepines (Valium/diazepam is frequently used). Extremely unpleasant withdrawal effects. Can be dangerous if mixed with alcohol or stimulants. Short-term memory loss.

Ketamine

Street slang name: Ket, K, special K, vitamin K, cereal.

Effects: Used medically as a dissociative anesthetic, sometimes for animals. Users take a fraction of the medical dose to achieve a mental and body high. Can feel very connected to objects or other humans. High doses cause a "K-hole"—feeling removed from reality and set adrift in a dream-like world, often involving complete dissociation.

Risks: Severe confusion, nausea, vomiting, susceptibility to accidents (from uncoordination and change in perception of body and time). Frightening distortion of reality. Depression of heart rate and respiration. Bladder problems. Psychologically, but not physically, addictive.

Magic Mushrooms

Psilocybe semilanceata or "liberty cap" and amanita muscaria or "fly agaric."

Street slang name: Liberties, magics, mushies, shrooms.

Effects: Similar to LSD. Distortions of perception. Emotionally sensitive. Can feel very connected to others. An experience outside in nature tends to be more pleasant.

Risks: Fly agaric is more potent and more risky. Can have bad trips leading to disorientation and ensuing flashbacks. Eating the wrong mushrooms can lead to illness and death. Can exacerbate mental health problems.

Moving on to responsibility
the world of work

My son is not "work ready." What can I do to help him?

There is a specific set of skills that will help your son do well no matter what job he goes for. These include attending every day unless he's sick, arriving on time, appearing clean and tidy, and listening to instructions then following them through. Being polite and friendly is also helpful.

If your son genuinely wants the benefits of a job, such as more money, establishing a work history, and gaining a positive reference, then he may be receptive to your help. Work with him on an action plan to establish work habits. Include practical ideas about timekeeping, appearance, and attitude. For example, calculate when he'd need to be up in order to be at work on time, then give him a "You've got a job!" gift of an easy to use, very loud, alarm clock. Help pick out a work wardrobe. It may include clothes he wouldn't be seen dead in at other times, but are appropriate for the job. Discuss with him whether he's prepared to be told what to do. This can be difficult, since in school he's encouraged to question and challenge, but in a first job he will probably have to take direction. Whatever he does, remind him to smile. If he's pleasant he may be forgiven some mistakes while he finds his feet.

How can I help my child with job applications?

To get a job, your teenager needs to make an impact on potential employers through her written application. Getting across her achievements and the key points relevant to a particular job, without being too wordy, takes practice. Preparation for written applications can be in the form of filling in mock application forms and through building up a brief, honest, and easy-to-read résumé. These allow her to practice expressing her qualifications and skills and organizing them well on the page. Try several styles of résumés and applications until she finds her style. She'll find plenty of examples to work from in books and websites. A school career advisor may be able to give you examples to try out, too.

I'm angry that my son used my card for online purchases.

Online shopping is a temptation to anyone, and your teenager is not immune—but it should not be you, via your credit card, who foots the bill without your knowledge. If he used your card, react as you would if he'd taken money from your purse. Get him to

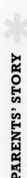

PARENTS' STORY

What to wear
a good impression

I know that first impressions really make a difference so I wanted my teenager to have a smart interview outfit. However, she likes to express her quirkiness through her appearance so we had to find clothes that reflected her personality and also showed a degree of formality. I vetoed anything revealing or with a controversial logo, which she accepted. Before her interview we checked the organization's dress code, so she matched her outfit with their expectations.

Because we bought new clothes for the event she wore them a few times before to make sure they were comfortable. I didn't want her to seem ill at ease in her outfit or be fidgeting with an itchy collar because that could have been really off-putting and taken the focus off her answers.

ESSENTIAL INFORMATION: TEENS

Preparing for work
Reducing interview stress

Facing the prospect of her first formal interview can be seriously daunting to your teenager. Help her prepare to reduce stress on the day.

✻ Investigate: Prompt your teenager to find out as much as she can about the company or college and the role before her interview. Asking to visit in advance and knowing the context of the work can shape her answers and impress the panel.

✻ Timing: Locating the interview venue can be almost as stressful as the interview itself. Coach your teenager through finding the place on a map and planning her journey. Have a trial run of the trip together. For example, try out the quickest bus route with the least changes and see how long it takes to walk from the bus stop to the venue. This way she can get her timing right and has one less thing to worry about on the day.

✻ Practice: Find a quiet, private place and offer to take part in a practice interview. It can feel awkward but it will help on the day if your teen has had a go at answering simple interview questions such as "Why do you want this job/place at college?" and "What are the personal qualities you can bring to the job/studying?" If she's too embarrassed to do this with you then write out the questions so she can practice with a friend.

✻ Sell herself: Your teenager may find it uncomfortable talking about all the things she is good at, perhaps seeing this as boasting. Reassure her that she should say positive things about herself and answer questions with plenty of detail about the knowledge, skills, and personal qualities she has to offer.

✻ Be honest: There is no doubt that many people find interviews stressful so don't pretend they're a breeze. Remind your teenager that most interviews are over within 30 minutes and reassure her you have confidence she can cope with that.

RESEARCH: Knowing about the company, what they do and the role might entail will all impress the interviewer and reassure them that your child is keen and willing to work.

PREPARATION: Help your teenager work on her body language, so that during the interview she can try to maintain eye contact and a calm, confident manner. This will impress the panel and may make her feel reassured.

Money management
An essential life skill

Budgeting, saving, and bank fees may not be top of your teenager's list of favorite discussion topics, but she'll thank you later if you give her a good start in money management.

✶ Comfortable with banking: Managing her own bank account gives your teenager an insight and practice in money management that she can't gain in any other way. Involve her in the decision about which bank and account will suit her needs, and open up the account with her. Visiting the bank, in person and online, will ensure she's familiar with handling her account in both arenas.

✶ The saving habit: It can be hard for your teen to delay getting what she wants, but teaching her to budget and save for a large item is essential if she's to keep spending under control. A regular savings plan, such as committing a portion of her allowance or wages to be stashed in her bank account each week, sets up a good saving habit.

✶ Budgeting: The urge to splurge is probably strong in your teenager, and is understandable when she first gets her hands on an allowance or paycheck. Once the initial thrill has worn off,

try to encourage a bit of planning. Ask her to make a list of the things she wants to use her money for and match these to her income. Create a simple balance sheet so she can see what money is coming in and where it is going. This way, she can make choices that keep her within her budget.

✶ Security: Handling money well isn't just about budgeting: Keeping cash and cards safe and secure is a skill in itself. Teach your teenager some basic rules such as limiting the amount of cash she carries around, keeping bank cards in a safe place, managing her account online, and checking regularly to make sure there are no purchases or charges she can't account for. Impress upon her that she must never give her PIN to anyone or record it so that others can find it.

✶ Model good money management yourself: Use a budget plan yourself to keep family spending under control. Save up when you need a big household item, rather than making an impulse buy. Pay bills on time, and let your teenager see that you check bank statements to make sure they're correct.

BUDGETING: Help your child draw up a budget of his income and expenditures. Rewards for good management, such as a contribution to an expensive item, may help to motivate him.
PRACTICAL: Allow your teen to do part of the weekly food shopping with your money to help him to develop both responsibility and money awareness. Start with small amounts at first.

return the goods, repay the money, and accept a consequence such as limited online access. Discuss what the theft has meant to you, revisit the values you want the family to share, and establish rules about taking things without permission. For example, he must ask before buying anything, use his own bank account, and save for large purchases. You may be tempted to hide away all your credit cards, but this won't rebuild trust. Instead, let him know you expect him to respect your property but, as trust is being rebuilt, you will check your account regularly to confirm he is keeping his word.

My daughter didn't get the job she wanted even though she practiced hard for the interview. What can I say to comfort her?

How disappointing after all that preparation—but what a great learning experience too. Each interview gives your daughter a wealth of information about how to give herself a better chance next time. Even though it can be daunting, encourage her to reflect on her performance and ask for feedback, including what she did well and where she could improve. When she's ready, role-play the interview together. Practice with her as the job applicant trying out different responses, then swap roles so she can ask you the questions and see the process from the interviewer's perspective, too.

Whatever the outcome, reaching the interview stage is an achievement. Remind her that the whole process, from preparing her résumé and written application to the face-to-face interview, is great practice for the next time.

Just because it's his money, does it mean he can spend it as he likes?

It can be quite a struggle if your son is splashing his cash on frivolous purchases when you recognize he needs to save for driving lessons, college fees, and so on. However, if he has earned the money himself you are not in a position to take it away from him, even if he doesn't spend it wisely. Your best approach to this

problem is trying to negotiate that he volunteer to put a proportion of his weekly wage aside in a savings account. Be clear that you will not be loaning him the money later, when a big expense comes up!

It is a different matter if he is using his earnings for illegal or harmful purchases, such as drugs or alcohol. This needs to be addressed as high-risk behavior rather than a concern for his spending habits. Set about understanding why he feels the need to spend in this way, and work with him on an agreement about what is acceptable to you as a family. For more ideas see pp. 238–243.

My teenager wants to buy everything on credit. How do I help her see that she'll pay more?

A practical exercise can help your teenager make an informed choice about buying on credit. Use her latest "must have" item as an example and ask her to work out the cost if she saves up and buys it with cash. Then calculate the amount if she has to use credit and pay interest. Once she has this figure, work out how many extra chores, or hours in her weekend job, she has to do to buy in advance. You can extend the scenario by asking how many items on credit would use up all her weekly income? Is she prepared to have less to spend each week because of credit payments? What would happen if she lost her job? Guiding her through these aspects of a "buy now pay later" decision means she can make a choice fully understanding the consequences rather than acting on impulse.

Most jobs are won or lost on the first impression your teenager gives, rather than the answers she provides

Glossary

Anemia A lack of hemoglobin, or iron, in red blood cells, usually the result of insufficient iron-rich foods in the diet.

Animism A stage in a child's development, between the ages of about two and seven years, when she sees inanimate objects as having life; she believes that the objects can feel, react, and act.

Attention deficit disorder (ADD) A term previously used to describe a child with attention and/or concentration difficulties, now more correctly referred to as attention deficit hyperactivity disorder (ADHD).

Autistic spectrum disorder (ASD) A neurodevelopmental disability that affects the way a child understands the world and relates to others. The term includes autism, high-functioning autism, and Asperger's syndrome.

Autistic savant A child with an autistic spectrum disorder who displays brilliance in one particular area, for example, music or mathematics, that is in marked contrast to her limited social and emotional functioning.

Baby signing A system of sign language developed to assist communication with a person suffering from deafness or learning difficulty that can also be used with babies from about the age of six months.

Bonding The neurochemical and emotional connection between a mother and her newborn.

Case worker A person chosen to help parents organize, coordinate, and manage a care program for a child with special needs.

Cerebral palsy This is a non-progressive physical disability caused by damage to the motor control center of the brain at or before birth.

Chronic condition A condition or illness that persists for a long time, in some cases for life, for example, diabetes.

Cognitive behavioral therapy (CBT) A therapy based on the idea that how a person thinks affects emotional reaction. CBT aims to help people challenge their current thinking patterns, therefore altering how they feel and behave.

Cognitive skills Mental skills used in the process of acquiring knowledge. For example, reading and writing cannot develop without memory, attention, symbolic thinking, and self-regulation.

Colic This describes bouts of unexplained crying in young babies up to the age of three months, usually in the late afternoon or early evening. Typically the baby's face becomes very red and she draws her legs up toward her abdomen.

Congenital abnormality An abnormality or deformity existing from birth, usually arising from a damaged gene, the adverse effect of certain drugs taken by the mother prior to or during the pregnancy, or the effect of some diseases in pregnancy.

Cortisol Hormone produced by the body in response to stress.

Co-sleeping Sleeping with your baby in the same bed.

Curriculum The set of courses, and their content, offered by a school.

Cyberbullying Victimizing another person through emails, text messages, or online forums to harm, damage, humiliate, or isolate that person.

Dethroned To no longer be in the prime position, for example, an older child when a new sibling is born.

Developmental coordination disorder (DCD) Also known as dyspraxia, this affects a child's ability to plan, coordinate, and perform certain purposeful movements, gestures, or thoughts.

Developmental delay A term used to indicate that a child has delayed achievement of one or more developmental milestones. Global developmental delay is used to refer to children with delays in all areas of their development.

Down's syndrome Also called trisomy 21, this is a condition in which a child is born with an extra copy of one chromosome in some or all of her body's cells. The child has 43 chromosomes instead of the normal 42. This results

in certain physical characteristics and some level of learning difficulty.

Dyscalculia A condition that affects the ability to acquire arithmetical skills.

Dyslexia A difficulty that mainly affects the development of literacy and language-related skills.

Dyspraxia See *developmental coordination disorder (DCD)*

Emotional intelligence A person's potential to feel, assess, manage, understand, and explain her own emotions as well as those of others.

Emotional literacy An ability to identify and communicate feelings.

Energy drinks Beverages, often containing high levels of caffeine, that claim to provide more energy compared to a typical drink, therefore improving physical activity of the drinker.

Estrogen The principal female sex hormone.

Extrovert A person who is outgoing and socially confident.

Flathead syndrome Also called positional plagiocephaly, this can be the result of your baby spending a lot of time in one position, usually lying on her back. Flathead syndrome does not affect brain development.

"Flight, fight, or freeze" response The body's reaction to a stressful situation. Hormones are released, causing the heart to beat faster, breathing to quicken, and sweating may increase.

Holophrase To use one word to carry the meaning of a sentence. Children use this as a means of communication when learning to speak.

Hormones Chemical messengers released by certain body cells in one part of the body that affect cell function in other parts of the body.

Hygiene hypothesis The theory that lack of exposure to infectious agents, especially in early childhood, is thought to increase susceptibility to allergies.

Hyperarousal An excessive reaction, for example, to stress.

Incubator Thermostatically controlled closed cabinet, or crib, in which a preterm baby may be cared for.

Intelligence quotient (IQ) A score resulting from standard tests used to measure intelligence.

Interpersonal psychotherapy (IPT) A therapy that is based on the belief that social context can affect psychological difficulties, therefore working on a person's history and interpersonal skills assists recovery.

Introvert A person who prefers their own company to that of others.

Isotonic drink Water that contains glucose and minerals designed to replace the fluids and salts lost through sweating.

Kangaroo care A method of caring for a baby by giving her skin-to-skin contact with her parent, most commonly the mother, for several hours a day.

Learning disability A relative and significant weakness in a particular type of learning or expression regardless of intelligence.

Mainstream school Any school other than a special school.

Mind map A diagrammatic study aid. Words, ideas, tasks, or other items are linked to, and arranged around, a central key word.

Mindfulness Ability to focus on the "here and now" to minimize worries, guilt, fear, and regret. It can be used to treat some physical and mental-heath problems.

Mirroring Reflecting a child's emotions, but in a milder, less intense version.

MMR vaccine Immunization against measles, mumps, and rubella (German measles), recommended for every child around the age of 13 months and again at about age four.

Myelin An insulating material that forms a layer, referred to as a myelin sheath, around neurons.

Nature–nurture debate Discussion as to whether physical and behavioral traits are formed by genetics (nature), experiences (nurture), or by a combination of these two categories of influence.

Neurodevelopmental disorder A disorder that results from impairment of the growth and development of any part of the brain or central nervous system, leading to emotional, behavioural, or physical problems.

Non-directive therapy Also known as client-centered or Rogerian therapy, this approach works on the premise that, through exploring thoughts and feelings with a warm and empathic listener, a person can understand and resolve difficulties.

Nurse specialist A nurse with an advanced degree in a particular aspect of patient care, for example, a diabetes nurse.

Obesity A condition in which a person has too much body fat for her height and weight.

Object permanence The point in a child's development when she realizes that an object exists even when she cannot see it. It generally occurs when a baby is about eight or nine months old.

Occupational therapist Works with a child to help overcome the physical effects of a disability so that she can participate in everyday activities.

Pediatrician Doctor who specializes in the care of children.

Parentese A form of speech used by parents when talking to their babies, combining a high-pitched musical tone of voice with strong facial expressions.

Phobia An extreme, irrational fear of something.

Physiotherapist Identifies and helps to improve movement and function in any part of the body following illness or injury.

Postpartum depression A depressive illness that can develop after having a baby.

Postpartum psychosis A severe form of postpartum psychopathology. Symptoms include delusions, hallucinations, and being unable to think clearly. In some cases a mother may reject her baby.

Prolactin Hormone that triggers the production of breast milk.

Psychodynamic therapy A therapy based on the principle that a person can benefit by gaining an understanding of conscious and unconscious experiences, often through play, art, and drama.

Psychology Academic and medical studies concerned with the scientific investigation of mind and behavior, including mental illness.

Psychotherapy Treatment of a mental illness by psychological rather than medical means, using a variety of different techniques based on relationship-building, dialogue, communication, and behavior change.

School phobia/school refusal A fear of going to school that can range from mild apprehension to crippling anxiety.

Separation anxiety The distress shown by a child in anticipation of, or during, an attachment figure's absence.

Speech and language therapist Person trained to help children and adults who have speech problems and/or language communication difficulties.

Sudden infant death syndrome (SIDS) Sudden, unexplained death of an apparently healthy baby. Previously referred to as "crib death."

Swaddling Wrapping a newborn baby firmly in a blanket so that her head and arms are held close to her body, to mimic the sensation of being in the womb.

Synapse A connection between neurons or other types of cells that have biochemical messages passing through them, allowing the nervous system to connect to and control other systems of the body.

Testosterone The principal male sex hormone, although produced in small amounts by the ovaries too.

Resources

Mental health and child development

American Academy of Child and Adolescent Psychiatry
www.aacap.org

American Academy of Pediatrics
www.aap.org
(847) 434-4000

American Education Research Association
www.aera.net

American Psychological Association
www.apa.org
(800) 374-2721

Association for Psychological Science
www.psychologicalscience.org

Consortium of Social Science Associations
www.cossa.orgindex.shtml

Foundation for Child Development
www.fcd-us.org

International Society for the Study of Behavioural Development
www.issbd.org

International Society on Infant Studies
www.isisweb.org

National Association of School Psychologists
www.nasponline.org

National Association for the Education of Young Children
www.naeyc.org

The National Child Traumatic Stress Network
www.nctsnet.org
(310) 235-2633

Society of Clinical Child and Adolescent Psychology
sccap.tamu.edu/

Society for Developmental and Behavioral Pediatrics
www.sdbp.org

Society of Pediatric Psychology
www.societyofpediatricpsychology.org

Society for Prevention Research
www.preventionresearch.org

Society for Research on Adolescence
www.s-r-a.org

Society for Research in Child Development
www.srcd.org

Zero to Three
www.zerotothree.org

Physical health

Advisory Committee on Heritable Disorders and Genetic Diseases in Newborns and Children
www.hrsa.gov/heritabledisorderscommittee/

American Academy of Family Physicians
www.aafp.org
(800) 274-2237

American Academy of Pediatrics
www.aap.org
(847) 434-4000

American Heart Association
www.americanheart.org
(800) AHA-USA-1 (800-242-8721)

Canadian Paediatric Society
www.cps.ca/english/
(613) 526-9397

National Dissemination Center for Children with Disabilities
www.nichcy.org
(800) 695-0285 (Voice/TTY)

National Institutes of Health
www.nih.gov

National Institute on Deafness and Other Communication Disorders
www.nidcd.nih.gov

World Health Organization
www.who.int/en

Caregivers and caregiving

The Annie E. Casey Foundation
www.aecf.org
(410) 547-6600

Child Welfare League of America
www.cwla.org
(703) 412-2400

National Center for Youth Law
www.youthlaw.org
(510) 835-8098

National Center on Fathers and Families
www.ncoff.gse.upenn.edu
(215) 573-5500

National Family Preservation Network
www.nfpn.org
(888) 498-9047

The National Resource Center for Family-Centered Practice and Permanency Planning
www.hunter.cuny.edu/socwork/nrcfcpp/

National Women's Law Center
www.nwlc.org
(202) 588-5180

General education resources

National Education Association
www.nea.org
(202) 833-4000

International Technology Education Association
www.iteaconnect.org
(703) 860-2100

National Art Education Association
www.naea-reston.org
(800) 299-8321

Speech, language, and learning

American Association on Intellectual and Developmental Disabilities
www.aamr.org
(800) 424-3688

American Speech Language Hearing Association
www.asha.org
(301) 296-5700

Council for Exceptional Children
www.cec.sped.org
(703) 620-3660

Council for Learning Disabilities
www.cldinternational.org
(571) 258-1010

Division for Learning Disabilities
www.dldcec.org

International Dyslexia Association
www.interdys.org
(800) 222-3123

Learning Disabilities Association of America
www.ldaamerica.org
(412) 341-1515

National Institute for Literacy
www.nifl.gov
(800) 228-8813

ProLiteracy Worldwide
www.proliteracy.org
(888) 528-2224

Reading, language, and literacy

Learning Disabilities Association of America
www.ldanatl.org
(412) 341-1515

Multilingual Children's Association
www.multilingualchildren.org
(415) 690-0026

National Association for the Education of Young Children
www.naeyc.org
(202) 232-8777

Autism and Autism Spectrum Disorders

Autism Society of America
www.autism-society.org
(800) 328-8476

National Autism Association
www.nationalautismassociation.org
(877) 622-2884

US Autism & Asperger Association
www.usautism.org
(801) 816-1234

Internet safety

Boys and Girls Clubs of America
www.bgca.org

Family Online Safety Institute
www.fosi.org
(202) 572 6252

International Crimes Against Children Task Force
www.icactraining.org
OJJDP ICAC Task Force
Fox Valley Technical College
c/o University of New Hampshire
(877) 798-7682

Internet Keep Safe Coalition
www.ikeepsafe.org
(703) 536-1637

Kids Health for Parents
kidshealth.org/parent/positive/family/net_safety.html

National Center for Missing and Exploited Children
www.missingkids.com

NetSmartz Workshop
www.netsmartz.org

Wired Kids
www.wiredkids.org
(201) 463-8663

Index

Acknowledgments

Author's acknowledgments

Dr. Claire Halsey AFBPsS, ClinPsyD, MSc, has been a consultant clinical psychologist for over 25 years, specializing in work with children and families. She has a strong academic background and has recently completed research on the subject of parenting at Britain's University of Sheffield. Claire is a journalist and author in the field of child psychology, parenting, and child development, and recently co-authored *Your Child Year By Year*.

Claire would like to thank Vicki McIvor and her family Michael, Rupert, Toby, and Dominic.

Dr. Matthew Johnson PhD, ClinPsyD, BSc (Hons), has worked as a clinical psychologist for seven years, and has over 10 years experience of working with children, young people, and their families. He completed a PhD at Keele University on parenting stress in fathers before undertaking clinical training. Matthew has a particular interest in the social, emotional, and behavioral difficulties experienced by children and young people with disabilities. In addition to his work with families in the community, Matthew leads a school-based service for students attending special schools. For the last two years he has served on the committee of the British Psychological Society—Division of Clinical Psychology: Faculty for Children and Young People.

For my wife Trish and my son Alex who make all things possible and worthwhile. With thanks to my family, friends, colleagues, all at DK, and the many wonderful children, young people, and their families whom I have had the pleasure to work with over the years.

Dr. Joanna Grave ClinPsyD, MSc, is an experienced consultant clinical psychologist specializing in child and adolescent mental health. She has been very involved in the development and dissemination of parenting programs and accessible psychological therapies for children.

For Michael, Josh, and Leo, with love.

Professor Tanya Byron PhD, PsychD, MSc, BSc, (foreword writer) is a consultant clinical psychologist specializing in child and adolescent mental health. She has made television programs about child and family behavior and writes regularly for a number of magazines. She has a weekly column in the British newspaper *The Times*, and is the author of several books. She is Chancellor of Edge Hill University.

Publisher's acknowledgments

DK Publishing would like to thank Salima Hirani for proofreading, Sue Bosanko for the index, Isabel de Cordova for design assistance, Jenny Baskaya and Romaine Werblow for assistance with images, Meliza Myburgh for photography assistance, and Suhel Ahmed for editorial assistance.

Picture credits